The Starr Report **DISROBED**

The Starr Report DISROBED

Fedwa Malti-Douglas

COLUMBIA UNIVERSITY PRESS

NEW YORK

Columbia University Press
Publishers Since 1893
New York   Chichester, West Sussex

Copyright © 2000 Columbia University Press

Library of Congress Cataloging-in-Publication Data
Malti-Douglas, Fedwa.
  The Starr report disrobed / Fedwa Malti-Douglas.
    p. cm.
  Includes index.
  ISBN 0–231–11932–1 (cloth : alk. paper) — ISBN 0–231–11933–X (pbk. : alk.
paper)
    1. Starr, Kenneth, 1946– Referral from Independent Counsel Kenneth W.
Starr in conformity with the requirements of Title 28, United States Code, sec-
tion 595(c).   2. Clinton, Bill, 1946– — Impeachment.   3. Clinton, Bill,
1946– — Sexual behavior.   4. Lewinsky, Monica S. (Monica Samille), 1973–
5. Political corruption — United States — History — 20th century.   6. United
States — Politics and government — 1993–   7. Governmental investiga-
tions — United States.   I. Title.

KF5076.C57 M35 2000
973.929'092 — dc21   99–044094
                                    ∞

To My Maine Coons and My Main Squeeze

Contents

Acknowledgments

Intellectual space and freedom of inquiry were essential for the growth of *The Starr Report Disrobed*. I have been fortunate to be associated at Indiana University with two academic units that treasure these all-too-rare commodities: Gender Studies, where I hold an appointment, and the School of Law, where my research paths have led me on more than one occasion.

Gender Studies has provided me with an academic home that can only be described with laudatives: incredibly supportive friends and colleagues whose encouragement is unconditional, palpable excitement that comes from the process of scholarly inquiry and discovery, seriousness of academic pursuits. And this is not to speak of the consistent and solicitous attention of the at-once patient and efficient staff: Jean Person, Karen Hayden, and most recently Stephanie Brown. To all of this is always added a dose of necessary laughter. Judith Allen, chair of Gender Studies, is responsible here. Astute and insightful, she combines an unflagging confidence in her colleagues with uncompromising scholarly standards to produce an environment in which research flourishes.

The School of Law has provided a different sort of intellectual harbor. To attempt to capture the vision of Dean Alfred C. Aman, Jr., with a few words would do him grave injustice. A Renaissance man, he is a courageous and undaunted explorer whose mere presence expands horizons. Lucky is the humanist who can have the good fortune of participating in the dynamic and stimulating environment that Dean Aman has created. I have been one of those lucky few.

The Starr Report Disrobed results from this serendipitous double association with gender and law. If I had not been invited to participate in a conference at the School of Law, to publish in one of its journals, or to attend one of its reading groups, I might never have had the courage to tackle a text like *The Starr Report*, a highly gendered narrative parading also as a legal text.

At the same time, well-deserved credit must be laid at Peg Brand's door. With her customary energy and infectious enthusiasm, Peg Brand had the brilliant idea of organizing a panel discussion on *The Starr Report* immediately after its appearance. I participated with friends in Gender Studies—Judith Allen, Peg Brand, Helen Gremillion, and Stephanie Sanders—in an evening of discovery and genuine merriment. I have always felt that scholarship must be first and foremost a source of enjoyment and delight. That evening convinced me that I was indeed lucky to be professionally surrounded by like-minded friends and colleagues. Other Gender Studies faculty deserve credit for friendship and encouragement: Laurel Cornell, Carol Greenhouse, and Jeanne Peterson.

My contribution that night on the peregrinations and transformations of *The Starr Report* made me realize that a book was in the making. I had long been interested in narratives of sex and gender, in the textual strategies employed with these culturally central areas, in short, in how one writes about them. There could not have been a more propitious moment for *The Starr Report* to appear on my scholarly horizons.

I must confess that writing *The Starr Report Disrobed* was sheer fun. The fact that an electronic version of the *Report* itself existed alongside the printed ones functioned almost as a security blanket. It meant that one could outsmart one's memory: every fact, every incident, every name could be verified and reverified instantaneously and at will.

But there is a long distance between a manuscript and a book. *The Starr Report Disrobed* would not be where it is now without Jennifer Crewe, editorial director of Columbia University Press. At once patient, energetic, encouraging, and exuberant, Jennifer has been nothing less than a guardian angel, from the moment I initially approached her about the project on September 23, 1998, roughly two weeks after the appearance of Judge Starr's *Report*. The support staff at Columbia University Press has been an author's dream. And the book would not be what it is without the exacting and diplomatic reading of my copy editor Sarah St. Onge.

Producing *The Starr Report Disrobed* had numerous salutary effects. It solidified my commitment to a wider conception of the academy. It made me understand the critical importance of putting cracks in the walls of the ivory tower so that ideas can hopefully reach a wider public. It made me more conscious of the political and cultural currents I am immersed in on a daily basis. But, more importantly, it made me aware of the unconditional generosity of friends and colleagues whose versatile intellects transcend disciplinary boundaries.

Through their generosity with their time and knowledge, these friends and colleagues renewed my faith in the intellectual enterprise. To them goes my deep gratitude for reading all or part of the manuscript. Their comments and suggestions have only improved the text: Judith Allen, Fred Aman, Stephanie Kane, Michael Klein, Marshall Leaffer, Judith Roof, Susan Williams.

It was Fred Aman, however, who paid me the highest, and most unexpected, compliment. After perusing the draft of the manuscript, he invited me to make a presentation on *The Starr Report Disrobed* at a School of Law faculty seminar. John Applegate was the wonderful and patient facilitator who then made it all happen. I am deeply touched by those faculty members at the School of Law who read selections from the book and discussed it with me, allowing me to benefit from their legal experience. I thank especially Jeannine Bell, Hannah Buxbaum, Perry Hodges, David Williams, and Susan Williams.

Patricia Meyer Spacks stands in a category by herself. Without her insightful reading and encouragement, the book would never have seen the light of day. Henry Louis Gates, Jr., provided essential and crucial support when it was needed. To him and Pat Spacks, I owe more than words can express. There are also friends and colleagues, other than those who read the manuscript, whose continued support over the years has been a great comfort. Rather than naming some who might prefer to remain unnamed, I have decided to err on the side of caution and not mention specific names. Nevertheless, those whose confidence in me has been critical know who they are, and, even more, they know how indebted I am to them.

I make an exception in the case of Joelle Bahloul and Marshall Leaffer. A great deal of discussion and debate about legal issues took place at their home. It was through them that I renewed my delightful contact with Wendy Schoener, who had patiently and cheerfully helped me navigate the shoals of publishing in a law school journal. It was through them that I met Elisabeth Zoller, who, writing in French, casts a different light, that of comparative constitutional law, on Judge Starr's *Report*. In Paris, Professor Zoller generously called to my attention a recent issue of the journal *Droits* that had a special section on the Lewinsky scandal. Tim Jon Semmerling, in his worldwide rovings, was instrumental in getting me a copy of *The Starr Report* in French.

I could not have survived the intense period that produced *The Starr Report Disrobed* without Allen Douglas. He has spoiled me over the years not only with his incisive criticism but with his uncompromising intellect. Every word I write benefits from his unparalleled acumen, logic, lucidity, and knowledge. As I embarked on the marathon journey that would lead to the book, he was there beside me, providing support and encouragement and dispelling any hesitations I had about the project. I will never be able to repay the variety of debts I have accumulated with him over the past few years.

What can I say about my other companions, those in the P.-T. family: S., D., and A.? They have looked over me and sat beside me as I conceived every sentence, every argument in the book. They sometimes even debated with me by inserting their own material into the text. A source of beauty, inspiration, and laughter, their presence has helped me to better understand and readjust life's priorities. Their calm and comfort have been necessary antidotes to the harried universe of today's academy.

Note

This book has been prepared with a minimum of scholarly apparatus. When quoting from the "Notes" to the *Report*, the references in the *Report* itself (e.g., dates of testimonies, phone records) have been omitted for ease of reading, with such omissions indicated by my unlabeled ellipses.

Since *The Starr Report* is available in different formats (including electronic), each of which features different pagination, I have included no page references to the text. Nevertheless, I have provided enough data to permit readers to find easily the incident or quotation in question.

Wherever possible, I have respected the punctuation, ellipses, emphases, and brackets in the quotations from *The Starr Report*. Only added brackets, ellipses, or emphases are noted. All translations in the text are my own.

Introduction

The American presidency under William Jefferson Clinton came in for a legal jolt as the multiyear and multimillion-dollar investigation by the independent counsel, Kenneth W. Starr, culminated in a referral to Congress arguing in favor of President Clinton's impeachment. What came to be known as *The Starr Report* has become a central document in contemporary America, if not the world. Before the emergence of the *Report*, few people outside Washington had ever heard of Judge Kenneth Starr. But the *Report* has propelled him to international fame as he has become, at the end of the investigation into President Clinton's activities, indelibly attached to the subject of his investigation.

Alan Dershowitz in his *Sexual McCarthyism* considered the investigation at the time it was being undertaken "the most important criminal case in recent American history." Certainly, the case has generated an enormous corpus of texts from both sides of the political spectrum. William J. Bennett and Ann Coulter, to name but two on one side, joined the ranks of Dershowitz and James Carville, to name but two on the other side.

The Starr Report Disrobed recognizes the central role of Kenneth Starr's *Report*. And now that the removal of President Clinton from office is no longer a possibility, it is time to understand what *The Starr Report* is all about. It is a book that will surely go down in the annals of American history as one of the country's more influential texts, if nothing else because of the effect it has already had on the American presidency and the legacy of William Jefferson Clinton. It is a book whose modest label of "report" belies great power. (Would most readers assume that a "report" would comprise over several hundred pages of prose?) For Dershowitz, the report is "a constitutional bastard."

"Constitutional bastard" or not, Kenneth Starr's text, on its birth, sparked a flurry of magazine articles and newspaper editorial pieces. Prominent names such as Joan Didion, Stephen Greenblatt, Toni Morrison, Cynthia Ozick, and James Wood took up the verbal lance and charged forward with brief pieces commenting on some of the literary attributes of this *Report* (all have been useful, but Wood comes closest to anticipating some of the concerns of *The Starr Report Disrobed*).

These discussions, brief though they are, signal the significance of *The Starr Report* beyond its legal position as a document arguing in favor of the impeachment of an American president. Their existence testifies to the centrality of the text as a cultural phenomenon. The subtitle of the *Report—The Independent Counsel's Complete Report to Congress on the Investigation of President Clinton*—only hints at the complexities of the stories within.

The Starr Report was a textual event with no real precedent in American history, and its effects were crucial in the evolution of a political and constitutional crisis. But the importance of the *Report* also stems from the way it was conceived, assembled, and constructed. Judge Starr could have made a narrowly focused legal argument, but instead he chose to cast his points in far broader cultural and political terms. In doing so he brushed up against an extraordinary number of American issues and problems. The material in *The Starr Report* is unique in its combination of high politics, legal and constitutional importance, and extraordinarily detailed description down to physical detail of the private behavior of the president in public space.

All this makes the *Report* an extremely important cultural object for what it reveals and for what it juxtaposes. In this sense, *The Starr Report* acts as a mirror of American society. A mirror, of course, does not reflect perfectly. Rather, it shapes and distorts in its own ways. *The Starr Report Disrobed* will demonstrate that the referral's hesitation between legal and far broader cultural materials has led to some highly revealing textual peculiarities.

There is much sexually explicit material in *The Starr Report* and much analysis of it in *The Starr Report Disrobed*. The purpose of this discussion is neither to hold the *Report* up to opprobrium on that account nor to argue that there is something inherently wrong in sexual explicitness. Instead, *The Starr*

Report Disrobed seeks to investigate the relative weight of the sexual material in the *Report* and its effects on the political and legal arguments in Judge Starr's referral and to examine how sexuality is treated and what this treatment says about images of sexuality in America today. This is all the more important because it is the thesis of *The Starr Report Disrobed* that, among other things, the sexual material in the referral to Congress is part of a coherent (whether conscious or not) strategy to use the physical and moral frailties of Bill Clinton, the man, to politically delegitimize William Jefferson Clinton, the president. In the process, the referral paints a picture of a multifaceted masquerade.

Much as Judge Starr's referral announces itself as an investigation, so *The Starr Report Disrobed* also announces itself as an investigation, this time of *The Starr Report* itself. Yet if the goal of *The Starr Report* is to argue for a particular result in American politics, such is not the goal of *The Starr Report Disrobed*. *The Starr Report Disrobed* will explore the textual strategies inherent in *The Starr Report* but will not represent a plea or an argument in favor of one or another partisan political position.

The Starr Report Disrobed works from the premise that *The Starr Report* itself is a sufficiently complex and culturally revealing work that it repays rigorous attention in its own right. As television viewers feasted on the congressional hearings starring Independent Counsel Kenneth Starr, they surely noticed Judge Starr lovingly holding his referral, the image of a proud father who felt that his textual offspring had to share the limelight with him. This performance was also a guarantor of the importance of *The Starr Report*, a sign of its veracity and its ability to withstand the vicissitudes of congressional assault.

And what is this strange book, this *Starr Report*, which can bring the American presidency to its knees? The quick forays into the text by professor-pundits and public intellectuals have led to provocative assessments that whet the readers' appetites but leave them unsatiated. Part of the reason for this is the nature of *The Starr Report* itself. What initially captivated the attention of some of these critics was the magical word "narrative." Rare is the critic able to resist the temptation of this "narrative" advertising itself with the help of the sexual act as the central and one easily accessible component of the *Report*. (In the discussion that follows, the section Starr so labeled will be identified as "Narrative" while the word lowercased refers to the telling of a series of events.)

As will become evident, however, this product of the Office of the Independent Counsel is not so simply circumscribed. It is a complex work whose text is both unstable and permeable. The work is capable of changing form and in the process altering its relationship to the reader. "The Mighty Morphin Report" (chapter 1) investigates the permutations of *The Starr Report* on its way to becoming a global textual phenomenon. From the referral to the United States House of Representatives through the Internet and newspapers to independent volumes, the *Report* traveled the globe. The iconography of both English-language and foreign-language covers demonstrates how the visual and verbal messages joined forces to comment on America.

This ability of *The Starr Report* to change form, to morph, is related to another aspect of the text: its organization. Organization is, of course, the way in which the building blocks that constitute a work are arranged to yield the resulting product. "Organization as Obsession" (chapter 2) takes the reader on a literary walk through *The Starr Report*. Along the way, the function of certain components, such as the dates and names that herald the beginning of the text, will become evident. Textual neighbors are key in defining a narrative. What precedes and follows the telling of a specific episode can alter the reading of that event as much as the content of the episode itself. More to the point, the frequently repetitive organization of *The Starr Report* reflects its obsessive nature.

This detailed walk through *The Starr Report* will also lead into another world, one not normally encountered in a narrative, and that is the world of the "Note." The "Notes" call attention to the fact that this tale of sex and secrecy follows different textual rules, has other textual ambitions, apes other forms of authority. But something else plays into this organizational complexity as well, and that is the role of the narrator(s) in this convoluted tale. Narrative voices switch and play musical chairs throughout *The Starr Report*.

No matter what its guises or its games, however, *The Starr Report* tells of a relationship between two people. The illicit nature of this relationship subjects it to different rules. "He Loves Me, He Loves Me Not: The Geographies of Lust" (chapter 3) investigates the various geographies in which the protagonists are involved. To move from the spatial to the personal, this relationship is, of course, defined by its being part of a love triangle. From this perspective, *The Starr Report* demonstrates that all angles need not be equal. And the lesser angle comes in the figure of Hillary Rodham Clinton. At the same time, the potential love story of Monica Lewinsky and Bill Clinton is complicated by the trappings of power and politics. These two elements combine to create an explosive mixture, a mixture in which the gaze plays a very important part.

An illicit couple in these situations normally benefits from a go-between, a mediator, someone who helps to join two people motivated by political or other circumstances to keep their relationship secret. Enter Betty Currie, who plays the role of the great facilitator in this contemporary story (chapter 4). In this sexual drama, Betty Currie becomes party to more than just the sexual intrigues, as she joins forces with Clinton and Lewinsky to create a fascinating ménage à trois.

This unfolding drama involves a number of intimate encounters between Bill Clinton and Monica Lewinsky (chapter 5). *The Starr Report*'s portrayal of these encounters lures the reader into a strange sexual world. The meetings as a totality of events elucidate the linked universe of sexuality and corporality in *The Starr Report*.

Of all the intimate encounters, it is no doubt the one featuring the by-now-infamous blue dress that leads the sexual parade. Here, the starring roles are not only those of Bill Clinton and Monica Lewinsky but also Betty Currie. An in-depth exploration (chapter 6) of the account in the "Narrative" section of *The Starr Report* highlights a number of aspects of the sexual event: the spatial dynamics, the ways the bodies are circumscribed, the discourse of semen. The discursive "Notes" add to, and complement, the "Narrative." As a corollary, the investigative task extends to the variant telling of this encounter in the section of the *Report* that outlines the grounds for impeachment (chapter 7). This version is not identical to that in the "Narrative" and plays its own games with the variety of available discourses.

Kenneth Starr, the name behind the *Report*, proclaimed "I love the narrative!" (chapter 8) There are, in fact, a variety of narratives in the referral, all of which emanate from the primary narrative whose task is to reveal the sexual exploits of Monica Lewinsky and Bill Clinton: narratives of denial, narratives of aggression, narratives of victimization, and narratives of desire—many with "his" and "hers" variants. Some of these narratives even serve as narratives of resistance to the primary narrative.

No matter what the narrative, however, bodies are central to *The Starr Report*. But these bodies are not so clear-cut. The text plays various, and interesting, games with gender and the body. "My Body, My Gender" (chapter 9) demonstrates a side of *The Starr Report* that speaks to a contemporary American preoccupation, that with the instability of gender roles, if not gender confusion. But at stake in all this is the president's two bodies, his "body politic" and his "body natural," and an attempt on the part of the referral to destroy the first by means of the second.

Judge Starr's *Report* is more than the tale of the sexual exploits of an American president and the arguments in favor of his impeachment. *The Starr Report* functions on a deeper level as a depository of Western cultural values and artifacts (chapter 10). The text glides from classics like Walt Whitman's *Leaves of Grass* and Shakespeare's *Romeo and Juliet* to contemporary erotica like *Vox*. With its multileveled narrative and panoply of cultural objects, *The Starr Report* proves to be symptomatic of today's postmodern age.

This legal and cultural monument etches its own map of contemporary America. The issues it addresses participate in broader and more general discourses. Gender, sexuality, disability, politics: they are all hopelessly intertwined as the president's "body politic" and his "body natural" become the targets of the *Report* in a wide-ranging cultural and textual masquerade. It is not just one president's two bodies but America's multiple bodies that are addressed, as *The Starr Report* discloses more about contemporary America than America would want to reveal.

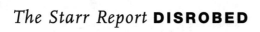

The Starr Report **DISROBED**

1

THE MIGHTY MORPHIN REPORT

Kenneth W. Starr has become synonymous with a volume that bears his name, *The Starr Report*. This *Report* was a national sensation even before its appearance. But *The Starr Report* itself has a changing nature, and the packaging and covers of the various editions affect the nature of the text, often telling their own stories. In this day of global culture, this quintessentially American product has traveled the world, taking on new identities in the process. Not surprisingly, analysis reveals that despite its numerous identities, the *Report*, no matter what its form, still serves as a powerful commentary on America.

Readers need to remember that *The Starr Report* is a constructed text. It is culled from volumes of material collected by Judge Starr's office, the Office of the Independent Counsel, in the process of its in-depth investigation of President Clinton. The material spans testimony, electronic mail, photographs, objects, and so on. Even the most superficial reading of the testimonies presented in the supplementary volumes and appendixes to the referral will show that the author(s) of the *Report* selected their details from a large variety of data and occasionally divergent versions of the same information. The chosen materials have then been encased in a veneer of prose that turns the text into the manufactured product that it is, a product for the consumer society in which all Americans live. The packaging and distribution of this product become then just as important as its contents.

Like any product intended for consumption, the existence of the *Report* preceded its appearance, providing the *Report* with a gestation period. The world heard about the report before seeing it or reading it. But it is not only the gestation period that is important. The delivery is as well. (The corporal images are by no means accidental.) The awaited *Report* finally came into the world with maximum visibility and much fanfare as Americans were shown two vans delivering thirty-six boxes of materials from Kenneth Starr's office. Yet the public was not told how big these boxes were. And anyone familiar with the compilation of materials for promotion at American universities knows that they can be arranged with more or less bulk. The printed version of Judge Starr's documentation, prepared by the House of Representatives, takes up less than two feet on a library shelf. And much of the material included, like excerpts from periodicals, is of dubious legal relevance. The overt strategy here is to legitimize this text with the immense quantity of weight behind it. The method is metaphorical: physical weight for intellectual, legal, and political weight.

But a form of mobility is also created: is *The Starr Report* that these vans delivered the several-hundred-page document that would bear this title, or is it the boxes and boxes of supplementary materials? The news had initially concealed the fact that the two vans had delivered not one copy of Kenneth Starr's materials but two. Starr's office had proudly given birth to twins. And these twins were far from being stillbirths. Instead, precocious as they were, they went forth and multiplied. From the Internet through newspapers to books, the twins cloned themselves. Savvy consumers know, however, that the quality of a product, its attraction, certainly begins with the packaging.

The *Report* in its newspaper appearance is perhaps the most fragile. Starr's text in the newspaper becomes subordinated to the newspaper itself, its identity subsumed to that of the newspaper. Newspaper print is normally small, and a newspaper is normally large. These two factors work together to create a reality whose effect is the shrinking of the mass that is the *Report*. More important is the limited life of the *Report* in that form. Once read, a newspaper is most often discarded, turning the *Report* in the process into a digestible object that once consumed can be thrown away and, most importantly, forgotten.

That is, unless the newspaper has an electronic life. In this day of electronic communications and in a period when electronic publishing is becoming a reality, there are crucial differences between a text as a bound entity, as a book, and a text in electronic format. It is not only the superficial aspect that changes but the reading process as well.

In its electronic manifestation, Kenneth Starr's work is a most fascinating creature. It is veritably a product of its age, able to live with and in contemporary media at the same time that it seems to have been created with those media in mind. In its electronic form, the *Report* can be manipulated simultaneously both by Internet providers and by Internet consumers.

The providers play interesting games with the *Report*, games that call attention to the protean quality of this contemporary document. The text can be commented on, directing the reader to one or another interpretation of the material. The text can be illustrated or not. "Investigating the President," CNN's banner title, is a provocative example of this. A close-up shows Clinton's eyes on the right side of the banner at the same time that two busts, one of Monica Lewinsky facing the reader and another of what looks like Kenneth Starr looking away from her and toward the president, grace the left side of the banner. This interactive form of CNN boasts a column on the lefthand side of the screen that features other links, running from headline news and politics through weather and books to travel and food. What a way to digest *The Starr Report*. The commodity aspect of the text is aggravated by the advertisements that proliferate on the Web and normally appear in other banners on the screen. The CNN site is only one of many locations on the Internet where one can browse through Starr's work in all its glory. Other sites provide news commentary. And yet others may be more sober, such as that of the Oklahoma Department of Libraries, which provides the "Report of Independent Counsel Starr" without any flourishes. There is, however, a potent warning placed directly below this title: "Note: Some of the material in this report contains graphic descriptions of sexual encounters." Most Americans know this already. By posting the warning, this particular Web site is highlighting the prurient content of *The Starr Report*.

The *Report* evolves as the material surrounding it changes and, in the process, redefines it. The ability of the Internet to help a product transform itself visually is enormous. More importantly, the appearance of the *Report* as an electronic commodity permits its morphing not only by the Internet itself but by every individual accessing the document through that medium. A font or a printing style will affect the way a text is read. On the Internet, a reader can alter the text to appear in different typefaces, with some that emphasize the more serious aspects of the document. The electronic text can be played with and divided into sections that do not have to be identical to the sections in the *Report*. One can look for given words and read only those sections that contain them. The ability to repeat the search over and over again translates into yet another way in which an individual can transform the text, by turning it into nothing but repeating segments. And this is not to speak of the capacity users have to download documents to a computer file and dissect them in any number of possible ways.

The electronic medium proves even more provocative for a work like *The Starr Report*. The bulk of the text is made up of two sections, the "Narrative" and the "Grounds" (on which more in chapter 2). Because the story in the two sections repeats itself (but not consistently, as this study will demonstrate), the electronic nature of Starr's work permits the two sections to be juxtaposed and compared more effectively.

If the electronic medium allows the text to morph, by contrast a book may not appear at first glance to be as magical. But a book has other virtues, not the least of which is accessibility to an audience that may not be at home with the world of the Web. Books are familiar products, even comforting in this familiarity. An item that can be held, pages that can be turned: a book can be admired as an independent and self-sustained object.

But there is more to a book as a cultural product. The French critic Gérard Genette, in a brilliant work, *Seuils*, discusses the other accoutrements of a text, such as the cover, the dedication, and sundry other materials that clothe a narrative and affect its reading. Genette is speaking about books. For *The Starr Report*, with its multiple editions and translations, these extratextual components, like the text itself, change as the cloning process evolves.

The American public has been blessed with multiple editions of Kenneth Starr's master work. And each edition, in its own way, is as complex a purveyor of cultural data as the next. Several English editions will be compared with a French and a German edition to see how the book crosses linguistic and cultural borders on its global journey.

The materials that Kenneth Starr amassed in his investigation of President Clinton formed part of a "Communication" from his office, transmitting "A Referral to the United States House of Representatives." The referral comes surrounded with multivolume appendixes and supplemental information. The entirety of the documents submitted to the U.S. House of Representatives are printed by the U.S. Government Printing Office. This referral is what constitutes the original version, if one may call it that, of the

Report. The subsequent printed editions of the *Report* represent reprintings of this referral, sometimes with supplementary materials.

A book cover can be as potent a purveyor of information, at once ideological and cultural, as the book itself. To "read" a book cover is to decode its images, its colors, the way the page is arranged: the entirety in the process transmitting a clear message to the reader that conveys information beyond the verbal content of the book itself.

To gauge the varieties of book covers and their ideological impact, one needs to start at the beginning, with the initial referral submitted to Congress. Printed on a beige to light-brown paper, almost the color of cardboard, the cover contains a border within which the information on the referral is transmitted. Outside the border on the top is the official label linking the document to a government agency: "105th Congress, 2d Session" sits on the left, joined by dashes to the words on the right, "House Document 105–310." Within the border are four horizontal registers. The first, flush right and in uppercase letters, reads: "Referral from Independent Counsel Kenneth W. Starr in Conformity with the Requirements of Title 28, United States Code, Section 595(c)." A short centered line separates this register from the next containing the essential information on a number of lines, all in uppercase letters, with some centered and some flush right: "Communication from Kenneth W. Starr, Independent Counsel transmitting A Referral to the United States House of Representatives filed in conformity with the requirements of Title 28, United States Code, Section 595(c)." Below this register and above the last is the American eagle, centered in the space. The last register is in a combination of upper- and lowercase letters and contains the following: "September 11, 1998. — Referred to the Committee on the Judiciary pursuant to H. Res. 525 and ordered to be printed."

Three elements stand out as one looks at this cover: the word "Communication," isolated and centered, and the words "Kenneth W. Starr, Independent Counsel," also centered but on two lines, one for the name and one for the title. This information appears in the largest uppercase print on the page.

This cover speaks the language of an official document. The light brown color of the cover paper combined with the American eagle tells the holder of the document that he or she is in contact with Uncle Sam. The only visual element on the cover is the eagle, a powerful sign that stands for the U.S. government. Notice that nowhere does the document bear the title *Report*. Outside the border, the volume is a House document. Inside the border, it is first a "Referral" (in the upper register) and then a "Communication" (in the second register); it is also something transmitted (in the second register) and then once again a "Referral" (in the second register), as well as something "Referred" (in the bottom register).

This cover does not simply speak volumes about the existence of the document as something official. It also links itself to the House of Representatives, as befits such documents. Kenneth W. Starr, as independent counsel, becomes merely the vehicle of transmission for this all-important referral. His is the power to communicate, to transmit. Nothing more, nothing less. The back cover adds no other information, simply the sales label from the Government Printing Office. The triple ownership of this volume — by the House of Representatives, the Independent Counsel, and the Government Printing Office — is also an official ownership, divided between different bodies of the political entity that is the United States government.

Starr's document begins its life as an official report. Its protean aspect is linked to this independent identity, an identity that survives not only in the printed editions but on the Internet as well. Forum, an imprint of Prima Publishing, presents its reader with a copy of *The Starr Report* that attempts to speak officialese along the lines of the Government Printing Office. A navy blue background boasts the words "The Starr Report" in big, white uppercase letters, lined up in three registers with Starr's name as the dominant register. Below this is the seal of the Department of Justice, with the eagle. And on a register below are three lines describing the document: "The Official Report of the Independent Counsel's Investigation of the President." A banner in gold with blue lettering on the top of the page features three words, in uppercase bold and separated by stars: "official, unedited, complete."

The back cover repeats that upper banner with its three words separated by stars. Then come the words of the title, "The Starr Report," below which is a blurb advertising the work. The beginning words say it all: "This is the complete, official, unabridged edition of *The Starr Report*." More material describes the impact that the volume will have, followed by a second paragraph. "Here, for the first time, you will have the opportunity to review, for yourself, all of the evidence against the president and make your own determination about the moral and legal ramifications of his actions." The name of the publisher with the Web address follows in gold and then, below and to the left, the seal of the Department of Justice.

Forum/Prima wants its reader to view its cover as the official government publication, replete with the seal of the Department of Justice, a seal that appears twice, once on the front and once on the back. The gold color recalls the light-brown cover of the House Document, published by the U.S. Government Printing Office. Notice that the word "official" occurs twice on the front cover and twice on the back cover, once in the upper banner and once in the other material. *The Starr Report* becomes "The Official Report." Of that there is no doubt.

This Forum edition draws readers into the process of judging the president. The back cover of the book takes them by the hand and addresses them with the second-person singular pronoun, attempting to seduce them into purchasing the product. "Here, for the first time," the reader is told "you will have the opportunity to review, for yourself, all of the evidence against the president." For the first time? Possibly. But it is not only an evaluation that a reader can undertake but the making of his or her "own determination about the moral and legal ramifications of his actions." In the first paragraph, the prospective buyer had already been told that here were "allegations of perjury, obstruction of justice, and abuse of power." Not only that, "the report will have a profound effect on the Clinton presidency as well as on the country and the world as a whole."

The "official" nature of the cover transcends its mere claim to being "The Official Report of the Independent Counsel's Investigation of the President" to become the means for the reader, the "you," to make a judgment on the president's actions. The name of the publisher may well follow these words, but the Department of Justice also becomes a signatory through the seal that is placed strategically below all this material. There is an urgency to this back cover, as the buyer/reader is beseeched to make a determination that includes the "moral and legal ramifications" of the president's actions. A tall order, but the assurance with which the "you" is encouraged to make this determination minimizes this mighty task.

Pocket Books takes a different tack. The cover of this mass-market paperback is quite provocative and uncovers yet another layer of signification in the packaging of *The Starr Report*. Three horizontal stripes cut the cover. A thin horizontal blue stripe on the very top is echoed by a much larger blue stripe on the bottom. Between the two blue stripes and toward the bottom third of the cover lies a red stripe. The larger blue stripe on the bottom sports in white lettering the words: "With an Introduction by Phil Kuntz." Between the top blue stripe and the red one lie the words "The Starr Report," in uppercase red letters on a white background. Then between the red stripe and second blue one appears the following: "The Independent Counsel's Complete Report to Congress on the Investigation of President Clinton." This latter is in the uppercase letters distinctive of a subtitle. The blue letters on the white background are a reverse image of the white letters on the blue background of the bottom stripe. In the middle of the thick red stripe rests the round official "Seal of the President of the United States," proudly bearing the American eagle. On the upper righthand corner of the front cover is a brown circle with jagged edges informing the potential reader/buyer that the book "includes the preliminary rebuttal from the White House." This circle looks like something pasted on the cover, although it clearly has not been.

Red, white, and blue speak to a host of patriotic ideas, not excluding the American flag. But the flag nowhere appears. Nor do the stars (with one "r" that is) that signal this flag and distinguish it from, say, the French flag or even the Dutch flag, depending on whether the stripes are horizontal or vertical.

Yet if stars are absent on this cover, such is not the case of the seal of the president of the United States. The seal, with the eagle, all in full color, is there and labeled, but the president is nowhere to be seen. The seal is a sign that more is going on with this seemingly innocuous cover whose patriotic subtext seductively beckons the buyer and reader. Surely, any red-blooded American would want to own me, the cover seems to say. Even better, since any red-blooded American would know of the sexually provocative content of the book, the cover performs another function. It dispels any hesitation a reader might have about the sexuality inside the book and foregrounds the patriotic over the sexual.

But that is not all. The words "The Starr Report" are emblazoned in uppercase red letters above the presidential seal: shades of Hester Prynne in *The Scarlet Letter*, sexual impropriety harking back to a colonial past. The president, one begins to realize, is on the cover. He is implicated by those red letters placed directly over his seal. Adultery looms large on this cover.

The back cover of the book confirms the negative assessment the buyer/reader should draw from the front. The top of the page contains a defined box that sports a lengthy quote from Kenneth Starr's "letter to Congress." It is well known that when people are confronted by a mass of information, they more easily retain the beginning and the end of it. How interesting it thus is that the last word quoted — and a word that sits alone on a line, drawing incredible attention to itself — is "impeachment." Below the box are once again those uppercase red letters: "The Starr Report." The message is clear: the reprehensible action is symbolized on the front cover and its consequence on the back. The voluminous book stands as evidence of the message its cover transmits.

Clearly, then, the iconography of book covers carries a host of ideas about *The Starr Report*, as this report changes. PublicAffairs (one word) Reports, "a member of the Perseus Books Group," flaunts yet a different cover, this one with fascinating semiotic content. Over a white background, stands a black text with the word "Starr" in larger uppercase red letters. A first register containing the words "The Starr Report" on three lines is separated from the second register by two gold-colored bars, one thinner than the other, with the thicker one facing the second register below. The second register appears in a number of lines, subdivided effectively into three visual sections. The first reads: "*The* Findings *of* Independent Counsel Kenneth W. Starr *on* President Clinton *and The* Lewinsky Affair." This text is framed by the gold-colored bar above and an identical one below. The two bars, though separated by the text in the second register, nevertheless form a visual unity, since the thicker ones face each other, at once highlighting and separating the message in the second register. The text in this second register is further visually broken by the "on" preceding "President Clinton" and the "and" preceding "The Lewinsky Affair." Reading only the block uppercase print that reaches out visually from this middle register, one gets: "Findings Independent Counsel Kenneth W. Starr" in the first section, "President Clinton" in the second section, and "Lewinsky Affair" in the third section. Below this, in yet another register separated by the gold-colored bars, is the statement "With Analysis by the Staff of *The Washington Post*."

Here, again, are the red letters of adultery. This time they are restricted to the word "Starr," completely in uppercase letters and by far the most visible word on the page. In the upper righthand corner of the cover is a red banner with gold borders containing the following words in white uppercase letters: "The Complete Text and the White House Response." The red of the banner speaks to the red of Starr's name and reinforces its message. And to the "Complete Text" of Starr's *Report* is added almost as an afterthought the "White House Response."

But what a curious arrangement is this cover with its black letters on a white background dressed by gold trim. Oddly enough, it reads like a wedding invitation. Starr invites you to the wedding of President Clinton and Monica Lewinsky, which will take place at *The Washington Post*.

This would certainly be a historic event! And, sure enough, the back cover of this volume emphasizes the historical. A long description that begins with "The Starr Report" in uppercase red letters continues with black print, the entirety on a white page. Again, the content is described as the "complete text" along with the White House response "and exclusive analysis and commentary by the Pulitzer-prize winning staff of the *Washington Post*." The reader is told that this is a "historic document," which "will become the central instrument in the House of Representatives' investigation that could lead to President Clinton's impeachment." The *Report* in this version becomes "essential reading for all citizens concerned about the fate of the presidency and our nation."

The back cover reinforces the invitational mode of the front cover. The reader is not being addressed with a pointing finger through the invasive "you" of the Forum/Prima cover. Instead, the PublicAffairs Reports edition turns the act of reading the *Report* into a function of the citizenry "concerned about the fate of the presidency and our nation." Notice the "our." The book cover sees its function as one of unifying "all citizens." There are no eagles here, no seals, nothing official: just a plea on behalf of "our nation," a powerful message, indeed.

Two of the covers analyzed mentioned the White House response to *The Starr Report*. The examination of the Pocket Books edition already called attention to the afterthought nature of the way this information is presented in the upper righthand corner of the cover. The cover presented by the PublicAffairs Reports goes further in this direction, presenting the "White House Response" in the same banner that it declares the comprehensive nature of its "Report": "The Complete Text and the White House Response." On both these covers, the White House reaction is subordinated to Starr's product.

This is not the case with another edition of the report, this one "Published by toExcel [again, one word]: The People's Press." The front cover of this particular version is distinctive and, not surprisingly, transmits yet another message. Once again, there are three registers. But these registers are different from those on the other covers. The middle register is an enormous photograph of the Capitol that takes up more than half the space and dominates it. The top register, a black background with white letters, divides its contents into four lines. The first line contains the words "The Starr Report" in uppercase letters. The second line states "Complete with," followed by the third line in uppercase, reading "The President's Rebuttals." The fourth line bears the following: "September 10th–12th, 1998." This top register is separated from the dominant photograph by a band of three colors: red, white, and blue. The bottom register, also with black background, carries the publishing information: "Published by toExcel: The People's Press." This appears in white uppercase letters but for the word "toExcel," printed in yellow.

The back cover of this edition is a black background with white print, except for the word "toExcel," in yellow. The multiparagraph speech on the back cover tells the prospective consumer about toExcel and its publishing policy. This statement is important because it addresses some of the issues already analyzed above:

> too many great ideas go unpublished because of the politics or economics of traditional publishing. . . .
>
> With the help of the Internet and the latest print on demand technology toExcel can economically publish books one at a time. . . . We believe that new thinking and new ideas need to be available to everyone, not just people with Internet access. . . . With these ideals in mind, we will endeavor to publish out of print books that should not be out of print. We will publish foreign language books heretofore available only in their native countries. We will publish academic works with small audiences. And through our People's Press, we will publish individual's [sic] and public domain books on virtually any subject [ellipses added].
>
> This report to the House of Representatives is one that we believe needs to be published. We offer it to the public at our cost as a demonstration of our commitment to publishing what the people themselves think is important . . . without editorial censure or comment.

This is followed by "information on toExcel" and how to access the Web site. The entirety is capped by a "Thank you."

To begin with the back cover, the editorial statement by toExcel engages a number of critical issues, most important of which is the Internet. The Internet is one of *The Starr Report*'s loci. ToExcel recognizes the significance of the Internet, though this importance is not directly linked to *The Starr Report*. At the same time, access to the Internet is highlighted, as toExcel claims to address precisely this issue.

Once the publishing philosophy is delineated, toExcel can move directly to the book at hand. Notice how the volume is identified: "This report to the

House of Representatives." This is not Kenneth Starr's *Report*, not the *Report* of the independent counsel. This is the "report to the House of Representatives." The elimination of any reference to Starr on this back cover is not accidental. His presence is diluted between the reference to the House along with the allusions to the "public" and the "people." The mention of "editorial censure or comment" is extremely provocative in this context, intimating that there has been censure in the case of the "report to the House."

All this rhetoric is compounded with the use of the first-person plural pronouns "we" and "our." There is always an inherent relationship between the first-person pronoun and the second-person pronoun, the first-person usage invariably implying the existence of a second person, the "you." And, sure enough, the text on the back cover graciously ends with the words "Thank you." The "you" here is, of course, the prospective reader. This "you" is radically different from the "you" on the Forum/Prima back cover. There, the "you" was isolated without the reassuring presence of the first-person plural pronoun. That "you" had the task of making a determination on the president's actions. Its obligation was much more serious.

The deemphasis on Starr on the back cover of the book is compounded by the emphasis on the U.S. Congress on the front cover. What looms large on the front is the image of the Capitol, the building that houses both the Senate and the House of Representatives. To make sure that the reader of this volume gets the point, the top register gives equal billing to "The Starr Report" and "The President's Rebuttals," both of which appear on their own lines and are printed in identically sized lettering.

Unlike the other covers, that of the People's Press features the name Starr only once, in the words "The Starr Report." Nowhere is there any indication that he is the independent counsel, as he is labeled on the other editions. By ignoring this function, the People's Press cover highlights the overcoding of the other covers. There, not only did one get "The Starr Report" both on the fronts and backs of the covers, but one was provided, in addition, with Kenneth W. Starr's official title, "Independent Counsel."

The absence of an overcoded independent counsel helps the People's Press to transmit both its verbal and its visual messages. The two parties in the controversy are equal, it argues. This is in opposition to the two editions that included the White House response as a mere addendum and not as an equal player. One concludes that the United States Congress, there through its physical building, will determine the outcome of "The Starr Report" and

"The President's Rebuttals," a determination the Forum/Prima edition asked individuals to make.

The English-language editions of *The Starr Report* obviously carry more or less the same verbal content within their covers. It is their external packaging, the iconography of their covers, that provides them with the power, both visual and verbal, to convey an ideological message. And this message, true to the dictates of a consumer society, does not have to be overt. Rather, its strength comes precisely from what may appear initially to be its seeming transparency and almost banal nature. No matter the content, however, the message remains deeply American.

Crossing linguistic borders sets the American signifiers in new cultural contexts. The examination of two different covers will reveal the visual and verbal languages of *The Starr Report* as it ventures beyond its home territory.

The German translation of *The Starr Report*, *Der Starr-Report*, advertises itself as the unabridged German edition. The cover of this edition is divided into segments. The top of the page is a composite photograph with the smiling face of Monica Lewinsky filling the left third. The remainder is occupied by President Clinton. While she smiles at the reader, lips in red, white teeth exposed, Clinton holds his right hand on his face, looking away from Lewinsky and shielding his eyes from both her and the reader/buyer. Clinton and Lewinsky are superimposed on the White House, replete with flowers. His dark jacket and her dark hair merge and become a transparent unity through which appear the columns of the White House. The "Der" of "Der Starr-Report" sits between Clinton and Lewinsky on the flowers, in large, red uppercase letters. The hyphenated words "Starr-Report," also in large, red uppercase letters, fill almost the entirety of the width of the cover directly under Clinton and Lewinsky. Below these hyphenated words sit two centered lines: "The Unique Document of the Times on the Scandal in the White House." Below this verbal register are two more items. On the right is a small photograph of Lewinsky hugging Clinton. Once again, she faces the reader/buyer while Clinton has his back turned. To the left of the photograph, and in an oval-shaped red space, are the white words: "Unabridged German Translation," and below, the name of the publisher.

This German cover, by stretching the visual borders of its American cousins, has redefined *The Starr Report* and set it in a non-American context. The words "Starr Report" are there, identifying the product for German readers. But unlike the American covers, the German one labels the events in the

White House as a "scandal." And to make the scandal more lurid, the two parties are visually represented for the edification of the reader/buyer: Clinton and Lewinsky. But notice that they are not identified. A German reader is expected to know who they are. Even more provocative are the poses the two take in the photographs. In both, Lewinsky's face is clearly visible, as she smiles. Clinton, on the other hand, does not show his face. In the lower picture, his back faces the viewer, as the young woman's hand on his shoulder draws him away, reinforcing the sense that he has turned his back not only to the viewer but also to the world. In the top picture, his right hand largely shields his face. Although Clinton takes up more of the composite picture, Lewinsky nevertheless dominates in a close-up: as her eyes look squarely at the viewer, he averts his gaze. While the young woman expresses happiness and joy, the older man hides his face and literally hangs his head in shame. The White House, with its transparent covering of the two figures, looks almost as if it has been shrouded in black. The iconography of the cover is echoed on the spine. The red letters "Der Starr-Report" are wedged between two large photos taken from the top register of the front cover, but in mirror image: Lewinsky's close-up is over the text, the shame-faced Clinton below it.

What is marketed here is the "scandal" in the White House. It is not the independent counsel's referral. It is not anything attached to patriotism. It is purely and simply scandal. And lest the buyer be unaware of the major characters in the scandal, they are there to titillate the prospective reader. The red of Starr's name, which spelled out a different message in the American editions, is here diluted by the red lipstick Lewinsky wears as well as by the red flowers gracing the front of the White House. For a non-American and non-Puritan audience, this cover reads flashy rather than adulterous. The hints at impropriety are instead transmitted by the powerful shame in Clinton's body language and the word "scandal." The sensationalism of the German front cover is softened somewhat by a back that appeals to a more serious kind of curiosity. "Millions of people have clicked on to the Internet, in order to get to know the complete wording of The Starr Report," it begins. Yet the German text goes on to suggest that many such readers might not have the requisite English to appreciate "the juristic fine points of the Report," a *Report* that shows "the methods and powers of the Special Counsel" while exposing the daily life of the president and his advisers. The twelve-line text ends with the reinvocation of the "document of the times" and the proposition that the *Report* will define the meaning of the Clinton administration.

Interestingly enough, a French-language edition (published in Belgium) plays similar games. An enormous American flag forms the background for the Francophone cover on which the various elements take their place. On the top of the cover and over the stars of the flag, sit the words "Clinton vs Lewinsky" to the left. To the right and superimposed on the flag is Monica Lewinsky, looking as though she is bursting from the stars of the flag. She is wearing some sort of jacket whose white merges with the white stripes of the American flag. Below this top register and dominating the rest of the cover is Bill Clinton. He is standing at a lectern, holding papers in his two hands, mouth slightly open, looking as though he is about to deliver a speech. His wedding ring is ever so slightly visible on his left hand. Directly on the left side of his torso is the remainder of the title words in white. The first line reads "Kenneth" and the second, "Starr." This name, in large letters, is underlined. Under the name on two lines are the words: "The Report That Is Shaking America." In the bottom right-hand corner is a red triangle with white letters announcing: "Complete Text." On the left of the cover and sideways is the name of the publisher.

The back cover of the French version is as eloquent as the front. The American flag from the front cover comes around the left side of the back and stops about a quarter into the space, the rest of which is composed of white background with black print and black-and-white pictures: three pictures at the top, three at the bottom. These small pictures show the faces and a bit of clothing here and there. Each of the characters is identified with a name and a description under his or her picture. The top pictures show, left to right, Kenneth Starr, The Prosecutor; Linda Tripp, The Spy; and Vernon Jordan, The Negotiator. The bottom pictures, again from left to right, show: David Kendall, The Lawyer; Sidney Blumenthal, The Aide; and Betty Currie, The Faithful One. Betty Currie's name has been gallicized to Bettie Curie, promoting her to the family of distinguished French atomic scientists. The top three have smiles on their faces, the bottom three are not so happy. Between these two registers of visual materials lies a verbal text that will sell the volume, promising the complete biographies of all the actors in this "politico-mediatic saga." Here, it says, are the detailed summaries of the sexual encounters "of the President of the United States, all the events, hour by hour, in the heart of the White House." The consumer is told that this work reads "like a novel."

Between the verbal text and the bottom register of photographs are choice quotations in italics. "I have lied all my life" (Monica Lewinsky, *Newsweek*). "I have cheated people, including my wife" (Bill Clinton, CNN). "I owe the truth to the American people, the whole truth, nothing but the truth. And I must find it without any fear" (Kenneth Starr).

If the German cover still had some pretense to being close to its American cousins, at least by calling the *Report Der Starr-Report*, the French translation makes no such pretense. The American flag is the dominant background for all the iconography, both verbal and visual. It is the medium that transmits the most basic of the messages here: this is America. But this is not the America of the White House, as it was on the German edition. From the front cover to the back cover, the visual and verbal languages of the French edition speak of melodrama with its cast of stock characters. Indeed, the French version takes this idea further on the inside of the volume, when it replaces Starr's "Table of Names" with "Un Casting de Rêve": a dream cast.

But what a melodrama! This is a melodrama wrapped in the symbol of America, its flag. Americans will surely recognize the photograph of Lewinsky as being of a later period than the one that graces the German edition: gone are the bangs and gone is the longer hair. This Monica Lewinsky looks much more serious. Her lipstick has become darker, her mouth is closed as she looks away from the viewer. Clinton is the one with the mouth open, looking as though he is about to speak. The title tells it all: "Clinton vs Lewinsky." The drama unfolds and centers on an adversarial relationship between two individuals, Clinton and Lewinsky. Kenneth Starr is there, but much smaller. He is the author here not of a document entitled "The Starr Report" or "Der Starr-Report" but of a hybrid entity titled "The Report That Is Shaking America." Note the use of the present tense, which, while common in French, nevertheless transmits the sense that this is a process that is continuing, at least at the time of the publication of the work. And by restricting the action of the verb to a specific locus, America, the verbal message keeps the "shaking" at bay. No global effects from "Clinton vs Lewinsky" on this cover.

The dominance of the visual on the front of the French cover is such that it can influence the back cover. The verbal text here is nothing compared to the six photographs. The cover effects a social balancing act. Two men and one woman at the top, two men and one woman at the bottom. One man, Kenneth Starr, wearing glasses at the top. One man, Sidney Blumenthal, wearing glasses on the bottom. One African American on the top. One African American on the bottom.

These pictures, combined with the choice sayings on the back cover, transport the *Report* from one cultural domain to another. In the American context, Starr's referral started from its government state to evolve into other editions, all of which emphasized the seriousness of the project. The French-language edition does no such thing. The work "reads like a novel," the back cover proclaims. But, in fact, this is not a novel. And, most assuredly, anyone who has read the entirety of the *Report* will know that it does not read like a novel. The photographs on the back cover, coupled with the one-word descriptions under the names, turn the individuals in question into characters in a melodrama. Each will play his or her defined role in the story.

The scandal of the German cover has been transformed into an adversarial relationship in the French-language edition. Indeed, the "scandal" in the White House of the German book also takes on larger proportions in the Belgian edition, as the "Report" in question shakes America. This is a much larger, more engulfing claim. The melodramatic aspect of the French translation redefines not only the "scandal" of the German rendition but the American book covers as well. The lower-cultural referents (scandal and melodrama) of these European editions contrast with the patriotic highmindedness of their American cousins. This difference is reinforced by the fact that both translations were rush jobs, linguistically clumsy and omitting or failing to translate major sections of the *Report*.

The Starr Report turns out to be an extremely malleable product. Yet these constantly shifting forms of the *Report*, from the dual delivery vans through the Internet to American and international book covers, represent so many packagings of the same story. Each packaging is an attempt on the part of different individuals and organizations in this fundamentally political process to control the *Report*, to define it in different ways.

At the same time, to dress in alternate clothing is to take on a different identity, to masquerade. As the independent counsel's referral becomes a melodrama, it effects a stunning change in identity. But this masquerade, no matter how radical, does not detract from the essence of the *Report* as an American product, tied in a most fundamental way to the country and the culture that gave it birth.

2

ORGANIZATION AS OBSESSION

The Starr Report may be subject to permutations and transformations. It may appear in book form. It may surface in an electronic version. It may travel the globe. But the story it tells is the same no matter how it is clothed. The plot is by now familiar to anyone who cares enough to know it. A middle-aged married man meets a younger woman and they engage in improper sexual activity, including oral sex, phone sex, and anal sex. The two exchange gifts and carry on this secret relationship. But after the demise of their affair, the ill winds of fortune blow their way, and their private liaison becomes public.

A banal enough story, perhaps. Except that the middle-aged married man happens to be the president of the United States, Bill Clinton, and the younger woman, initially a White House intern, Monica Lewinsky. As for the winds of ill fortune, they are embodied in that Aeolus of the 1990s, Independent Counsel Kenneth W. Starr. His investigation leads to *The Starr Report*, this chameleonlike textual creature.

The ability of the *Report* to mutate is related to more complicated aspects of the text. The most visible of these is its organization, the way in which its building blocks are put together. Names, dates, and notes: these are but a few of the elements that this chapter will investigate. But more significant than the components themselves are the techniques hidden behind the composition of the work, techniques that turn the *Report* into a text of obsession. Obsession is understood here (setting aside its psychoanalytical implications) as something showing the marks of being dominated by an inordinate fixation that escapes rational control. This obsession manifests itself not only in the organization of Judge Starr's referral but also in both the narration and the technique of repetition so privileged in this convoluted text. Repetition, of course, is natural — even inevitable — in all narrative and argument. In *The Starr Report*, however, it goes far beyond what is necessary to deliver the text's points. This is true of the most common form of repetition, that of events, as well as the reiteration of formulae.

The long document that parades as *The Starr Report* is a compilation of materials drawn from the voluminous array of evidence collected by the Office of the Independent Counsel, onto which has been grafted a narrative of sorts. This the reader knows already. It is the way in which the *Report* lays out its parts that is provocative (the names of these parts will be capitalized and surrounded with quotation marks). Beginning with a chronology of "Key Dates" and a "Table of Names," the *Report* continues with an "Introduction." Following this, the reader faces the two major sections of the *Report*, the "Narrative" and the "Acts that May Constitute Grounds for an Impeachment." These two sections will be referred to in the following analysis as the "Narrative" and the "Grounds." Enriching these two sections is a set of "Notes." The entirety of the text is sealed, in some of the printed versions, by a "Conclusion."

The structural principle that underlies this distinctive organization could be characterized as "There you go, again, Mr. President," unless it should be "There you go, again, Judge Starr." Or to use a technologically obsolete comparison, *The Starr Report* reads like a broken record with a scratch that keeps sending the needle back to the beginning. The "Key Dates" succinctly carry the reader through the entire scandal. Then "The Table of Names" evokes the same events, in a nonchronological presentation. And the events are evoked again, in largely chronological order, in the "Introduction." The "Narrative" begins at the beginning and continues to the end, chronologically speaking, only to be followed by the "Grounds," which goes over substantially the same material, but from a topical perspective. This is an obsessive organization.

The "Key Dates" surface as two columns. The one on the left of the page displays the dates, whereas the one on the right sets out the events in telegraphic form. The dates begin in November 1992 with Clinton's election to the American presidency and end on September 9, 1998, the day on which the Office of the Independent Counsel submits its referral to Congress. Note that the beginning is simply a month followed by a year, whereas the submission of the referral is attached to a specific date in the month of September. This is hardly irrelevant. A quick perusal of the "Key Dates" reveals that the majority of dates are specified with the month and the day.

The first event to which a specific day is attached is that of November 15, 1995. On this date, the "President begins sexual relationship with Lewinsky." This is clearly a major development, the date singling itself out as the first one with full specificity in the chain of "Key Dates." But even more interesting, there is no alleged event here, no supposed accusation of impropriety. Yet the certainty regarding the sexual relationship is attached to a specific date. The "Key Dates" stand on their own, depicting these events as though their protagonists were isolated from other world or political events. Hence, for example, President Clinton is elected and reelected to office, has the *Jones* lawsuit filed against him, has his "sexual relationship" with Monica Lewinsky. The political universe that the president of the United States normally inhabits is largely missing, as a major world leader becomes but a pawn of sexual-textual games. In the "Key Dates," William Jefferson Clinton has no existence other than that bestowed on him by the "sexual relationship."

This seemingly innocuous beginning is certainly designed to impress the reader. The dates lined up with the events look quite authoritative, especially ending as they do with the submission of the Referral to Congress "pursuant to 28 U.S.C. 595(c)." The discourse defines itself as official, and *The Starr Report* is on its way.

But the dates are not enough to begin this game of political cat and mouse. The "Table of Names" plays a role here as well. This list of names functions as a parallel to the "Key Dates." It boasts two columns: to the left is a name and to the right a title and/or a description of the individual's position. The inquisitive reader will surely wish to count the names that will presumably surface in *The Starr Report*. The cast of characters boasts 153 individuals, from "The Principals" and "The First Family," through the "Presidential Aides/ Advisors/Assistants," "Other White House Personnel," "Department of Defense Employees," "Monica Lewinsky's Friends/Family/Acquaintances," "Monica Lewinsky's New York Employment Contacts," and the "Secret Service," and finally to "Lawyers and Judges," the "Media," "Foreign Dignitaries," and "Other." This list bespeaks thoroughness. After all, here are the members of Monica Lewinsky's entourage and a list of lawyers and judges that should impress any red-blooded American.

Certainly overwhelming but not necessarily accurate. Striking at first glance is the fact that this list of names stands in sharp contrast to the individuals who appear in the "Key Dates." There, in alphabetical order, were Betty Currie, President Clinton, Monica Lewinsky, Paula Jones, Kenneth Starr, and Judge Wright. From six major players in the chronological background, the list inflates to 153 actors who should supposedly perform on the stage of *The Starr Report*.

All is not as it would appear, however. This cast of thousands may impress the reader, but all the characters are not given roles in this drama. Some surface but once, others never. Three names chosen at random will illustrate the precarious nature of this list of names. Everyone knows that Chelsea Clinton is the daughter of President Clinton and Hillary Rodham Clinton. So it would seem essential that she should be listed in the "Table of Names" as she will surely be in the *Report*. But, in fact, Chelsea's name is completely absent from Starr's text. The Clinton daughter appears only once in the entire text, and without a name, as an individual who is ill and by whose side the President must stay. Chelsea's presence in the "Table of Names" speaks to the sacred nuclear unit that is the "Family" and of whose disruption Clinton and Lewinsky are guilty.

Two other names will illuminate the artificial nature of the "Table of Names" in *The Starr Report*: Ron Brown and Yitzak Rabin. Ron Brown, identified as "Former Commerce Secretary" and listed under "Other," appears but once in the *Report*. Monica Lewinsky tells that she had asked the President "if he was doing okay with Ron Brown's death." The well-informed reader will surely remember the tragic death of Ron Brown, but *The Starr Report* does not shed any light on this issue for the reader whose memory might be failing. As for Rabin, identified as "Former Prime Minister of Israel" (a questionable appellation, since Rabin was assassinated while in office), he may be listed under the category of "Foreign Dignitaries," but that does not keep him from being completely absent in the text. Rabin's place on the list (combined with his absence in the text) contrasts ironically with the fact that Palestinian Authority Chairman, Yasser Arafat, who is in the text of the *Report*, is absent from the "Table of Names." An accident, or would an Israeli Prime Minister be a more damning reference than the much more controversial head of the PLO?

This tantalizing game of peekaboo with the names is but another ruse on the part of *The Starr Report* to enrich the text and broaden its political impact.

The presence of all these figures might convince a gullible reader that Clinton's indiscretions have had an effect beyond the American public. More importantly, the "Table of Names" at the beginning of the text calls attention to an aspect of *The Starr Report* that will emerge repeatedly throughout the subsequent analysis: that of a masquerade. The names hint ever so gently at this notion: things are not at all what they seem to be.

Onomastic games do not end here. Chapter 9 below elucidates the broader gender games inherent in name-calling in the *Report*. For the moment, however, the list of names opening the text is what stands out. The 153 names stretch from the personal to the legal. The various lawyers and judges are named, including the attorney for Betty Currie, Linda Tripp's former attorney, a former "Deputy White House Counsel," and so on. Yet oddly missing from this list is the coterie of attorneys, legal figures, and other support staff swirling around the Office of the Independent Counsel (with the exception of Robert Bittman, "Deputy Independent Counsel"). The name of Kenneth Starr does not grace the list, and perhaps it should not since he is the authoritative voice behind the *Report*. But the absence of almost all the members of the oic is as eloquent, if not more eloquent, than the presence of the other names.

There are certainly more powerful ways for the Office of the Independent Counsel to make itself visible in the *Report*. And this is accomplished through narration. Part of what makes *The Starr Report* the convoluted text that it is are the verbal acrobatics in narration coupled with the different voices that surface in the text. Kenneth Starr's book boasts a multiplicity of narrative voices. Not only does the reader encounter the interspersed first-person narration by Monica Lewinsky, but he or she also hears other characters, such as Bill Clinton and Betty Currie, to name but two, speaking occasionally in the first person. This is to be expected, of course.

Far more interesting is the narrative voice of the Office of the Independent Counsel itself. At times, this appears as "this Office," at others, it is as "the oic." "This Office" personalizes the text and makes it almost self-referential. Even more provocative is the emergence of Kenneth W. Starr himself as a quasi-independent character. When Attorney General Reno petitions the Special Division of the United States Court of Appeals for the District of Columbia Circuit, it is "to expand the jurisdiction of Independent Counsel Kenneth W. Starr." This appearance removes, as it were, Kenneth W. Starr from the text of *The Starr Report* and transforms him from the putative author into simply another legal figure who happens to be involved in the activities the *Report* is outlining.

But it is when the text of Kenneth Starr speaks in the first-person plural that questions arise. There are numerous times when the "we" appears or when "our" surfaces. In explaining the details of the referral, the *Report* informs its readers: "We next set forth a series of 'Document Supplements.'" Or, again, "we urge review of the full transcripts of the testimony cited below."

Who is this "we," and what is the meaning of the first-person-plural voice? In fact, more is at stake than simply a multiplicity of narrative voices. The "we" (and the subsequent "our") creates a basic sense of corporative sentiment, of a tightly knit group of like-minded individuals who can speak in the first-person plural. The use of this pronoun demonstrates a unity and a basic solidarity in the positions enunciated or the actions performed.

The legal corporation behind *The Starr Report* then remains largely nameless. Its namelessness also has the additional advantage of rendering it genderless. The reader never discovers if the "we" refers to males, females, or a combination of the two. The force behind this association means that the group can be effectively pitted against the evil forces emanating from the sexual escapades of President Clinton and Monica Lewinsky, as the nameless narrators undertake the description of the encounters. This is not to say that other examples of "we" do not exist. There is the "we" of Clinton's attorney, David Kendall. But, in this case, the name is attached to the "we" in a conclusive manner. The "we" of the Starr team is pervasive, unidentified, and disturbing in its textual frequency.

This first-person-plural narrator, who surfaces at odd times in the text, is a reminder of the complexity of narrative voices in *The Starr Report*. The first-person-plural narrator is there in the "Introduction" to the referral and in the "Grounds," the more legally minded section of the *Report*. Nevertheless, and most often, the narrator in the *Report* appears as a third-person narrator, seemingly objective and outside the action. But a sophisticated reader always remembers, of course, that narrators are never innocent participants or observers in a text. Rather, they can manipulate or hijack a text to their own end.

This extraordinary manipulation will become quite evident in the detailed analysis of the sexual encounter with the blue dress (chapter 6 below). But the crafty third-person narrator in the *Report* is ever present and always willing to go the extra mile to direct the narrative. To take but one example (though others could be adduced), one of the sections in the "Grounds" spells out Sidney Blumenthal's testimony. An "Assistant to the President," Blumenthal asks Clinton to "explain alleged answering machine messages (a detail mentioned in press reports)." The president answers Mr. Blumenthal by saying that "the call he made to Ms. Lewinsky relating to Betty's brother was the 'only one he could remember.'" So far so good. But the narrator will immediately strike back. "That was false: The President and Ms. Lewinsky talked often on the phone, and the subject matter of the calls was memorable." One could argue that the narrator has the right to make a judgment about the veracity of Mr. Clinton's answer. But the same narrator states that "the subject matter of the calls was memorable" without any attribution to a specific source. In fact, the narrator simply kidnaps the narrative and delivers that testimony on his or her own authority, interpreting the material in the process. That the calls should be "memorable" becomes attributable to that narrator and no one else. It is as though he or she were eavesdropping on the conversations between Clinton and Lewinsky.

It is ultimately the narrator, be it he or she in the third or first person, who controls the narrative. And what a complex narrative is that of *The Starr Report*. The separation of the story into the "Narrative" and the "Grounds" is just a preliminary step for a convoluted text that is constantly being split and partitioned into segments. True, there is a chronological development, at least in the "Narrative," as the reader moves from event to event. But the narrative flow is continually interrupted as the work is consistently divided and subdivided into fragments, each of which is labeled and ends up being quasi-self-sustained.

Yet despite this intricate arrangement and order, all is not well with *The Starr Report*. First of all, the complicated outline with its intricate system of divisions and subdivisions is not identical in the "Narrative" and the "Grounds," showing minor discrepancies as one progresses deeper and deeper into the text. It could be argued — and perhaps correctly, though that is open to debate — that the reader is looking at two different sorts of texts and the *Report* is under no obligation to be completely consistent.

More disturbing is the fact that this overly complex organization provides the reader with a false sense of security and order. The outline that partitions the text into more and more descending categories calls up a scientific association, a rigorous system of organization of material: order, hierarchy, mastery, control. The only flaw in this system is precisely that it is not error-free.

Thus it is that in chapter 12 of the "Narrative," "December 19, 1997–January 4, 1998: The Subpoena," the section labels appear as follows:

A. December 19: Ms. Lewinski is subpoenaed
B. December 22: Meeting with Vernon Jordan
C. December 22: First meeting with Francis Carter
D. December 23: Clinton Denials to Paula Jones
E. December 28: Final Meeting with the President
E. December 28: Concealment of Gifts
D. December 31: Breakfast with Vernon Jordan
E. January 4: The Final Gift

While the dates and incidents follow in correct order, the letter labels do not. "E" follows "D" as it should but is then followed by another "E," after which the alphabet goes backward to "D" (the second one) and then forward again to yet a third "E." Clearly, the narrator lost track of the organization here, a lapse that is present in the original "Communication" to the House of Representatives and printed by the U.S. Government Printing Office. One of the other editions noticed this discrepancy and appropriately labeled it with a "*sic.*"

Of course, no one is perfect. And *The Starr Report* is there to demonstrate, in more ways than one, that that adage is absolutely correct. The mislabeled outline sections are only one sign that this tortured text ran away from its narrator. There are also section labels that do not reflect what is in those sections. In chapter 13 of the "Narrative," "January 5–January 16, 1998: The Affidavit," section K is entitled "January 15: The Isikoff Call." On Thursday, January 15, 1998, Betty Currie, according to her testimony, receives a call from *Newsweek's* Michael Isikoff. He wanted to know about courier receipts "reflecting items sent by Ms. Lewinsky to the White House." Betty Currie calls Vernon Jordan and seeks his advice for her response. Betty Currie's "concern" is confirmed by Jordan in his testimony. The narrator proceeds swiftly from material related to the Isikoff call to other matters that are completely unrelated, such as a recorded conversation on the same day, January 15, between Monica Lewinsky and Linda Tripp, in which "Ms. Lewinsky tried to persuade Ms. Tripp to lie by telling her that others planned to lie." In the process, Lewinsky states "that she did not think the President would 'slip up' at his deposition because she was not a 'big issue' like Gennifer Flowers and Paula Jones." From there, the narrator jumps to the testimony of one of Monica Lewinsky's friends, Natalie Ungvari, about Lewinsky's being implicated in the *Jones* case.

Under one label, "January 15: The Isikoff Call," the narrator has presented a smorgasbord of materials. True, Isikoff is there at the beginning of the section. But no sooner is he disposed of than the narrator moves to a telephone conversation that takes place on the same day. This might be understandable, but it is not excusable, given the pretensions of rigor in *The Starr Report*, since that conversation about lying is not related to the Isikoff call about courier receipts. But then that conversation, by a process of association, leads to Natalie Ungvari's testimony. The reader is now several levels removed from the Isikoff call that is parading as the unifying element for the entire section, which, after all, bears that title. Lest it appear that *The Starr Report* is being falsely accused of disorganization, the information presented will speak for itself. The "Note" appended to Ungvari's contribution in the text reveals the source for her statements, namely, her testimony to the grand jury on March 19, 1998, approximately two months after the Isikoff call of January 15, 1998.

The reader can certainly find reasons for the wealth of information presented here. Chronology plays a role, since both phone calls occurred on the same day. But association does as well, since that is the principle linking the call between Tripp and Lewinsky with Ungvari's testimony. Yet these reasons do not answer the fundamental questions. Is the narrator of *The Starr Report* so overwhelmed with facts and data that he or she desperately attempts to find linking principles that will allow the textual merger of different sorts of materials? Or is the narrator so obsessive that he or she must be certain to include every little detail, every little fact, out of fear that the reader might find the evidence not strong enough to warrant the impeachment of the president of the United States? Or is the narrator such a muddy thinker that he or she moves from fact to fact without much concern for the integrity of the narrative?

Another segment in the "Narrative" may help elucidate some of these questions. Section C of chapter 10 ("November 1997: Growing Frustration") bears the dramatic title: "November 13: The Zedillo Visit." "On Thursday, November 13," the section begins, "while Ernesto Zedillo, the President of Mexico, was in the White House, Ms. Lewinsky met very briefly with President Clinton in the private study." Exit President Zedillo and enter Monica Lewinsky and her visit, which she herself described as a "hysterical escapade." This "escapade" occurs after numerous attempts to see the president, involving phone calls to Betty Currie and notes to Bill Clinton. The two-page narration of this segment includes quotations from Lewinsky's notes to Clinton. The visit finally occurs, but not before a dramatic interlude in which Betty Currie informs the already-impatient Lewinsky that the president was out playing golf, in response to which Lewinsky "went ballistic." And if this verbal drama were not enough, more is to follow. Lewinsky is told by Betty Currie to wait for the president's return from the Army-Navy Golf Course in her car, but Lewinsky arrives at the White House only to find the car locked and has to wait in the rain. Eventually, Currie meets Lewinsky in the parking lot, and the two of them make a "bee-line" for the White House, "sneaking up the back stairs to avoid other White House employees." Lewinsky leaves gifts for the president and waits for him in the Oval Office Study. When he finally arrives, "they were alone for only a minute or two." In addition to giving him a gift, she "also showed him an email describing the effect of chewing Altoid mints before performing oral sex. Ms. Lewinsky was chewing Altoids at the time, but the President replied that he did not have enough time for oral sex. They kissed, and the President rushed off for a State Dinner with President Zedillo."

From A (Altoid mints) to Z (Zedillo), this incident is a masterful display of narrative deception. A reader could read and reread the section to try — in vain, one might add — to answer the question of why it is labeled "The Zedillo Visit." The president of Mexico may well open the segment, in the same way that he closes it, but his visit is nothing more than a stage prop, a curtain, in front of which the events involving Clinton, Currie, and Lewinsky unfold. The text does not reveal what Zedillo is doing in the White House or what he might be discussing with President Clinton. The political content and implications of the visit are completely absent. What does Zedillo have to do with the golf game? The reader does not hear whether he accompanied the president to the Army-Navy Golf Course. What does Zedillo have to do with Lewinsky's attempts to see the president? Or better still, what does Zedillo have to do with Lewinsky waiting in the rain? At most, one could say that the orality of the Altoid mints (both because they are being chewed by Lewinsky and because they refer to oral sex) links to the eventual dinner at which the president will be eating, an oral activity par excellence. (Orality looms large in *The Starr Report*.) At the same time, the Zedillo segment displays an interesting mixture of sex and politics, as President Clinton moves from an offer of oral sex that he rebuffs to a state dinner with a visiting head of state. But to name Zedillo and label the section in his honor is, at best, misleading.

The same phenomenon occurs with Yitzak Rabin, whose name incidentally appears next to that of Ernesto Zedillo in the section on "Foreign Dignitaries" in the "Table of Names." Remember that Rabin is completely absent from *The Starr Report*. The presence of these two world leaders, one absent and the other simply a stage prop, must be seen in the same light: as an attempt on the part of the *Report* to link the sexual encounters of an American president to larger global political issues, with which they apparently have no link whatsoever. Setting the tawdry escapades in the context of state visits renders them even more ignominious. These superficial allusions to politics also add a certain veneer to Starr's *Report*, a veneer designed to add respectability to the text, in an attempt to transport it from its American setting onto a more international stage.

These narrative disjunctions, these literary bumps, should serve to remind the reader that *The Starr Report* is a constructed text, some of whose parts fit well together and some not. And as a constructed text, it tells more about itself at times than it does about its purported subjects, the relationship between Clinton and Lewinsky and the grounds for the impeachment of the president.

Because the aim of *The Starr Report* is to substantiate the "Acts that May Constitute Grounds for an Impeachment" of President Clinton, how does President Clinton first appear as a voice speaking in the first person in the referral? The first time the president's voice is heard, he is being asked "to identify all women who were state or federal employees and with whom he had had 'sexual relations' since 1986." The president answers under oath: "None." The last words in the "Narrative" are also the president's. This time, in a public statement, his first-person voice, quoted in the *Report*, comes in loud and clear: "I want to say one thing to the American people. I want you to listen to me. I'm going to say this again: I did not have sexual relations with that woman, Miss Lewinsky. I never told anybody to lie, not a single time. Never. These allegations are false." These same denials are echoed, again in the first person, in the closing paragraph of the "Grounds," which is, of course, the last paragraph of the text of the referral.

With their appearance and reappearance, the president's denials call attention to a preponderant narrative characteristic of *The Starr Report*: repetition. Repetition was already programmed into the organization of the work itself. The external division into the "Narrative" and the "Grounds" facilitates the repetition, if only because the two sections constitute two different ways of telling the same story.

But the *Report* is not satisfied with this double recurrence of narrative details. The narrator is nothing short of obsessive when it comes to the presentation and re-presentation of materials. The obsession is perhaps most visible with the telling of the sexual encounters between Clinton and Lewinsky
(though the obsession is present in the discussion of the gifts exchanged by
Clinton and Lewinsky and in many other topics as well). The sexual encounters are obviously presented in the "Narrative." But they are also in the
"Grounds." Lest this not be enough, they are presented in the "Notes," too.
And, of course, this is not to speak of the specific descriptions of sexual activity by Lewinsky's acquaintances in their testimony.

Even in the "Narrative," however, the encounters surface more than once.
In the summary preceding each chapter, the narrator normally summarizes
the events in the chapter, only to furnish them in greater detail once again
after the initial abridgment is complete. One example will suffice. In chapter
2 of the "Narrative," "1995: Initial Sexual Encounters," the introductory paragraph establishes the start of Monica Lewinsky's position as an intern, her
having made "eye contact with the President," his having invited her "to his
private study, where they kissed," their having engaged in a sexual encounter
on that day, their having had yet another sexual encounter two days later, and
yet another on New Year's Eve. Thus this summary version effectively pre-
views the lurid details of the encounters themselves that will surface in their
full glory in the "Narrative."

The narrator is obviously aware that this repetition might seem dubious,
so he or she repeatedly takes special care to blame President Clinton for having to reexpose the reader to these details. Early on in the "Narrative," the text
graciously excuses itself: "The evidence of the President's perjury cannot be
presented without specific, explicit, and possibly offensive descriptions of
sexual encounters." Notice the "possibly offensive," a warning to the sensitive reader that has the advantage of at once disculpating the *Report* and moving the burden for the "offensive" to the president. This is clearly a problematic issue for the narrator. In the "Grounds," the reader is told that "the ten
incidents are recounted here because they are necessary to assess whether
the President lied under oath, both in his civil deposition, where he denied
any sexual relationship at all, and in his grand jury testimony, where he acknowledged an 'inappropriate intimate contact' but denied *any* sexual contact with Ms. Lewinsky's breasts or genitalia." Not satisfied that the reader
will be convinced by this blaming of President Clinton for more sexual de-

tails, the narrator will reemphasize the point. "Unfortunately," the text begins, "the nature of the President's denials requires that the contrary evidence be set forth in detail. If the President, in his grand jury appearance, had admitted the sexual activity recounted by Ms. Lewinsky and conceded that he had lied under oath in his civil deposition, these particular descriptions would be superfluous." So *The Starr Report* kindly informs its public that any criticism for the presence of its sexual narratives should be directed at the true source of the problem, Bill Clinton.

Looked at more closely, what emerges from this justification is a binary construction that pits the president's denials against the descriptions, the nature of the denials requiring detailed evidence. The details will serve, the argument goes, to demonstrate the falsity of the president's statements. The "unfortunately" is rather coy, showing remorse on the part of a narrator who has already provided ample sexual details. But as the argument moves from the "unfortunately" to the "superfluous," questions arise. After all, the text seems to be saying that had the president admitted the encounters, then the descriptions would be superfluous. Does this imply that *The Starr Report* would have provided the details but then it would be up to the reader to consider them superfluous or that no details would have been provided had the president confessed to his alleged crimes? The narrator's expressed remorse does not really serve to disculpate him or her. In fact, it is nothing but a sign of the obsession inherent in the multiple tellings not only of the sexual encounters but of other events and details as well.

The narrator did not need to present excuses for this obsessive repetition. And this is for a simple reason. Repetition is such an inherent characteristic of *The Starr Report* that its absence should be questioned rather than its presence. And not to bore the reader excessively, the narrator indulges in different sorts of repetition.

Here is, for instance, "The President's Grand Jury Testimony":

On August 17, 1998, the President testified to the grand jury and began his testimony by reading a statement admitting that he had been alone with Ms. Lewinsky:

When I was alone with Ms. Lewinsky on certain occasions in early 1996 and once in early 1997, I engaged in conduct that was wrong.

The President acknowledged being alone with Ms. Lewinsky on multiple occasions, although he could not pinpoint the precise number.

The opening sentence posits the information, which is then followed by the president's statement already summarized by the opening sentence. And following the president's direct narration in the first person comes the reformulation of this information.

This repetitive structure in which the narrator intersperses his or her words with the first-person narration of another character is quite common. This procedure is evident in the segments detailing the president's testimony:

> The President denied that he had asked Betty Currie to pick up a box of gifts from Ms. Lewinsky:
>
> Q: After you gave her the gifts on December 28th [1997], did you speak with your secretary, Ms. Currie, and ask her to pick up a box of gifts that were some compilation of gifts that Ms. Lewinsky would have —
> WJC: No, sir, I didn't do that.

Once again, the narrator opens with a summary of the information that will follow. The question reiterates the information, as does the answer.

Exploiting repetition in details does not preclude errors or inconsistencies. The account of the second sexual encounter, that of Friday, November 17, 1995, is a good case in point. In the "Grounds," the narrator states that "The President initiated the oral sex by unzipping his pants and exposing his genitals. Ms. Lewinsky understood the President's actions to be a sign that he wanted her to perform oral sex on him. During this encounter, the President also fondled Ms. Lewinsky's bare breasts with his hands and kissed her breasts." The account in the "Narrative" paints a different picture. First, there are the complexities of the events surrounding the encounter, including Monica Lewinsky's delivery of pizza to the president, a delivery that had already been preceded by mutual kissing ("she and the President kissed"). More importantly, the "Narrative" begins the description of the sexual encounter with another mutual act of kissing, this time expressed in the third-person plural: "they kissed." This is followed by the touching of Lewinsky's bare breasts. The president's unzipping his pants and exposing himself are actions that take place while he is on the phone following the erotic prelude. There is no semiotic reading by Lewinsky here, no "sign" to be interpreted as in the "Grounds."

Yes, there is repetition. But the repetition casts a different light on the same event. The same acts are there in both renditions: the kissing, the exposing of the genitalia, and the oral sex. But the reformulation in the "Grounds" changes the order of the actions and the image of the president. (Chapters 6 and 7 below examine in greater detail the manipulative techniques of the narrator in the "Narrative" versus the "Grounds" in the discussion of the sexual encounter with the blue dress.) Part of the tendentious nature of the account in the "Grounds" relates thus to the ordering of events in the encounter. The exposure by the president coming as it does as the first event, redirects the narration so as to turn the male into the sexual predator.

The chronology is not innocent either. The narrative situation created by the fact that a synopsis of a chapter opens the chapter to be followed by a detailed exposition of the summarized events translates itself not only into repetition but into a constant shift in chronological registers. A warning, however: these summaries at the beginning of the chapters do not necessarily encompass the entirety of the events in the chapters in question. Nevertheless, this situation with summaries occurs not only in the "Narrative" but in the "Grounds" as well. In the "Grounds," however, the précis at the beginning of a section or chapter appears preceded by legal terminology summing up the "substantial and credible information" regarding President Clinton's grave acts. A "Summary" in the "Grounds" ends the section/chapter, once again arguing for the president's guilt.

Most of the time, however, these chronological feats in *The Starr Report* deal with actions long past. After all, the referral outlines events that have taken place and requests future action from the United States Congress. There is an unsettling moment, nevertheless, when the *Report* sets up a fascinating chronological dissonance. The title of chapter 14 in the "Narrative" is "January 17, 1998–Present: The Deposition and Afterward." What is the "Present" here? In fact, this is the last chapter in the "Narrative," and the last event it recounts, dated Monday, January 26, 1998, is the president's public remarks coupled with his denials. On the other hand, the "Conclusion" to the referral (which will reappear momentarily) is dated September 9, 1998.

Is the "Present" the present of the "Narrative" (whose last event is January 26, 1998), or that of the date on which the referral is submitted to Congress (September 9, 1998), or finally that of the reader reading the text, which is, of course, not at all the present of the narrative or the submission of the referral? Whatever the "Present" may be, its use creates a provocative notion that the process continues to any present the reader may be in. An indefiniteness and nonclosure to that proposition and to that time frame make it appear as if the president's indiscretions, after all the subject of *The Starr Report*, are never-ending and will be there no matter when the present is. This present transcends the time-bound narrative of the *Report* itself to become applicable in an unspecified future.

Kenneth W. Starr's referral is happy dancing between the "Narrative" and the "Grounds." But its dance card would not be full if the "Notes" appended to the referral were not placed on it. Most striking about the "Notes" is their sheer quantity: over one thousand for the "Narrative" and almost five hundred for the "Grounds." A cursory examination of the "Notes" themselves shows that they are far longer and more frequent than is necessary for reference and clarification. One is reminded of the strategy of the fledgling scholar (or first-draft dissertation writer) making a show of industry and erudition.

These "Notes" do more than substantiate the information in the text. They take on their identity not just as appendages but as vital parts of the text. The "Notes" sometimes provide information otherwise not presented in the body of the text. For example, references to oral-anal contact between Clinton and Lewinsky surface only in the "Notes." The narrator may be showing a certain amount of prudery here. Or perhaps this narrator is playing a perverse game with readers, hiding materials and forcing them to go to the "Notes." Or perhaps the narrator realizes that some of the information may not be critical to the referral and is better kept in the "Notes."

There may, however, be a touch of voyeurism on the part of the narrator that surfaces in these "Notes." In the account of the March 29 sexual encounter in the "Narrative," for example, Monica Lewinsky speaks in the first person: "I wanted him to touch my genitals with his genitals," only to be interrupted by the third-person narrator who finishes the sentence for her by stating "and he did so, lightly and without penetration." The "Note" appended to this verbal display elaborates: "Ms. Lewinsky testified that their genitals only briefly touched: '[W]e sort of had tried to do that, but because he's so tall and he couldn't bend because of his knee, it didn't really work.'" Clearly, the "Note" here is explaining Lewinsky's assertions regarding genital-to-genital contact between herself and President Clinton. Her comments on Clinton's height and his knee could be considered superfluous and hence to be relegated to the "Note." Notice, however, that the subject of penetration does not appear in her testimony, either in the text or in its attached "Note," whereas the third-person narrator in the "Narrative" is anxious to break into her first-person account and add that comment.

While the information in this particular "Note" *modifies* the text, other

"Notes" provide information that may actually *alter* the data in the body of the text. For example, before President Clinton goes on vacation, Ms. Lewinsky asks that he bring her a T-shirt from "the Black Dog, a popular Vineyard Restaurant." The "Narrative" tells the outcome: "In early September, Ms. Currie gave several Black Dog items to Ms. Lewinsky. In an email message to Catherine Davis, Ms. Lewinsky wrote: 'Well, I found out from Betty yesterday that he not only brought me a t-shirt, he got me 2 t-shirts, a hat and a dress!!!!' " The president seems a generous patron! Like a miracle, the T-shirt has multiplied and been transformed into several gifts. This miracle, however, is explained in the "Notes": "According to the President and Ms. Currie, he gave the Black Dog items to Ms. Currie to distribute as she wished; he did not bring them specifically for Ms. Lewinsky. . . . Ms. Currie acknowledged, though, that in presenting the items to Ms. Lewinsky, she might have implied that President Clinton had gotten them especially for her." The mystery in the "Narrative" is resolved. But from a reading of the "Narrative" alone, one would be convinced that President Clinton had gone out of his way to please Monica Lewinsky, whereas in the "Notes" it becomes clear that he gave Betty Currie carte blanche to do with the Black Dog items as she wished. If the text in the "Narrative" culpabilizes President Clinton, the text in the "Notes" disculpates him. The "Notes" in *The Starr Report* may present additional data not in the text, or they may redefine material already in the body of the text. They create an alternate narrative.

Confronting these different sorts of materials only serves to argue in favor of the complexity of *The Starr Report* as a text and, by extension, of the possibilities of reading that it engenders. Ideally, of course, the *Report* would wish that its readers digest its every word from beginning to end, including the "Notes." But the construction of the *Report*, its organization, permits a great deal of liberty in the reading process. One can delve into the "Narrative" and read it by itself or with its attached "Notes." The same procedure is applicable to the "Grounds." Or one can simply read the "Notes" on their own. This is what distinguishes *The Starr Report* from the discourses of rigorous scholarship and scientific inquiry that it apes. No one would cheerfully choose to read through the notes to a scientific monograph. But the "Notes" in *The Starr Report*, the reader discovers over and over again, belong to another species altogether.

More important, if one chooses to read just the "Narrative" or just the "Grounds," there are different ways of reading these as well. The summaries at the beginning of each chapter that purport to sum up the chapter can be read as a sequence on their own. They push the plot forward quite effectively without need of the subsequent details. For example, the opening paragraph of chapter 5 in the "Narrative," entitled "April–December 1996: No Private Meetings," is anxious to inform its reader that Monica Lewinsky "had no further physical contact with the President for the remainder of the year." Does this mean that "physical contact" will go on the next year? Tune in. The curious reader can forgo the following details that constitute the bulk of chapter 5 and jump directly into the opening summary paragraph of chapter 6, "Early 1997: Resumption of Sexual Encounters." There, the narrator clarifies that the two culprits had "further private meetings" that included some sexual encounters.

Or, for the individual who does not enjoy reading, there are always the "Key Dates" and the "Table of Names." The dates are a very brief summary of the major events in the life of the Clinton-Lewinsky duo. No details are available here, but, nevertheless, this material brings the entire ensuing story into another realm, that of the theatrical, that of drama. (Few narratives take on as their task the introduction of all the characters prior to the text, whereas this is a much more common procedure in drama.)

The "Key Dates," the "Table of Names," and the "Notes" in *The Starr Report* are leading a parade of erudition. But they also participate in that process of obsession that will permit Kenneth W. Starr's *Report* to become a text that is overwritten and repetitive and in which the essential sits alongside the trivial. This is not to say anything of the errors that are part of the document, this permanent piece of the American political record.

And here is where the "Conclusion" to *The Starr Report* enriches the argument. Under the proud label of "Conclusion" sits the following: "This Referral is respectfully submitted on the Ninth day of September, 1998," followed by the name of Kenneth W. Starr and his title, "Independent Counsel." Some of the editions bear his signature as well. This is not really a conclusion. Did the *Report* need any conclusion at all? The "Conclusion," it would appear, is nothing more than this simple statement that establishes the date on which the referral was submitted to Congress. In truth, however, this "Conclusion" also establishes Kenneth W. Starr as the ultimate authority behind the text. Not the Office of the Independent Counsel, not "this Office," not that intrusive global first-person-plural pronoun, "we," but Starr himself. The "Conclusion" does therefore serve a function. It brings Kenneth W. Starr back into the text and possibly explains his absence from the "Table of Names."

3

HE LOVES ME, HE LOVES ME NOT: THE GEOGRAPHIES OF LUST

No matter what its guises or its games, *The Starr Report* still tells of a relationship between two people or, more correctly, of a relationship whose motivating driving force is sexual encounters. The precise physical boundaries of what constitutes "sexual relations" become themselves subject to a legal definition and are debated as such in the *Report*. The nature of the encounters between Clinton and Lewinsky is partly dictated by the complicated world of power and politics that the president of the United States by definition inhabits. The illicit nature of this relationship between an older married man and a single younger woman also means that the question of being alone becomes central. Who is where and when become critical. It is the geography of the encounter, as this geography intersects with issues of space and time, that will usher in one of the central concerns in the sexual escapades of the Clinton-Lewinsky duo: the gaze. The gaze will, in turn, lead the reader quite naturally down the paths of exhibitionism and voyeurism, corollaries of the gaze. The geographies of lust in these encounters englobe a third party, Hillary Rodham Clinton. Present and yet absent, Hillary Clinton will bring in a different sort of geography at the same time that she also engenders a discourse of heterosexual marriage.

The narrator of the *Report* is best placed to summarize the nature of the sexual contact between President Clinton and Monica Lewinsky. After all, this narrator has practiced the art of telling and retelling these various materials over and over again. Here is one summary from the "Notes" to the "Grounds":

> The President and Ms. Lewinsky had ten sexual encounters that included direct contact with the genitalia of at least one party, and two other encounters that included kissing. On nine of the ten occasions, Ms. Lewinsky performed oral sex on the President. On nine occasions, the President touched and kissed Ms. Lewinsky's bare breasts. On four occasions, the President also touched her genitalia. On one occasion, the President inserted a cigar into her vagina to stimulate her. The President and Ms. Lewinsky also had phone sex on at least fifteen occasions.

Ten sexual encounters plus phone sex. The reader knows from the "Key Dates" of the *Report* that this relationship spanned the period between November 15, 1995, and March 29, 1997.

How did the most public figure in America, namely the president, carry on this involvement and keep it hidden? By attempting to be alone with Lewinsky, of course. The convoluted discourse of "being alone" is almost as pivotal to the Starr referral as the sexual escapades themselves.

Like the question of what constitutes sexual contact, the issue of "being alone" must undergo endless definition. Not surprisingly, the president debates the meaning of this concept. In one of its discursive "Notes," the *Report* quotes the president: "It depends on how you define alone"; "There were a lot of times when we were alone, but I never really thought we were." Clinton further explains that "when I said, we were never alone, right . . . I meant that she [Ms. Currie] was always in the Oval Office complex, in that complex, while Monica was there."

Betty Currie will not only be mentioned by the president. Instead, she will enter the linguistic arena alongside the other characters. In the text of the "Narrative," she is presented as having

> testified that there were several occasions when the President and Ms. Lewinsky were either in the Oval Office or in the study without anyone else present. Ms. Currie explained that she did not consider the President and Ms. Lewinsky to be "alone" on such occasions because she was at her desk outside the Oval Office; accordingly, they were all together in the same "general area." Ms. Currie testified that "the President, for all intents and purposes, is never alone. There's always somebody around him."

Currie will also make it clear that "I was always there. And I considered them not to be alone. . . . I always thought that my presence there meant that they were not alone."

To be or not to be alone, that is the question. Other personnel, such as Secret Service officers, participate in the debate, adding their testimony on whether Bill Clinton and Monica Lewinsky were ever alone. Not only that, this is a question that everyone seems to dance around. Secret Service Officer Fox, for example, "testified that the President and Ms. Lewinsky were alone." But is that really true? No. His certainty is redefined. Officer Fox's "sworn testimony on this point differs from the public statements of his attorney, who told reporters that Officer Fox did not know whether the two were alone."

The conversation on the question of being "alone" is much more fundamental, however, than a mere linguistic definition of whether or not the president was alone with Monica Lewinsky. After all, this is a mystery that will be solved in the "Grounds" with the president's grand jury testimony on August 17, 1998, when he reads "a statement admitting that he had been alone with Ms. Lewinsky."

Rather, this is a debate that enters the domain of appearances: what looks proper and improper for the president of the United States.

> Elsewhere in her testimony, Ms. Currie appeared to have a different understanding of "alone." She testified that, on one occasion, because others observed Ms. Lewinsky in the Oval Office complex, Ms. Currie accompanied Ms. Lewinsky into the Oval Office, where the President was working. Ms. Currie explained that she waited in the dining room while Ms. Lewinsky and the President met in the study so "[t]hey would not be alone." . . . Ms. Currie testified that she did not want people who had observed Ms. Lewinsky enter the Oval Office to think that she and the President were "alone" [ellipsis added].

Betty Currie has foregrounded a central concern. Appearances become crucial. What one sees is not what one sees. Or at least, what one sees will be redirected so that it is not what one thinks it is. The issue of masquerade arises yet once more.

But the company the president keeps constitutes a domain that transcends the lurid experiences of one president to address the behavior of the holder of the highest office in the land. Here, *The Starr Report* brings in Leon Panetta, "Former White House Chief of Staff," who describes the "precautions taken 'to protect the President's office and protect his integrity,' including preventing President [*sic*] from meeting alone with female acquaintances in circumstances that 'could be misinterpreted.'" "Meeting alone with female acquaintances" is clearly a danger from which the male president (note that he is unspecified and unnamed here) must be protected. Observe also the grammatical slip of saying: "preventing President." This slip signals in Starr's referral either an absent article ("a" president or "the" president) or a personal name. The absence of specificity leaves the issue open: Panetta could be speaking about a generalized holder of the presidential office or about a specific president, possibly Clinton. This nonspecificity has the additional advantage of generalizing the "precautions" at the same time as disculpating the particular president under discussion, William Jefferson Clinton. All this, of course, is not to speak of the inherent heterosexist assumption that sexual danger comes from women. Equally important, the president has been conflated with his office, since protecting the two becomes but one act.

Perhaps the most naive individual in all this is Monica Lewinsky, one of those "female acquaintances" that Panetta mentions. In the "Narrative," Monica Lewinsky "expressed confidence that her relationship with the President would never be discovered. She believed that no records showed her and the President alone in the area of the study." In fact, the opposite is the case.

The Starr Report is anxious to share with its readers White House logs that record in minute detail the president's various activities, including the arrival and departure of his visitors. But, not surprisingly, time was used to advantage when possible. Thus it is that Betty Currie can explain that "when Ms. Lewinsky visited the White House on weekends and at night, being spotted was not a problem." The narrator had already graciously informed the reader that after the first two encounters, the others "generally occurred on weekends, when fewer people were in the West Wing." The sense of collusion, the sense of covert activity, particularly as these intersect with time, are well served in Starr's *Report*. A call in the middle of the night fits in well with encounters that take place on "weekends."

But the "being spotted" that Betty Currie mentions is also a matter of the spatial configurations of the encounter. Americans all know that the president lives in the White House. But this White House, *The Starr Report* reveals, has fascinating spaces, some of which are more private than others.

When denying his involvement with Monica Lewinsky during the *Jones* deposition on January 17, 1998, the president speaks of curtains and blinds: "[t]here are no curtains on the Oval Office, there are no curtains on my private office, there are no curtains or blinds that can close [on] the windows in my private dining room." The configuration of these spaces might well lead the reader to imagine that nothing is private in the Oval Office.

The president's words aside, the geography of space takes on its own life in the *Report*. The Oval Office area, the narrator explains in a "Note" in the "Grounds," encompasses "the study, dining room, kitchen, bathroom, and hallway connecting the area." According to the "Narrative," "the sexual encounters most often occurred in the windowless hallway outside the study." The study turns out to be, from an appended "Note," "one of the most private rooms in the White House." In two separate "Notes" in the "Grounds," Monica Lewinsky is credited with saying that "the hallway outside the Oval Office study was more suitable for their encounters than the Oval Office because the hallway had no windows" and that "many of her sexual encounters with the President occurred in this windowless hallway."

The sketching of the hallway as a supremely secluded and private space becomes part of the repetitive discourse of the geography of the sexual encounters. Over and over, the reader will discover that this was a favored locus for the illicit sexual activity. But that does not prevent the manipulation of this geography. The narrator mentions that "the President ordinarily kept the door between the private hallway and the Oval Office several inches ajar during their encounters, both so that he could hear if anyone approached and so that anyone who did approach would be less likely to suspect impropriety."

A hallway, no matter how elegant, remains a hallway, and it adds to the tawdry aspect of these furtive encounters. But as one learns more about the enclosed spaces in which Clinton and Lewinsky conducted their peccadilloes, one may be surprised that the bathroom will reign supreme here as well. *The Starr Report*, in fact, goes so far as to refer to one of the encounters as a "bathroom encounter." If the study is "one of the most private rooms in the White House," how much more private is a bathroom, the space where one's most private bodily functions are performed?

These enclosed spaces, these geographies of privacy, are clearly essential to the evolution of the sexual encounters. One moves further and further into spaces without windows, just as one moves at night without fear of "being spotted."

"Being spotted." Being seen. The gaze plays a central role in *The Starr Report*, as the geographies of space intersect with other corporal and moral issues. Who sees whom? Who or what should not be seen? What does seeing imply? The gaze is a multilayered phenomenon. There is the gaze as the primary tool of attraction, there is the gaze to be avoided, and there is the gaze as instrument for the judgment of others. Hearing comes in as well, but its role, no matter how important, is secondary to that of the gaze.

In the referral, the initial gaze is the primary instrument of attraction between Clinton and Lewinsky. It is not accidental that what sets off the entire affair between the president and the then-intern is that in the months following the beginning of her internship in the office of the Chief of Staff, she "made eye contact with the President" at "White House functions." It is not only the details of this that will follow but also the revelations Lewinsky makes to a friend that "there was some mutual eye contact." This mutual eye contact is not an isolated event, and "according to Ms. Lewinsky, a Senior Adviser to the Chief of Staff, Barry Toiv, remarked to her that she was getting a great deal of 'face time' with the President." It is the corporality, the face, that ties up the actual act of seeing to making contact with President Clinton.

The importance of the gaze was not alien to Monica Lewinsky. She admitted that "she tried to position herself to see the President." Being seen was an important step in moving the plot forward: "[U]sually when I'd see him, it would kind of prompt him to call me. So I made an effort. I would go early and stand in the front so I could see him."

Perhaps it should not come as a surprise that Ms. Lewinsky should try to defend herself against the notion that she was a stalker: "[P]eople were wary of his weaknesses, maybe, and . . . they didn't want to look at him and think that he could be responsible for anything, so it had to all be my fault . . . I was stalking him or I was making advances towards him." Certainly, the idea of Lewinsky as stalker is not hers alone, as chapter 8 will demonstrate. What is significant here is that her pursuit of the president was not innocent of the power of the gaze.

Once the plot is set in motion, once the sexual relationship develops, the gaze signals transgression and must be avoided. The transgression is initially that of Monica Lewinsky, but it also becomes transformed into one that inextricably ties together Clinton and Lewinsky.

The young woman's initial transgression is spatial, as she enters geographical spaces where she should not be. This is where the time issue comes in, when White House entries on weekends or at night meant that "being spotted" was not a problem, when, to quote Betty Currie, "there would be no need to sneak." Simply, that would be a time when avoiding the gaze would be possible. Currie's position is well displayed in her statement that "I don't want the impression of sneaking, but it's just that I brought her in without anyone seeing her." This avoidance goes further. "From some of the President's comments," Monica Lewinsky "gathered that she should try to avoid being seen by several White House employees."

While attempting to keep Lewinsky out of the gaze of others, Betty Currie herself does not forgo her own gaze. In her testimony, she "also maintained that the President and Ms. Lewinsky were '[n]ever out of eyesight.' . . . The President, however, acknowledged 'inappropriate intimate contact' with Ms. Lewinsky on February 28 and testified that, to the best of his knowledge, Ms. Currie never witnessed any such encounters between himself and Ms. Lewinsky." Currie's unequivocal statement that "the President and Ms. Lewinsky were '[n]ever out of eyesight'" can be reversed to state that Currie always had them in her eyesight, that she was always watching. At the same time, however, and in the same "Note," the president states that "to the best of his knowledge, Ms. Currie never witnessed" the inappropriate encounters that took place.

The two negations, the two "nevers," one uttered by Currie and the other by the president, are obviously contradictory. If Betty Currie never had the two out of eyesight, and that is her "never," then that would mean that nothing out of the ordinary occurred. On the other hand, if she never witnessed any of the "intimate contact" that occurred, and that is the president's "never," then she must have had the two out of her sight at some point or other. Currie's gaze constitutes an act of always watching that contradicts the president's interpretation of that same gaze, which is never witnessing.

The clear discomfort that this contradiction embodies is there in part of the president's testimony. The following colloquy is cited in the "Grounds":

Q: . . . you would not have engaged in those physically intimate acts if you knew that Mrs. Currie could see or hear that, is that correct?
WJC: That's correct.

Currie's gaze notwithstanding, the spatial configurations already discussed, those windowless hallways, those private spaces, are reinforced with the attempt to avoid the gaze. Once the culprits are in their enclosed space, the transgression is no longer that of Lewinsky alone but that of Clinton as well.

> According to Ms. Lewinsky, the President was concerned that the two of them might be spotted through a White House window. When they were in the study together in the evenings, he sometimes turned out the light. Once, when she spotted a gardener outside the study window, they left the room. Ms. Lewinsky testified that, on December 28, 1997, "when I was getting my Christmas kiss" in the doorway to the study, the President was "looking out the window with his eyes wide open while he was kissing me and then I got mad because it wasn't very romantic." He responded, "Well, I was just looking to see to make sure no one was out there."

Clinton's fear of being the object of the gaze translates itself either into turning "out the light" or into leaving a room. The transgression can even destroy a romantic interlude such as a "Christmas kiss." The president is looking out the window while kissing Lewinsky, and she gets mad. How did she know he was looking outside? Unless her own eyes were open, how could she tell that the president's were not closed?

This incident displays a complicated game with the gaze. The duo is fearful that someone will see them. But their precautions are based on their own vision, their own attempts to see if anyone is seeing them. This double game with the gaze is not an isolated incident. Monica Lewinsky described her visit with President Clinton on July 4, 1997, as "very emotional." For purposes of this analysis, it is not the verbal content of the discussion or the events leading to it that are in question but the game with the gaze. "Ms. Lewinsky began weeping, and the President hugged her. While they hugged, she spotted a gardener outside the study window, and they moved into the hallway by the bathroom." How interesting that it should be a gardener once again who is at the center of the gaze (these are the only two instances in the entire referral in which gardeners appear). Clearly, the gaze of others can be averted if one sees them early enough to move from one space of transgression into another. From being the initial tool of attraction, to becoming the sign of transgression, the gaze can transform itself and be turned into the means for the denial that a transgression has taken place. Monica Lewinsky enunciates this view quite eloquently. Speaking to Betty Currie: "On one occasion, Ms. Lewinsky said of herself and the President, 'As long as no one saw us and no one did — then nothing happened.' Ms. Currie responded: 'Don't want to hear it. Don't say any more. I don't want to hear any more.'"

But the savvy narrator expands the referential universe of the gaze by appending a "Note" to this exchange between Lewinsky and Currie. Here, the argument is made that "according to Ms. Lewinsky, the President at one point told her similarly that 'if the two people who are involved [in a relationship] say it didn't happen — it didn't happen.'" For the narrator, it would seem at first that the essence of the initial interchange between the two women concerns the denial of the relationship, and that would be where the "similarly" comes in. In fact, the president's words also appear in the text of the "Narrative." In her statement to Starr's office, Lewinsky wrote that the president "also said something to the effect of if the two people who are involved say it didn't happen — it didn't happen." The "Note" attached to this text, however, brings in the gaze: "Ms. Lewinsky once told Betty Currie: 'As long as no one saw us — and no one did — then nothing happened.'"

The net effect of these repetitions and cross-references is to link the gaze not only to Lewinsky's statements but to those of the president as well. Her viewpoint is clearly dependent on the gaze and its ability to eliminate the transgression: "If someone looked in the study window, it's not me," she is quoted as saying. The president's viewpoint that referred simply to the verbal denial of an existing relationship was not linked to the gaze. Instead, it is the narrator who performs this operation through the manipulation of materials in the text and the "Notes."

Monica Lewinsky's assertion that were someone to look in the study window it would not be she is simplistic in its naïveté. For her, the power of the gaze to identify a culprit can just be willed away. She directs the denial to her actions and to herself. The identity of the culprit is no longer her problem.

The president, on the other hand, is much more englobing — and in his own way much more moral — when he links the gaze to his actions. "I did what people do when they do the wrong thing. I tried to do it where nobody else was looking at it." Bill Clinton's two sentences tell a host of things. The president, come to discover, did what others do "when they do the wrong thing." This is, of course, an admission that Clinton did "the wrong thing." But every American already knows that from his testimony. What he is emphasizing here is the locus of the wrong action, defined as a negative space for the gaze, as a space where nobody is looking. And since this is "what people do," conclusions can be drawn not only about the power of the gaze but about its general applicability to individuals other than the president who also do "the wrong thing."

It is evident, then, that the all-powerful gaze creates different discourses in whose conception three of the "principals," Currie, Lewinsky, and the president, participate. In its multiple transformations and mutations, the gaze permits the invention of other, and infinitely more provocative, sexual discourses, such as exhibitionism and voyeurism.

President Clinton himself raises the issue of exhibitionism. In the "Note" appended to his statement about doing "the wrong thing," *The Starr Report* adduces the following: "I'd have to be an exhibitionist not to have tried to exclude everyone else." This denial concords with Clinton's already familiar testimony, in which he states that he would not have "engaged in those phys-ically intimate acts" if Betty Currie "could see or hear." The president's state-ment about exhibitionism goes beyond Currie, however, to encompass a much broader audience, represented by "everyone else." Starr's referral reit-erates Clinton's assertion in the "Grounds": "Indeed, he acknowledged that he would have to have been an 'exhibitionist' for him not to have been alone with Ms. Lewinsky when they were having sexual encounters."

These two statements may have the word "exhibitionist" in common, but their nuances are not identical, despite the fact that they emanate from the same reference in *The Starr Report*. One represents the president's own words, quoted by the narrator, and the second, the narrator's rephrasing of the president's statement. In his allusion to exhibitionism, the president places the emphasis on the process of exclusion. The narrator, on the other hand, concerned with the issue of being "alone," has redefined that process to include the possibility of exhibitionism. According to Bill Clinton, if one does not exclude, then one is an exhibitionist, whereas according to the nar-rator, if one is not alone, then one is an exhibitionist. (The difference would be the involuntary or unknowing presence of another.) Both versions of ex-hibitionism, interestingly enough, place the action in the positive and not the negative form: how to be an exhibitionist rather than how not to be an exhi-bitionist, and for the narrator it is easier than for the president.

Exhibitionism may be an overt category in *The Starr Report*, but its corol-lary, voyeurism, is not. And yet, voyeurism is alive and well in the referral. This is voyeurism in the most direct sense: the willful viewing of sexual acts. There is, of course, a second type of voyeurism in the *Report*, that induced by making the reader witness to graphically described sexual episodes.

The presentation in the "Grounds" of the third sexual encounter, which oc-curred on Sunday, December 31, 1995, generously offers an appended "Note." "After the sexual encounter," Monica Lewinsky "saw the President masturbate in the bathroom near the sink." The sexual encounter of Sunday, January 21, 1996, has a similar "Note." This time, "as Ms. Lewinsky departed, she observed the President 'manually stimulating' himself in Ms. Hernreich's office." The narrator mentions when presenting the testimony of "Debra Finerman," Lewinsky's aunt, that she "testified that Ms. Lewinsky described a particular sexual encounter with the President." In the "Note," more is to come: "She testified that the encounter concluded with the President masturbating into a bathroom sink. . . . Ms. Finerman indicated that 'it was something I didn't want to talk about,' and Ms. Lewinsky 'sort of clammed up' thereafter."

These references to masturbating both occur in the "Notes" to the "Grounds." They could be understood as afterthoughts on the part of the narrator. Or the narrator could simply be playing coy with the subject, as he or she did with oral-anal contact, relegating that to the "Notes" as well. Perhaps Finerman's words are most applicable to the narrator here when she states, "it was something I didn't want to talk about." Her reactions may be that of many a reader. Yet the narrator does talk about this, albeit furtively.

The reader is not told to which masturbation Finerman's testimony pertains. The answer to this dilemma is almost irrelevant. What is relevant is that the telling of the president's act of self-gratification is repeated. And, as with other repetitions, the narrator changes the vocabulary used to describe the event in subtle but significant ways, from masturbation to manual stimulation. The spatial configurations also change. One of the references states that Lewinsky "saw the President masturbate in the bathroom near the sink." Finerman testifies that "the encounter concluded with the President masturbating into a bathroom sink." "In the bathroom near the sink," on the one hand, versus "into a bathroom sink," on the other. Perhaps memory is responsible for the inexactitude, though obviously there is a sink involved as there is a bathroom.

At issue here is really the gaze. It is none other than this gaze, in its voyeuristic form, which permits Lewinsky to observe the president undertaking this act. At the same time, one wonders about the president's exhibitionist tendencies, as he masturbates, now in "Ms. Hernreich's office" and now in the bathroom, whether near the sink or into it being beside the point. Why did he not close the door to these spaces? Was Lewinsky invited to remain and watch as he reached his physical climax? Assuming she was not, did the president know that she was even there watching him? The narrative silences in this context are as eloquent as Finerman's expressed desire not to want to talk about the incident.

Whether the president was "alone" while masturbating or whether he was "alone" with Lewinsky creates a provocative association with the notion of being "alone." Voyeurism expands the semantic field of aloneness, permitting it to go beyond the strict domain of whether or not Bill Clinton was ever alone with Monica Lewinsky and tying it to a broader sexual geography.

At the same time, the president in an odd twist transports the idea of being "alone" into yet another realm, that of his future marital state. Monica Lewinsky mentions that in their July 4, 1997, meeting, the president said: "I don't know, I might be alone in three years." The core of Clinton's statement on his marital status traveled through Monica Lewinsky and appeared in the testimony of her friend Neysa Erbland. President Clinton is supposed to have "confided in Ms. Lewinsky that he was uncertain whether he would remain married after he left the White House. He said in essence, '[W]ho knows what will happen four years from now when I am out of office?' Ms. Lewinsky thought, according to Ms. Erbland, that 'maybe she will be his wife.'" Not to worry, however. Between Monica Lewinsky's ability to tell her friends and the narrator's love of repetition, the "Note" alludes to the testimony of another friend of Lewinsky, Catherine Davis.

But this discourse on heterosexual marriage is not the sole property of the president in *The Starr Report*. Lewinsky herself articulates a fixation and fascination with the president's marriage to Hillary Rodham Clinton. This fascination, not surprisingly, is linked to the gaze. In a "Note," the narrator brings in a fragment — that reads like something from a romance novel — from a deleted file on Lewinsky's computer in which she addresses the president: "I don't care what you say, but if you were 100% fulfilled in your marriage I never would have seen that raw, intense sexuality that I saw a few times — watching your mouth on my breast or looking in your eyes while you explored the depth of my sex." The conclusion about the president's marriage is based on visual information. Notice that the act of seeing is overcoded by Lewinsky as she comments on the "sexuality" and as she watches the president's mouth and eyes. Her gaze allows her to draw conclusions about the president's marriage.

It is this kind of conclusion that can permit the interchange with Vernon Jordan after Lewinsky is served with her subpoena, when she asks him "about the future of the Clintons' marriage." As is customary in *The Starr Report*, variants on this essential question appear and reappear. This version is that of the third-person narrator. In transmitting to the president the essence of his meeting with Monica Lewinsky, Vernon Jordan testified: "I told him what she said to me about whether or not he was going to leave the First Lady at the end of the term." "According to Vernon Jordan," in the appended "Note," "the President listened with 'some amazement' when Mr. Jordan recounted the conversation." The narrator's mania for cross-referencing means that the interchange between Vernon Jordan and Monica Lewinsky will weave its way into the "Note" supporting the Neysa Erbland discussion. Not only that, but it will reappear in the president's grand jury testimony, when Bill Clinton was "asked whether he recalled that Mr. Jordan told him that Ms. Lewinsky appeared fixated on him and hoped that he would leave Mrs. Clinton."

The president may express "amazement" when hearing about Lewinsky's future hopes. But Vernon Jordan had a much better grasp of the situation when he told Lewinsky: "You're in love, that's what your problem is." And this certainly is the picture that Monica Lewinsky draws. Sure, she may express frustration and anger, but her "love" for the president is a central element, as is her belief that "he loved her too."

The discourse of heterosexuality and heterosexual marriage that pervades the relationship is quite powerful, as Lewinsky fantasizes about replacing Hillary Rodham Clinton. "On two occasions she asked the President if she could go upstairs to the Residence with him. No, he said, because a record is kept of everyone who accompanies him there." This action is interpreted as fear of discovery both because of the president's statement and the way this statement is presented in the *Report*. Nevertheless, it is significant because it means that Clinton kept Lewinsky out of his private quarters. Nor does he give in to her desire for sexual intercourse. Rather, it is the opposite. "He responded that he could not do so because of the possible consequences. The two of them argued, and he asked if he should stop calling her. No, she responded."

More provocative is a "Note" in the "Narrative" that speaks about Dick Morris who "believed that Ms. Lewinsky's credibility was in question based on a claim by a *USA Today* reporter that there was an occasion when the President and Mr. Morris spoke on the telephone while they each were involved in a sexual encounter. The President was reportedly 'having sex' with Ms. Lewinsky while Mr. Morris was allegedly involved with a prostitute at the Jefferson Hotel." Whatever the veracity of this claim, it creates an analogy between the two men engaged in parallel activity while on the telephone to one another. While Clinton is "having sex" with Lewinsky, Morris "was allegedly involved with a prostitute." But the narrative result of an analogy is its uncanny ability to compare the parts of the analogy. The comparison between Lewinsky and the prostitute is not flattering. That Lewinsky should write the president and say that she felt "disposable, used and insignificant" might not come as a surprise. These last sentiments are a far cry from the feelings of a woman who thought she could replace a spouse.

Hillary Rodham Clinton, the "First Lady of the United States," appears in the "Table of Names" as a member of "The First Family," next to Chelsea Clinton, "Daughter of the President and First Lady." As the married woman whose husband is having an affair with a younger woman, as the third angle in this traditional triangle, Mrs. Clinton, one assumes, will play a substantial role in this story. But, in fact, Mrs. Clinton is more often an absence than a presence in the *Report*. The reader is already well aware that Monica Lewinsky's fantasies revolve around the president's leaving Mrs. Clinton. This departure would mean the obliteration of Hillary Rodham Clinton from the life of William Jefferson Clinton, turning her into an absence. This, on the one hand. On the other hand, in the case that sets in motion the entirety of the *Report*, that of Paula Jones, the First Lady is inscribed as difference: "One request sought documents sent to President Clinton by any woman (other than Mrs. Clinton) with whom President Clinton had sexual relations." The key phrase is "other than," a phrase that defines the individual in question as the principle of exclusion, as outside the action.

Yet Hillary Clinton will add still another sort of geography to those under investigation here. As Bill Clinton and Monica Lewinsky merrily gamble through their sexual encounters, Mrs. Clinton becomes the representative of America around the world. When the narrator bothers to drag her into the world of the encounters, it is to state that she is in Athens, or Ireland, or Africa. Her geography in these cases is international. Nevertheless, and very much like Yitzak Rabin and Ernesto Zedillo, the First Lady will appear on the international scene, but as an absence. She may be in Greece or Ireland or Africa, but it is her absence from Washington that makes her presence in these international locations noteworthy.

Is the reader to surmise that Mrs. Clinton's travels are what set the events in motion? The moral is clear: a wife should be by her husband's side. In the sexual-moral world of *The Starr Report*, the liberated-woman First Lady has her share of responsibility in the affair. Thus it is that the narrator remarks that: "During the fall 1996 campaign, the President sometimes called from trips when Mrs. Clinton was not accompanying him. During at least seven of the 1996 calls, Ms. Lewinsky and the President had phone sex." From Mrs. Clinton's absence on the campaign trail, one progresses to phone calls to Lewinsky and from there to phone sex.

Lest the reader not draw the correct conclusion, the clever narrator is there to make it obvious: "In Ms. Lewinsky's recollection, she and the President also had phone sex on May 21, July 5 or 6, October 22, and December 2, 1996. On those dates, Mrs. Clinton was in Denver (May 21), Prague and Budapest (July 5–6), Las Vegas (October 22), and en route to Bolivia (December 2)."

In fact, Mrs. Clinton's presence "in town" surprises Monica Lewinsky when the president calls her. In Andrew Morton's book, Lewinsky makes it clear that she "followed Hillary Clinton's daily movements on the news." Hillary Rodham Clinton's absence from the relationship detailed in *The Starr Report* is, in fact, double. She may well be a part of this triangle by definition, but she is an absent part. When she is mentioned, it is to stress her absence.

Does this mean that heterosexual marriage is beyond redemption? Absolutely not. Like a knight in shining armor, Hillary Rodham Clinton will ride in on her white horse and defend her husband, William Jefferson Clinton, the president of the United States. She is there to help President Clinton offer "an explanation for the President's meetings with Ms. Lewinsky." This she does with Sidney Blumenthal on January 21, 1998. Then, on January 27, 1998, "Mrs. Clinton forcefully denied the allegations."

It would seem that the First Lady has an uncanny ability to know when to reappear. There may be a geography of absence associated with her that is predominantly international, but she will come into sight at a critical moment in an attempt to help obliterate those other geographies of lust created with the help of her absence. This she does, along with the president, for example, when they attempt to explain Lewinsky's meetings with Clinton. And since the meetings represented a geographical transgression that led to other transgressions, including those of the gaze, Mrs. Clinton becomes a player in the geographies of privacy and lust from which she was so conveniently absent in *The Starr Report*.

4

THE GREAT FACILITATOR; OR, HOW TO "CURRIE" FAVOR

If Hillary Rodham Clinton is a dominant absence in *The Starr Report*, such is far from the case with Betty Currie. Defined in the "Table of Names" as "Personal Secretary to the President," Betty Currie has the dubious honor of appearing as one of "The Principals" in the case. The referral recognizes the important role that Ms. Currie plays as an intermediary between Bill Clinton and Ms. Lewinsky. But, as will become evident, she is much more than a mediating principle, as she participates not only in the intricate discourses of geography just analyzed but in the much more precarious discourses of sexuality. Her role in *The Starr Report* may be perceived to be largely that of an intermediary, but she is an intermediary who will redefine her own actions, placing them in a moral universe. At the same time, her facilitating of calls and meetings is nothing next to her ability to develop into an active part of the Clinton-Lewinsky duo, creating in the process an interesting sort of ménage à trois.

The first time that Betty Currie appears in the "Narrative," it is in the context of the "Conversations and Phone Messages": "The President placed the calls himself or, during working hours, had his secretary, Betty Currie, do so; Ms. Lewinsky could not telephone him directly, though she sometimes reached him through Ms. Currie." This role as intermediary is the one that heralds Ms. Currie's entry into *The Starr Report*. As the intrigue develops, the referral will expand this role.

The modalities of Currie's function as intermediary for calls are delineated in the *Report*. In a section entitled "*Role of Betty Currie*," a subdivision reads "*Arranging Meetings*." This subdivision, while giving priority to the arrangement of meetings, also emphasizes Currie's position as facilitator for calls in general:

> According to Ms. Currie, Ms. Lewinsky would often call her and say she wanted to see the president, sometimes to discuss a particular topic. Ms. Currie would ask President Clinton and, if he agreed, arrange the meeting. Ms. Currie also said it was "not unusual" for Ms. Lewinsky to talk on the phone with the president and then call Ms. Currie to set up a meeting. At times, Ms. Currie placed calls to Ms. Lewinsky for President Clinton and put him on the line.

Being an "intermediary" for calls is one thing. Betty Currie clearly went beyond this as far as calls are concerned. In a subsection entitled "*Secrecy*," the *Report* makes it clear that "Ms. Currie helped to keep the relationship secret." Rather than going through White House operators "who keep logs of presidential calls made through the switchboard," Betty Currie "would dial the call herself." Or she did not log the call at all. Or she "avoided writing down or retaining most messages from Ms. Lewinsky to the President." When Monica Lewinsky "once expressed concern about records showing the President's calls to her," Betty Currie "told her not to worry."

The calls processed through Betty Currie (unlike the direct calls that the president himself made) are able to lead to the meetings that Lewinsky so clearly coveted. And Currie, once again, is responsible for the modalities leading to the meetings. She was, for example, the one who authorized Lewinsky's entry into the White House. Sometimes, as she herself acknowledged in the *Report*, she "would come to the White House for the sole purpose of having Ms. Lewinsky admitted and bringing her to see the President."

But Betty Currie is also the engineer behind the spatial movements not only of Lewinsky but of the president as well. Lewinsky might have to wait at the lobby or at the gate, but this would be at Currie's bidding. How much more dramatic it is when the president himself becomes a pawn in the space game. Betty Currie, for example, "instructed Officer Brent Chinery to hold Ms. Lewinsky at the lobby for a few minutes because she needed to move the President to the study." She is the active agent who moves the president, and he becomes the passive object being moved. This situation serves as an interesting alternative to Monica Lewinsky's "evaluation" that downplays and underestimates Currie: "Many White House staff members tried to regulate the President's behavior, but Ms. Currie generally did as he wished."

The meetings that Currie brings about need obviously to be preceded by entries into the sacred enclosure that is the White House. These entries, as chapter 3 has already made clear, are not simply a matter of having Lewinsky come in to see Clinton. They engender various games that partake of the discourses not only of geography but of transgression and the gaze as well. Betty Currie will also redirect the gaze and redefine the modalities of these meetings, inserting a moral twist on the entire activity in which she is a clear participant. She testified that "she once brought Ms. Lewinsky directly to the study, 'sneaking her back' via a roundabout path to avoid running" into White House employees who did not approve of her. And, again: "When Ms. Lewinsky visited the White House on weekends and at night, being spotted was not a problem — in Ms. Currie's words, 'there would be no need to sneak.'" And in a "Note," appended to some of this discussion, "Ms. Currie later said that 'I don't want the impression of sneaking, but it's just that I brought her in without anyone seeing her.'"

From the familiar gaze, Betty Currie has transported the narrative into the domain of "sneaking." Generally, the act of "sneaking" implies that the activity being undertaken is wrong. Currie has redefined her role as mediator and facilitator into an improper action that requires "sneaking." At the same time, the ability to navigate the geography in such a way as to avoid being seen is not too dissimilar from the manipulation of the phone logs so as not to leave a trace.

Alongside her role in "*Arranging Meetings,*" Kenneth Starr's referral gives Currie the dubious honor of being an "*Intermediary for Gifts.*" And gifts are so important to *The Starr Report* that they receive their own section in the first chapter of the "Narrative": "Nature of President Clinton's Relationship with Monica Lewinsky." The summary in this section presents the number of gifts exchanged, who gave what to whom, and the modalities of the exchange. Whereas Lewinsky gave the President "about 30 items," he "gave her about 18." "Many of the 30 or so gifts that she gave the President reflected his interests in history, antiques, cigars, and frogs" (this in the "Narrative"). In the "Grounds," the narrator ups the ante: "Ms. Lewinsky gave the President approximately 38 gifts; she says she almost always brought a gift or two when she visited." The discrepancy may not be significant since both numbers are approximate ("30 or so gifts" versus "approximately 38 gifts"). But it does place a question mark, like so many things in the *Report* do, next to the relia- bility of the narrator. The various articles they exchanged include items such as clothing, jewelry, and books, as well as sundry playful objects. But *The Starr Report* would not be the obsessive text it is did it not itemize the gifts for the delectation of its reader. More than simply gifts, the objects also produced their own language. For example, Monica Lewinsky "construed it as a sign of affection when the President wore a necktie or other item of clothing she had given him."

Betty Currie plays into this as well. Although *The Starr Report* does not de- lineate different paths for the gifts, these paths are nevertheless there. The trajectory of gifts followed a two-way street: from Lewinsky to Clinton and vice versa. Bill Clinton put it most eloquently. Even after the "intimate rela- tionship ended in 1997 . . . '[S]he continued to give me gifts. And I felt that it was a right thing to do to give her gifts back'" (ellipsis added). This seemingly polite statement in favor of proper etiquette is repeated in the "Grounds" ("it was a right thing to do to give her gifts back"). So one can imagine what this meant before the relationship ended!

Here is the trajectory of gifts from Lewinsky to Clinton:

> According to Ms. Currie, Ms. Lewinsky would call and say she was sending something for the President. The package would arrive addressed to Ms. Currie. . . . Evidence indicates that Ms. Lewinsky on occasion also dropped parcels off with Ms. Currie or had a family member do so, and brought gifts to the President when visiting him. Ms. Currie testified that most packages from Ms. Lewinsky were intended for the President.
>
> Although Ms. Currie generally opened letters and parcels to the President, she did not open these packages from Ms. Lewinsky. She testified that "I made the determination not to open" such letters and packages because "I felt [they were] probably personal." Instead, she would leave the package in the President's box, and "[h]e would pick it up." To the best of her knowledge, such parcels always reached the President [ellipsis added].

From this description, it would appear initially that Betty Currie, as an "inter- mediary," functioned almost as a mail slot into which the parcels to the pres- ident were deposited. That she determined not to open the packages from Lewinsky because she "felt [they were] probably personal" is perhaps just as well. After all, what would have been her reaction to a packet that included a "very erotic" Egon Schiele painting? Her discretion is echoed by Lewinsky who "suspected that Ms. Currie was not logging in all of her gifts to the President." This would be despite the fact that, as *The Starr Report* states, there are "White House procedures" for logging in "gifts to the President."

The other trajectory is that of the gifts from the president to Monica Lewinsky. The president was certainly not in need here of Currie's position as intermediary. He could simply give Monica Lewinsky objects during their meetings, as he did on July 24, 1997, when "they chatted for five to ten minutes" and President Clinton "gave Ms. Lewinsky, as a birthday present, an antique pin." Or Betty Currie might arrange a meeting, instigated by a request from Monica Lewinsky, to have the latter come to the White House and pick up her promised Christmas gifts, such as happened on December 28, 1997. But, in this case too, the president's gifts need no intermediary, being given directly to Monica Lewinsky.

The scenario of gift giving was not always so manifest. Chapter 2 above already outlined the complicated trajectory of the Black Dog gifts. There, however, the story of the gifts illustrated the convoluted narrative game in the *Report*. Here, the movement of those gifts illuminates the not-so-obvious nature of Betty Currie's role, defined by the referral as an "*Intermediary for Gifts*." The simple request from Ms. Lewinsky for a T-shirt is answered by a plethora of gifts from the Vineyard restaurant. But what the narrator leaves for the "Notes" is the fact that President Clinton had given all the items from the Black Dog to Betty Currie to distribute as she wished and she had simply given the entirety of the objects to Monica Lewinsky. In the process, "she might have implied that President Clinton had gotten them especially for her."

There is an irony to the items the president brings back from the Black Dog restaurant. The president gives them to Betty Currie. For whatever reason, she gives them all to Lewinsky, implying that they were "especially for her." Lewinsky, in turn, is ecstatic and sends an email to her friend Catherine Davis in which she waxes eloquent about the president: "Even though he's a big schmuck, that is surprisingly sweet." The role of intermediary can create interesting waves indeed.

But the greatest irony, without doubt, is embodied in the last gift that Monica Lewinsky gives to William Jefferson Clinton. The "Narrative" tells it this way: "On Sunday, January 4, 1998, Ms. Lewinsky called Ms. Currie at home and told her that she wanted to drop off a gift for the President. Ms. Currie invited Ms. Lewinsky to her home, and Ms. Lewinsky gave her the package.

The package contained a book entitled *The Presidents of the United States* and a love note inspired by the movie *Titanic*."

As is to be expected, the "Grounds" will relate the same incident but with some significant changes: "On January 4, 1998, Ms. Lewinsky left a book for the President with Ms. Currie. Ms. Lewinsky had enclosed in the book a romantic note that she had written, inspired by a recent viewing of the movie *Titanic*. In the note, Ms. Lewinsky told the President that she wanted to have sexual intercourse with him, at least once." Most intriguing about this last gift is the note. Described in the "Narrative" as "a love note" with no specific content, it metamorphoses in the "Grounds" into "a romantic note" with real content: Monica Lewinsky's desire for sexual intercourse. The reader knows that this desire will never be fulfilled. But the inspiration for the note is more eloquent than the note itself. The star-crossed lovers of the cinematic *Titanic* have become part of contemporary American culture. Romantic content notwithstanding, the *Titanic* tells the story of a sinking ship. The intertextual burden here is quite imposing and makes a powerful commentary on this doomed relationship, sinking fast. That the gift into which this note should be placed is a book entitled *The Presidents of the United States* (a title that only appears in the "Narrative") increases the irony. William Jefferson Clinton is the president of the United States, and he is given a book about his predecessors into which is slipped a "romantic note" inspired by a film about a sinking ship. That Lewinsky should then regret what she wrote in the note and that the president should concur does not detract from the power of this last gift.

Interestingly enough, however, Betty Currie's role in the saga of the Clinton-Lewinsky gifts goes beyond that of mere intermediary. Her function might initially seem to be more crucial when it came to gifts flowing from Lewinsky to Clinton. But, in fact, Betty Currie takes on an equally central position in the opposite trajectory, that of gifts from Clinton to Lewinsky. There, she is transformed from an intermediary to the final depository for gifts.

The objects that Clinton gave to Lewinsky become major players in the interactions between the three "principals," Betty Currie, Monica Lewinsky, and President Clinton. The précis preceding chapter 12, "December 19, 1997–January 4, 1998: The Subpoena," reads:

Ms. Lewinsky was served with a subpoena in the *Jones* case on Friday, December 19. She immediately called Mr. Jordan, and he invited her to his office. Mr. Jordan spoke with the President that afternoon and again that evening. He told the President that he had met with Ms. Lewinsky, that she had been subpoenaed, and that he planned to obtain an attorney for her. On Sunday, December 28, the President met with Ms. Lewinsky, who expressed concern about the subpoena's demand for the gifts he had given her. Later that day, Ms. Currie drove to Ms. Lewinsky's apartment and collected a box containing some of the subpoenaed gifts. Ms. Currie took the box home and hid it under her bed.

As is the custom in the referral, a detailed description of the events follows this précis. But, in fact, this summary does not tell all. Other events will grace the chapter, such as Monica Lewinsky's December 31 breakfast with Vernon Jordan and, more important, Lewinsky's delivery of her final gift for the president to Betty Currie's home, for her, in turn, to deliver to Bill Clinton. The contents of that gift have already been revealed: the book "entitled *The Presidents of the United States* and a love note inspired by the movie *Titanic*."

More telling, however, is the fact that of all the chapters in the referral, including both the "Narrative" and the "Grounds," this is the only one whose outline is mangled. Chapter 2 already noted this confusion, where outline elements displayed the following order: A, B, C, D, E, E, D, E. The first discrepancy occurs at the first repetition of E. And it might not come as a surprise that that culprit "E" labels a section entitled "December 28: Concealment of Gifts." This confusion, added to the fact that the opening summary paragraph of the chapter ends with Betty Currie's hiding of the gifts under her bed, indicates the problematic nature of the episode with the "concealment of gifts."

This episode in the Clinton-Lewinsky adventures appears troublesome for *The Starr Report*. In the section entitled "December 28: Concealment of Gifts," the narrator delivers the muddy saga of this "concealment." The end of the adventure, much clearer than its beginning, interestingly enough appears first, creating in the process one of the chronological breaks with which the *Report* is extremely comfortable: "In the afternoon of December 28, a few hours after Ms. Lewinsky's White House visit, Ms. Currie drove to Ms. Lewinsky's Watergate apartment and collected a box containing the President's gifts. Ms. Currie then took the box home and hid it under her bed. Ms. Lewinsky, Ms. Currie, and the President were all questioned as to why Ms. Currie retrieved the box of gifts from Ms. Lewinsky." Of course, the reader already knows the eventual resting place for the gifts from the opening paragraph of the chapter.

Of the collection and storage of the gifts there is no doubt. The uncertainties here relate to the Rashomon effect in the narrative. Each principal remembers the precollection events differently. As befits the "Narrative" sec-

tion of the *The Starr Report*, which concentrates on Monica Lewinsky's rendition of the melodrama, the young woman's account precedes that of the
other two characters involved. She credits the idea for the transfer to Betty
Currie who, according to Lewinsky, initiated the events with a phone call. Ms.
Lewinsky "put many, but not all, of her gifts from the President into a box.
Ms. Currie drove by her apartment and picked it up." Betty Currie's testimony, on the other hand, was "somewhat at odds with Ms. Lewinsky's." Currie "believed that Ms. Lewinsky had called her and raised the idea of the gifts
transfer." She could not shed any light on whether President Clinton was involved in "the transfer." As for the veracity of Lewinsky's statement that Betty
Currie had "in fact spoken to the President," Currie replied: "Then she may
remember better than I. I don't remember." As for the president, he "testified that he never asked Ms. Currie to collect a box of gifts from Ms. Lewinsky. He said that he had no knowledge that Ms. Currie had held those items
'until that was made public.'"

Three different memories, three different accounts. But no matter what
the variants in the portrayal of those initial events, there is no doubt that
Monica Lewinsky placed the gifts in a box and that Betty Currie picked up this
box whose top read "Please do not throw away!!!" and placed it under her bed.
This is how the "Narrative" presents this pivotal event, whose substance is repeated in the "Grounds," with a few minor changes.

For the curious reader, *The Starr Report* provides a list of the gifts that were
placed in the box. They included pieces of jewelry, some photographs, and
some clothing. Monica Lewinsky kept the gifts because of their sentimental
value, and she surrendered them to Betty Currie because this represented "a
little bit of an assurance to the President . . . that everything was okay."

The narrator's discomfort with this episode of the "concealment of gifts"
or "gifts transfer," manifested in the mangling of the outline in the "Narrative," may not be misplaced. The entire business of hiding the gifts should
raise some eyebrows. In its "Summary of Gifts," the text of the "Grounds" reiterates that Currie "stored them under her bed in her home." "Her bed"
would certainly be in her home and not, for example, in a hotel. "Her home,"
at the very least, personalizes the gesture.

It will, however, do more. This bump in the textual road should force the
reader to stop or at least to slow down. The first questions relate to the hiding place of the gifts. After all, why did Betty Currie have to hide them under
a bed in the first place? Why not a closet, garage, basement, or any of a num-

ber of places in a home in which one tucks boxes that will remain forgotten for decades? True, Betty Currie may not have had such spaces available to her. Then how about a storage locker outside her premises?

But the space remains a bed, and the gifts remain in a box. A bed is, of course, where one sleeps. It is also a space where couples can perform the sexual act. It is precisely the sort of space that Monica Lewinsky and Bill Clinton never get into. Their sexual escapades remain in the hallway or bathroom. And despite Lewinsky's desire to have "sexual intercourse" with the president "at least once," this is not to be. It is perhaps not accidental that this desire, expressed it will be remembered in the "love note" inspired by the movie *Titanic*, lies close to the "concealment of gifts" in both the "Narrative" and the "Grounds."

This placement of the box of gifts under a bed functions as a kind of surrogate consummation of the relationship of these two star-crossed lovers. At the same time, it represents a type of vicarious participation on Betty Currie's part in the relationship between Monica Lewinsky and Bill Clinton. After all, it is her bed; she lies on top of these objects every night. The virtual ménage à trois extends the eternal triangle into a contemporary quadrangle. That "under the bed" is a conjugal space certainly seems to have occurred to Starr's people, one of whom asked Currie in the course of her testimony (not in the *Report*) whether she had informed her husband of the placement of the objects under their bed.

This entire episode is also imbued with discourses of the public and the private that, at the same time, participate in the discourses of sexuality and transform them. In the "Narrative," the president is made to justify himself by saying that "he had no knowledge that Ms. Currie had held those items 'until that was made public.'" The argument in the "Grounds" that the president "encouraged the *concealment* and *non-production* of the gifts by Ms. Lewinsky" is buttressed by his statement that he "hoped that this relationship would never become public." This is a statement that serves the narrator of the *Report* well, since it is repeated in different contexts. For the purposes of this inquiry, however, it is its direct linkage with the hidden gifts that is central. It is the narrator who uses the notion that something has become public to bring together the information that Betty Currie "had held those items" and the "relationship." In the process, the gifts become the concrete symbol of that "relationship."

But no matter what the modalities of the relationship, the inconsistencies in the testimonies rankle the narrator. Here is the rationalization in the "Grounds" for why Monica Lewinsky's "testimony makes more sense than Ms. Currie's testimony":

> First, Ms. Lewinsky stated that if Ms. Currie had not called, Ms. Lewinsky simply would have kept the gifts (and perhaps thrown them away). She would not have produced the gifts to Ms. Jones's attorneys. And she would *not* have given them to a friend or mother because she did not want to get anyone else involved. She was not looking for someone else to take them.
>
> Also, Ms. Currie drove to Ms. Lewinsky's house to pick up the gifts. That was only the second time that Ms. Currie had ever gone there. More generally, the person making the extra effort (in this case, Ms. Currie) is ordinarily the person requesting the favor.

The reasons behind Monica Lewinsky's justifications are certainly tantalizing. Is it possible that she would have thrown away the gifts? She had not done so up to that point. Nor would she "have given them" away out of fear of involving others. But she has already "involved" people, including both friends and family members, in her affair with the president by confiding in them. A well-attuned reader will undoubtedly reread this passage that speaks of not giving the gifts "to a friend or mother." This statement implies a multiplicity of mothers. *The Starr Report* nowhere explains Monica Lewinsky's family situation, the fact that she does have two "mothers" if one wishes to throw her father's wife, her stepmother, into the mix. These relationships are explained, for example, in *Monica's Story*. Instead, the *Report* mentions Lewinsky's "family" as an abstract entity. For example, she "and her family attended the taping of the President's weekly radio address and had photos taken with the President." The narrator also mentions in the context of gift giving that on occasion "a family member" would drop off packets with Ms. Currie. These family members remain both unnamed and unspecified. The "father" appears but once, when Monica Lewinsky "testified that she would not actually have told her father about the relationship — she had already told her mother." Not only is the father unnamed, like the other family members, but he appears in the referral as an absence, very much like Hillary Rodham Clinton, as an individual to whom one would not tell something. It is worth noting here that *The Starr Report* is disingenuous in its "Table of Names." Under the category of "Monica Lewinsky's Friends/Family/Acquaintances," three family members are identified: Deborah (also spelled

"Debra" in the *Report*) Finerman, "Aunt of Monica Lewinsky"; Marcia Lewis, "Mother of Monica Lewinsky"; and Peter Strauss, "Husband of Marcia Lewis." While Finerman and Lewis appear in the *Report*, Peter Strauss is not to be found, either in the "Narrative" or in the "Grounds." Like others in the "Table of Names," he is an absent presence.

To return to the narrator's claim that Monica Lewinsky's testimony makes "more sense" than that of Betty Currie, it is the latter's actions that cause this savvy narrator to philosophize. What does it mean to say that: "More generally, the person making the extra effort (in this case, Ms. Currie) is ordinarily the person requesting the favor?" What is that favor anyway that Betty Currie is requesting here? These are questions that only the narrator can answer since the philosophizing remains his or her domain.

The retrieval of the gifts and their stowage under a bed make evident the important function of Betty Currie in this relationship. This function is also intimate, leading to a provocative sort of ménage à trois. It is not a ménage in which actual sexual relations take place, yet it is one in which the "principals" are bound one to the other in fascinating ways.

In her numerous phone pages to Monica Lewinsky, Betty Currie would leave messages requesting that she "call Kay." *The Starr Report* had already informed its readers that: "At some point, Ms. Currie and Ms. Lewinsky decided that they would use a code name — Kay — when leaving messages for each other."

A name is first and foremost something that identifies an individual. To use a code name is to adopt a different persona, to take on another identity, albeit temporarily. Here, two people who know and call each other use the same code name. There is no question but that this onomastic game sets up an identity between Betty Currie and Monica Lewinsky. The two share the same hidden identity through the identical code name and become interchangeable when it comes to leaving phone messages. This name game that creates a confusion of identity facilitates possible allusions to that ménage à trois that is always lurking behind the *Report*. It would be unfair to the referral to ignore a "Note" in the "Grounds." The narrator states that: "As the records reflect, Betty Currie used the name Kay or Kate when paging Monica Lewinsky." What the narrator has omitted here is the reciprocal part of the arrangement, that Lewinsky might use this code name as well, an omission that interestingly enough does not negate the statement in this "Note." Incidentally, the only "Kate" who appears in the entirety of the referral is a friend of Linda Tripp, Kate Friedrich. Chapter 9 will undertake the examination of more name games in *The Starr Report*.

Whether Monica Lewinsky's testimony makes "more sense" than that of Betty Currie does not in any way detract from Currie's importance in the referral and from the part she plays in the trio of Clinton-Currie-Lewinsky. Her presence makes possible one of the cover stories, that Lewinsky was visiting her, a story to be investigated in greater detail in chapter 8. Currie is also the one who facilitates the Vernon Jordan contacts. And she is the one whose opinion of Monica Lewinsky changes dramatically: "At first, she testified, she considered Ms. Lewinsky 'a friend' who 'had been wronged' and had been 'maligned improperly.' But '[l]ater on, I considered her as a pain in the neck, more or less.' The change of heart resulted in part from Ms. Currie's many phone calls in 1997 from Ms. Lewinsky, who was often distraught and sometimes in tears over her inability to get in touch with the President."

More than simply a weathervane that registers changes in Lewinsky's behavior, Betty Currie partakes of the emotional universe in which the Clinton-Lewinsky duo operated. A July 3, 1997, letter from Lewinsky to the president, described as "peevish" in the referral, ostensibly discussed Lewinsky's job situation but at the same time "obliquely threatened" the president with the revelation of the relationship. This letter led to the July 4 meeting that Monica Lewinsky described as "very emotional": "In Ms. Lewinsky's recollection, their meeting began contentiously, with the President scolding her: '[I]t's illegal to threaten the President of the United States.' He then told her that he had not read her July 3 letter beyond the 'Dear Sir' line; he surmised that it was threatening because Ms. Currie looked upset when she brought it to him." Here, it is Betty Currie's face that reveals her emotions to the president. From this, he then "surmised" that Lewinsky's letter "was threatening." Betty Currie does not need to speak. Her looking "upset" tells President Clinton all he needs to know. She is the emotional conduit between the two members of the sexual couple.

Behind this physiognomic exercise lies the fact, unspoken, that Currie read Lewinsky's missive to the president. In the discussion of Betty Currie's role as "*Intermediary for Gifts*," her testimony in the first person was adduced: "I made the determination not to open" such letters and packages because "I felt [they were] probably personal." In a "Note" clarifying this position, the narrator brings in Betty Currie again, this time from a different testimony before the grand jury, "testifying that she did not open sealed cards from Ms. Lewinsky to President [*sic*] but 'may have read' unsealed ones."

This universe in which the three principals circulated was also physical. At the end of a meeting on October 11, Monica Lewinsky said that "she and the President joined Ms. Currie in the Oval Office. The President grabbed Ms. Lewinsky's arm and kissed her on the forehead." All three inhabit the same space, with Currie being a sort of voyeur to Clinton's act of intimacy, a concept that will resurface momentarily. On another occasion, that of the December 28 meeting, after Monica Lewinsky "arrived at the Oval Office, she, the President, and Ms. Currie played with Buddy, the President's dog, and chatted."

And Lewinsky did not even have to be there for this ménage à trois to function. During the famous incident with the blue dress (to be discussed in chapters 6 and 7), the president gave Monica Lewinsky a hat pin as one of his "belated Christmas gifts" to her. This particular act of gift giving does not involve Betty Currie at all. Yet a "Note" appended directly to this action adds that "Ms. Currie testified that the President later asked her, 'Did Monica show you the hat pin I gave her?'" This testimony by Betty Currie is irrelevant to the act of gift giving, already clearly established in the body of the "Narrative." All the "Note" does is to tie Currie into something of which she might not otherwise form a part. Notice the chronological reference, the "later." This "later" remains unspecified: it might be a "later" that occurs directly after the encounter or a "later" far enough away from the sexual episode as to be completely isolated from it. This becomes almost irrelevant, since what the narrator does with the aside is to re-create the already familiar ménage à trois. In a section in the "Grounds," along with a "Note," the trio and the hat pin are brought together, this time more overtly, by the narrator.

One of the incidents most eloquent in its delineation of the intricacies of the trio's emotional universe is the one *The Starr Report* calls "The Northwest Gate Incident." In the "Narrative," this incident has subsections and takes up several pages. In the "Grounds," the incident makes no appearance at all. The incident is preceded by a section entitled "December 5: Christmas Party at the White House," which provides the historical and emotional background for the "Northwest Gate Incident." On December 5, Monica Lewinsky attended a Christmas party at the White House with a colleague of hers, at which she had "exchanged a few words with the President in the reception line." The narrator notes that this "reception encounter heightened Ms. Lewinsky's frustration," leading her to write an "anguished" letter to the president. She had also "purchased several gifts for him" and had already asked Betty Currie that Friday if the president could see her the "next day, but Ms. Currie said he was busy meeting with his lawyers."

Enter the Northwest Gate Incident. The narrator will relay the incident in all its complexities.

1. Initial Visit and Rejection

On the morning of Saturday, December 6, Ms. Lewinsky went to the White House to deliver the letter and gifts to the President. The gifts included a sterling silver antique cigar holder, a tie, a mug, a "Hugs and Kisses" box, and an antique book about Theodore Roosevelt. Ms. Lewinsky planned to leave the parcel with Ms. Currie, who had told Ms. Lewinsky that the President would be busy with his lawyers and unable to see her.

Ms. Lewinsky arrived at the White House at approximately 10:00 A.M. She told the Secret Service uniformed officers at the Northwest Gate that she had gifts to drop off for the President, but that Ms. Currie did not know she was coming. Ms. Lewinsky and the officers made several calls in an attempt to locate Ms. Currie. The officers eventually invited Ms. Lewinsky inside the guard booth. When Ms. Currie learned that Ms. Lewinsky was at the Northwest Gate, she sent word that the President "already had a guest in the [O]val," so the officers should have Ms. Lewinsky wait there for about 40 minutes.

While Ms. Lewinsky was waiting, one officer mentioned that Eleanor Mondale was in the White House. Ms. Lewinsky correctly surmised that the President was meeting with Ms. Mondale, rather than his lawyers, and she was "livid." She stormed away, called and berated Ms. Currie from a pay phone, and then returned to her Watergate apartment.

Hands shaking and almost crying, Ms. Currie informed several Secret Service officers that the President was "irate" that someone had disclosed to Ms. Lewinsky whom he was meeting with. Ms. Currie told Sergeant Keith Williams, a supervisory uniformed Secret Service Officer, that if he "didn't find out what was going on, someone could be fired." She also told Captain Jeffrey Purdie, the Secret Service watch commander for the uniformed division at the time, that the President was "so upset he wants somebody fired over this."

2. Ms. Lewinsky Returns to the White House

From her apartment, Ms. Lewinsky reached the President on the phone. According to Ms. Lewinsky, the President was angry that she had "made a stink" and said that "it was none of my business . . . what he was doing."

Then, to Ms. Lewinsky's surprise, the President invited her to visit him. She testified that "none of the other times that we had really fought on the phone did it end up resulting in a visit that day." WAVES records reflect that Ms. Lewinsky was cleared to enter the White House at 12:52 P.M. and exited at 1:36 P.M.

During their meeting, Ms. Lewinsky told the President that Mr. Jordan had done nothing to help her find a job. The President responded, "Oh, I'll talk to him. I'll get on it."

Ms. Lewinsky testified that, overall, she had a "really nice" and "affectionate" visit with the President. In an email to a friend a few days later, she wrote that, although "things have been crazy with the creep, . . . I did have a wonderful visit with him on Saturday. When he doesn't put his walls up, it is always heavenly."

3. "Whatever Just Happened Didn't Happen"

Later that day (December 6), the uniformed Secret Service officers at the Northwest Gate were told that no one would be fired — so long as they remained quiet. According to Sergeant Williams, Ms. Currie said that, if the officers did not "tell a lot of people what had happened, then nothing would happen."

The President told Captain Jeffrey Purdie, the Secret Service watch commander for the uniformed division at the time, "I hope you use your discretion." Captain Purdie interpreted the President's remark to mean that Captain Purdie "wasn't going to say anything," and he in turn told all of the officers involved not to discuss the incident. One officer recalled that Captain Purdie told him and other officers, "Whatever just happened didn't happen." Captain Purdie told another officer, "I was just in the Oval Office with the President and he wants somebody's ass out here. . . . As far as you're concerned, . . . [t]his never happened." In response, that officer, who considered the Northwest Gate incident a "major event," "just shook [his] head" and "started making a set of [his] own notes" in order to document the incident.

Captain Purdie recommended to his supervisor, Deputy Chief Charles O'Malley, that "no paperwork be generated" regarding the Northwest Gate incident because "Ms. Currie was satisfied with the way things were handled." According to Captain Purdie, Deputy Chief O'Malley agreed, and no record of the incident was made. Deputy Chief O'Malley testified that the meeting between the President and Captain Purdie was the only occasion he could recall in fourteen years at the White House where a President directly addressed a job performance issue with a uniformed division supervisor.

The President was questioned in the grand jury about the incident at the Northwest Gate. He testified that he knew that Ms. Lewinsky had become upset upon learning that Ms. Mondale was in the White House "to see us that day." He testified: "As I remember, I had some other work to do that morning. . . ." The President said that the disclosure of information that day was "inappropriate" and "a mistake," but he could not recall whether he wanted a Secret Service officer fired or gave any such orders. He thought that the officers "were . . . told not to let it happen again, and I think that's the way it should have been handled." When asked if he told Captain Purdie that he hoped that he could count on his discretion, the President stated, "I don't remember anything I said to him in that regard."

According to Ms. Lewinsky, the President later indicated to her that he had concerns about the discretion of the Secret Service uniformed officers. On December 28 she asked how Paula Jones's attorneys could have known enough to place her on the witness list. The President replied that the source might be Linda Tripp or "the uniformed officers."

The entanglements in this episode are quite telling. Note that the narrator divides the episode into three sections. The first two, "*Initial Visit and Rejection*" and "*Ms. Lewinsky Returns to the White House,*" both allude directly to Monica Lewinsky, whereas the third, "*Whatever Just Happened Didn't Happen,*" is a direct quote from a statement by the Secret Service watch commander. Not only is the trio of Clinton-Currie-Lewinsky participating actively in the events, but they do so in a completely open way, involving the Secret Service officers in the intrigue as well.

Beginning the narrative with a highly loaded word like "rejection" sets the emotional tone for what follows. There is no "rejection" here as such. Yet this word ushers in the tangled web of emotions that the narrator will describe. And, in its own way, the word serves to justify the subsequent — and otherwise unjustifiable — actions by Monica Lewinsky. In effect, as one reads the incident, it becomes clear that whatever is unleashed, including the possible firing of Secret Service officers, is the result of her feelings and actions. Monica Lewinsky was "livid" when she "surmised" that Clinton was meeting with Eleanor Mondale instead of his lawyers. A "Note" to the section kindly informs the reader that "Ms. Lewinsky suspected that Ms. Mondale was romantically involved with the President." So Lewinsky "stormed away, called and berated Ms. Currie from a pay phone." Again, in a "Note," Betty Currie's testimony attributes anger to the way Lewinsky addressed her ("Ms. Lewinsky angrily told her . . ."). And, not surprisingly, Currie adds that Monica Lewinsky "was not too happy . . . and words were exchanged" (ellipsis added). Even the president comments on Ms. Lewinsky's emotional state. In his testimony before the grand jury, he understates her reaction: "Ms. Lewinsky had become upset upon learning that Ms. Mondale was in the White House 'to see us that day.' "

That Betty Currie should also have an emotional reaction is not a surprise: "hands shaking and almost crying" is how the narrator describes her response. She is the one who receives the unjust and improper verbal whipping from Monica Lewinsky. But, in the long run, Betty Currie was "satisfied with the way things were handled."

As for the president, Betty Currie tells the Secret Service officers that he is "irate." She also informs "the Secret Service watch commander for the uniformed division at the time that the President was 'so upset he wants somebody fired over this.'" As for Lewinsky, she puts it this way: "the President was angry that she had 'made a stink' and said that 'it was none of my business . . . what he was doing.'"

The bystanders in this entire episode, and those who risk losing their positions over this lack of "discretion," are the Secret Service officers. The message relayed to them is: your "ass" or your job. And their job means learning that "whatever just happened didn't happen." The overt statement of this obliteration of the event that appears as the title of the third section signals the importance of this action, an importance reiterated over and over again. In fact, the silencing of the officers represents the opening act in the third section, the officers being "told that no one would be fired — so long as they remained quiet." This nontelling comes in with the second sentence as well: "Ms. Currie said that, if the officers did not 'tell a lot of people what had happened, then nothing would happen.'" Then there is the president advising discretion to the watch commander, interpreted by the commander that he "wasn't going to say anything." So "he in turn told all of the officers involved not to discuss the incident." And this is where the title of the section appears. "One officer recalled that Captain Purdie told him and other officers, 'Whatever just happened didn't happen.'" Another officer was advised: "As far as you're concerned, . . . [t]his never happened." There is the recommendation that "no paperwork be generated" and, as a result, "no record of the incident was made." After all this textual insistence and repetition that nothing happened, it is rather ironic that *The Starr Report* should not bring back this incident in the "Grounds." Chapter 8 below will return to this question of narrative absences.

Perhaps one should, for the moment, leave well enough alone. The "Northwest Gate Incident" was really sparked by Monica Lewinsky's fury at the thought that a competitor might be in the White House. When the president has his moment in court, so to speak, he verifies that Monica Lewinsky "had become upset." Notice, however, how he then turns the tables on her: her upset comes "upon learning that Ms. Mondale was in the White House 'to see us that day.'" Who is the "us" here? The president and the First Lady?

Bill Clinton and Betty Currie? The narrator does not elaborate. But that narrative twist, in its own way, discredits Lewinsky's reaction and in the process lends credence to the fact that "whatever just happened didn't happen."

The entanglements between the three principals are perhaps best seen in a meeting between Bill Clinton and Betty Currie. The statements the president made in this critical conversation became household phrases. Here is how the "Narrative" recounts the event:

> Soon after the deposition, the President called Ms. Currie and asked her to come to the White House the next day. Ms. Currie acknowledged that, "It's rare for [the President] to ask me to come in on Sunday." The President wanted to discuss Ms. Lewinsky's White House visits.
>
> At approximately 5:00 P.M. on Sunday, January 18, 1998, Ms. Currie met with the President. The meeting took place at her desk outside the Oval Office. According to Ms. Currie, the President appeared "concerned." He told Ms. Currie that, during his deposition the previous day, he had been asked questions about Monica Lewinsky. Ms. Currie testified: "I think he said, 'There are several things you may want to know.' " He proceeded to make a series of statements, one right after the other:
>
> * "You were always there when she was there, right?"
>
> * "We were never really alone."
>
> * "Monica [Lewinsky] came on to me, and I never touched her, right?"
>
> * "You can see and hear everything, right?"
>
> Ms. Currie testified that, based on his demeanor and the way he made the statements, the President wanted her to agree with them.

These four questions that are at the center of the meeting between Clinton and Currie and deal with Lewinsky lead to interminable parsing in *The Starr Report*. The president and his secretary are repeatedly asked about the implications and nuances of the statements, as the memory game is constantly replayed.

The parsing may be interesting in its own right but more relevant here is the way that the questions contribute to that discourse of the ménage à trois. While Monica Lewinsky is not physically present at the meeting, she is at the center of the questions. But before entering that investigative field, the analytical task should be complicated by seeing how the "Grounds" narrates the incident.

Shortly after 7:00 P.M. on Saturday, January 17, 1998, two and a half hours after he returned from the deposition, President Clinton called Ms. Currie at home and asked her to come to the White House the next day. Ms. Currie testified that "[i]t's rare for [President Clinton] to ask me to come in on Sunday."

At about 5:00 P.M. on Sunday, January 18, Ms. Currie went to meet with President Clinton at the White House. She told the grand jury:

He said that he had had his deposition yesterday, and they had asked several questions about Monica Lewinsky. And I was a little shocked by that or — (shrugging). And he said — I don't know if he said — I think he may have said, "There are several things you may want to know," or "There are things —" He asked me some questions.

According to Ms. Currie, the President then said to her in succession:

* "You were always there when she was there, right? We were never really alone."

* "You could see and hear everything."

* "Monica came on to me, and I never touched her, right?"

* "She wanted to have sex with me, and I can't do that."

Ms. Currie indicated that these remarks were "more like statements than questions." Ms. Currie concluded that the President wanted her to agree with him. She based that conclusion on the way he made most of the statements and on his demeanor. Ms. Currie also said that she felt the President made these remarks to see her reaction.

Ms. Currie said that she indicated her agreement with each of the President's statements, although she knew that the President and Ms. Lewinsky had in fact been alone in the Oval Office and in the President's study. Ms. Currie also knew that she could not or did not in fact hear or see the President and Ms. Lewinsky while they were alone.

In the context of this conversation, President Clinton appeared to be "concerned," according to Ms. Currie.

The four critical questions/statements posed by the president to Betty Currie are embedded in extra material that sets the chronological and spatial background for this predominantly one-way conversation. Notice that the president calls in Betty Currie on a Sunday, a rare event that is noted in both the "Narrative" and the "Grounds." But, after all, the president is the president, and his secretary dutifully responds.

So far so good. In the "Narrative," the narrator specifies that "the meeting took place at her desk." This locus gives priority to Betty Currie since normally a meeting between a superior and an inferior takes place in the office or at the desk of the superior. Here, the boss who calls the meeting in the first place has the meeting at the secretary's desk. This role reversal is not insignificant, signaling an important shift in the narrative and preparing the reader for what is to follow.

And what follows are the questions. The questions differ between the "Narrative" and the "Grounds," a fact indicated summarily by the narrator in a "Note" in the "Grounds": "At different points in the grand jury testimony, there are minor variations in the wording used or agreed to by Ms. Currie in recounting the President's statements."

"Minor variations" aside, the statements, in their own way, function as a set of signs on the road that is the relationship between Clinton and Lewinsky. They start with that all-important issue of being alone. The first two rhetorical questions in the "Narrative" address that question: "You were always there when she was there, right?" and "We were never really alone." In the "Grounds," those two are conflated into one, the president's first statement: "You were always there when she was there, right? We were never really alone." The remainder of the questions address, on the one hand, the aggressive role of Monica Lewinsky and, on the other, the ability of Betty Currie to hear and see everything. The "Narrative" foregrounds Lewinsky as aggressor, whereas the "Grounds" foregrounds Currie's ability to see and hear what is transpiring.

The variations in the role of Lewinsky as aggressor are quite telling. In the "Narrative," her action is restricted to coming on to the president, whereas in the "Grounds" she not only came on to him but also wanted to have sex with him. Even though her aggressive behavior is more detailed in one variant than in the other, the president's response is identical in all the cases and is expressed by a negative verb. He "never touched her," and he "can't do that," meaning "have sex."

Betty Currie's role in these statements is on the most superficial level that of verificatory instrument, there to reassure the president. At the same time, the reader of the *Report* is already sensitized to the fact that these allusions to seeing and hearing have a much greater role to play, participating as they do in those dominant discourses of sexuality, the gaze, exhibitionism, and voyeurism. All the statements allude, albeit not overtly, to a sort of voyeuristic relationship on Betty Currie's part, a sort of participatory role. After all, and to take but one example, how would she know that Monica Lewinsky came on to the president, wanted to have sex with him, and that he refused? Would her seeing and hearing everything mean that she saw and heard all that? If so, and the president's statements assume that this is the case, then voyeurism is certainly part of the formula. There is no question, however, of the president's exhibitionism: his negative actions testify to that. The addition of that "right" at the end of most statements is a further testimony to the fact that the president is attempting to create complicity between himself and his secretary.

Gender discourses are not alien here, either. The statements by President Clinton clearly delineated the progression of a relationship, beginning with the being "alone" and moving on to a possible sexual act. Nevertheless, the role of the women in these discourses is very telling. The expression of the president's actions with a negative verb highlights the actions of the female participants, which then appear with a positive verb, be it the woman as the sexual aggressor, as in the case of Monica Lewinsky, or as the proof of the man's innocence, as in the case of Betty Currie.

But this does not really call into question the gender implications of that role reversal in which the president, as the active agent, first summons his secretary, who appears, and then has a conversation at her desk, implying that she has a more powerful role. In fact, the president's words challenge the reversal created by the reverse spatial power configurations.

Betty Currie then returns to being a secretary. No matter what part she may have had in that provocative ménage à trois in *The Starr Report*, that role was but a passing fancy. In the process, she lost her privacy (and her private life). She is summoned on Sunday; she is called at home both by the president and Monica Lewinsky. The reader learns that her brother has died in the context of the fact that the president wishes to have her "come in over the weekend so that Ms. Lewinsky could visit and he could give her several Christmas presents." It is Monica Lewinsky who replies that "since Ms. Currie's brother had just died, perhaps they should 'let Betty be.'"

This last incident also speaks eloquently to the gender dynamics of the text. Monica Lewinsky is the woman who is portrayed as being sensitive to another woman's plight when that woman loses her brother. The man, President Clinton, has no problem calling his secretary and asking her to come in over the weekend, just for his personal convenience.

The trio, the ménage à trois, of Bill Clinton, Betty Currie, and Monica Lewinsky illustrates the complexities of a relationship in which only two of the three parties are overtly — or is it covertly? — involved. The third member, Betty Currie, becomes a textual part of the trio by virtue of a variety of discourses inhabiting *The Starr Report*, not the least of which revolve around gender and sexuality.

5

ARE WE HAVING FUN YET?

The cast of characters in *The Starr Report* participates, willingly or unwillingly, in a melodrama involving sexual encounters between Bill Clinton and Monica Lewinsky. As settings shift and as individuals move on and off the stage, the textual dynamics change. As Kenneth Starr's *Report* describes these encounters, differences arise between the "Narrative" and the "Grounds." The contents of the encounters themselves, the "Notes" that expand and redefine their corporal and textual boundaries, the phone sex: all these are critical in the referral's construction of the sexual encounters. It then becomes possible for the stars of the "Bill and Monica Show" to ask themselves: "Are we having fun yet?" This chapter centers on the narration of the sexual episodes as they are told as events in the relationship between Bill Clinton and Monica Lewinsky and not as information provided in the testimony of Lewinsky's friends, family, and acquaintances. Those testimonies are relegated to chapter 8, below.

An important element in the "Bill and Monica Show" is the definition of precisely what constitutes "sexual relations." How fortunate for the reader that "sexual relations" is a domain that enters the legal universe of *The Starr Report* with the definition set forth in the *Jones* case. This definition, repeated a number of times in the "Narrative" and in the "Grounds," establishes the rules of the game. Following in the footsteps of *The Starr Report*, that definition will be parsed in chapter 9, below. It does form, however, the background against which the plurality of narratives engendered by Kenneth Starr's referral will appear:

> Judge Wright accepted the following definition of the term "sexual relations:" [*sic*]
>
> > For the purposes of this deposition, a person engages in "sexual relations" when the person knowingly engages in or causes . . . contact with the genitalia, anus, groin, breast, inner thigh, or buttocks of any person with an intent to arouse or gratify the sexual desire of any person. . . . "Contact" means intentional touching, either directly or through clothing.

Buttressed by the legal system and its definition of "sexual relations," the narrator of *The Starr Report* is well on the way to presenting all the details that the *Report* is sure will convince any red-blooded American reader that all is not what it should have been with President Clinton. Lest the narrator of the *Report* feel slighted, two summary versions of the encounters will be adduced, one from the "Narrative" and the other from a "Note" to the "Grounds." Here is a summary from the "Narrative":

> According to Ms. Lewinsky, she and the President had ten sexual encounters, eight while she worked at the White House and two thereafter. The sexual encounters generally occurred in or near the private study off the Oval Office — most often in the windowless hallway outside the study. During many of their sexual encounters, the President stood leaning against the doorway of the bathroom across from the study, which, he told Ms. Lewinsky, eased his sore back.
>
> Ms. Lewinsky testified that her physical relationship with the President included oral sex but not sexual intercourse. According to Ms. Lewinsky, she performed oral sex on the President; he never performed oral sex on her. Initially, according to Ms. Lewinsky, the President would not let her perform oral sex to completion. In Ms. Lewinsky's understanding, his refusal was related to "trust and not knowing me well enough." During their last two sexual encounters, both in 1997, he did ejaculate.
>
> According to Ms. Lewinsky, she performed oral sex on the President on nine occasions. On all nine of those occasions, the President fondled and kissed her bare breasts. He touched her genitals, both through her underwear and directly, bringing her to orgasm on two occasions. On one occasion, the President inserted a cigar into her vagina. On another occasion, she and the President had brief genital-to-genital contact.

And here, for memory, is a summary from a "Note" in the "Grounds."

The President and Ms. Lewinsky had ten sexual encounters that included direct contact with the genitalia of at least one party, and two other encounters that included kissing. On nine of the ten occasions, Ms. Lewinsky performed oral sex on the President. On nine occasions, the President touched and kissed Ms. Lewinsky's bare breasts. On four occasions, the President also touched her genitalia. On one occasion, the President inserted a cigar into her vagina to stimulate her. The President and Ms. Lewinsky also had phone sex on at least fifteen occasions.

Notice that in the "Grounds," the sexual encounters bring in their wake phone sex. Phone sex, of course, while included in the domain of sexual activity does not necessitate an "encounter." Phone sex and its discourses will reemerge momentarily. But this seemingly natural association extends the parameters of the encounters into a larger sexual arena.

Narrating the ten sexual encounters, whose essence is already familiar to the reader of the referral, is one of the referral's central tasks. True, tawdry sexual details may of themselves hold the reader's interest, but variety will surely add a bit of spice to the telling. The *Report* clearly feels obligated to amass an enormous amount of data relating to these encounters and feed them to the unsuspecting reader. This material contains chronological information, including the dates and times of the encounters; White House records for the entries and exits of the various individuals involved; and even logs that substantiate phone calls around the times of the encounters. These sundry details are accumulated for the delectation of the reader in the "Narrative." In the "Grounds," the encounters are reduced to their bare essentials.

Each encounter in *The Starr Report*, whether it be in the "Narrative" or the "Grounds," presents itself as a self-contained unit. This unit begins with what can be called the evidentiary information, continues with the modalities of the encounter, including the encounter itself, and concludes with some kind of after-encounter materials. Nevertheless, and despite the apparent independence of the narrative units, the units themselves are intertwined in a complicated intertextual web not only with themselves but with the entirety of the *Report*. The narrative here is not the same as the story, the events seen in the order in which they would have occurred.

The chronological and evidentiary information in the "Narrative" normally precedes the actual encounter itself. The ubiquitous third-person narrator opens the narrative with Monica Lewinsky, who is there as the primary voice testifying to the events. She either "testified," or the following tale is "according to" her, whether this be preceded or followed by the chronological

placement of the encounter. Thus, for example, the "January 7 Sexual Encounter" opens with: "According to Ms. Lewinsky, she and the President had
another sexual encounter on Sunday, January 7, 1996." The "January 21 Sexual Encounter," on the other hand, is a variant on this: "On Sunday, January
21, 1996, according to Ms. Lewinsky, she and the President had another sexual encounter." The only exception to this type of beginning is the eighth sexual encounter: "On Easter Sunday, April 7, 1996, Ms. Lewinsky told the President of her dismissal and they had a sexual encounter." It may well be here
that the label for this entry tells it all: "Easter Telephone Conversations and
Sexual Encounter." The encounter itself is complicated by extraencounter
materials.

Monica Lewinsky serves as supreme authority. Not only does the opening
chronological setting begin with her, but after the White House records she
invariably returns once again, heralded by the familiar phrase "according to."
This, on the simplest level, argues in favor of her vision of the events. But it
is not just her testimony that dominates. Her view — and her memory reinforced through the telling — then becomes the ruler against which the president's testimony is measured. The third-person narrator, who controls the
narrative, is at times extremely generous, allowing Monica Lewinsky or Bill
Clinton to speak in the first person, in the process sharing the limelight with
that third-person narrator.

Once this evidentiary material, including White House logs, is presented,
the excitement can begin, as the narrator is free to indulge his or her skills as
a storyteller. The narration of the ten encounters varies from less to more
complicated scenarios. The complexities emanate from the fact that there are
constant allusions, chronological intrusions, or intertextual plays and echoes
that alter the otherwise potentially simple narration that, for each incident,
would provide the chronological information and then follow this up with the
actual sexual event. Two examples will demonstrate the textual intricacies in
the "Narrative" section of *The Starr Report* and how these intricacies transport
a single incident from its solitary existence into a participant in a larger web
of sexual and corporal discourses.

The first example is the "March 31 Sexual Encounter":

On Sunday, March 31, 1996, according to Ms. Lewinsky, she and the President
resumed their sexual contact. Ms. Lewinsky was at the White House from 10:21
A.M to 4:27 P.M. on that day. The President was in the Oval Office from 3:00 to

5:46 P.M. His only call while in the Oval Office was from 3:06 to 3:07 P.M. Mrs. Clinton was in Ireland.

According to Ms. Lewinsky, the President telephoned her at her desk and suggested that she come to the Oval Office on the pretext of delivering papers to him. She went to the Oval Office and was admitted by a plainclothes Secret Service agent. In her folder was a gift for the President, a Hugo Boss necktie.

In the hallway by the study, the President and Ms. Lewinsky kissed. On this occasion, according to Ms. Lewinsky, "he focused on me pretty exclusively," kissing her bare breasts and fondling her genitals. At one point, the President inserted a cigar into Ms. Lewinsky's vagina, then put the cigar in his mouth and said: "It tastes good." After they were finished, Ms. Lewinsky left the Oval Office and walked through the Rose Garden.

Three uncomplicated paragraphs seemingly move from one thing to the next without interruption. The opening segment has everyone tucked nicely in his or her own place, with Mrs. Clinton conveniently in Ireland. The second paragraph provides the events that will set the encounter in motion, including Monica Lewinsky's arrival, gift in hand. The third furnishes the details of the sexual episode and, at its conclusion, her departure.

But more lurks behind this simple structure. The first sentence transports this particular encounter from the mere world of a specific interlude that occurs on a given date into a broader universe of other sexual escapades. The narrator accomplishes this quite deftly with the simple phrase: "she and the President resumed their sexual contact." One obviously cannot resume something that has not already started. That means that other sexual encounters have occurred, whether the reader is familiar with them or not. Once that first sentence has been uttered, once the larger background established, the apparently simple linear event has been redefined in such a way that it can no longer be read in isolation.

The chronological context is only one way in which this particular encounter relates not only to its sexual neighbors but to other elements in *The Starr Report*. Monica Lewinsky's appearance on the stage is initiated by a phone call from the president, who "suggested that she come to the Oval Office on the pretext of delivering papers to him. She went to the Oval Office and was admitted by a plainclothes Secret Service agent. In her folder was a gift for the President, a Hugo Boss necktie." The entry of Lewinsky, at the suggestion of the president, is "on the pretext of delivering papers to him." The text of *The Starr Report* had already informed its reader that the delivery of papers was one of the stories used to facilitate Monica Lewinsky's entrance to the Oval Office.

> For her visits to see the President, according to Ms. Lewinsky, "[T]here was always some sort of a cover." When visiting the President while she worked at the White House, she generally planned to tell anyone who asked (including Secret Service officers and agents) that she was delivering papers to the President. Ms. Lewinsky explained that this artifice may have originated when "I got there kind of saying, 'Oh, gee, here are your letters,' wink, wink, wink, and him saying, 'Okay, that's good.'" To back up her stories, she generally carried a folder on these visits.

And this is precisely what occurs in this narration, down to the "folder" Lewinsky carries. This time, the contents of the folder are specified: "a gift for the President, a Hugo Boss necktie." The gift enters into the gift-giving games analyzed in chapter 4 above. Chapter 8 will examine what the *Report* calls the "cover stories" in the context of the multiple narratives that exist in the text. Suffice it to say that the "pretext" imbricates this particular episode in the larger discourses of the referral.

This is not enough, however. At the heart of the encounter is the physical "contact," as the *Report* sometimes describes these events, undoubtedly borrowing the terminology from Clinton's very own "inappropriate intimate contact." The reader can deduce what he or she wishes from the insertion of the obviously phallic cigar into Monica Lewinsky's vagina and Clinton's subsequent placement of this cigar in his mouth, topping the entirety with his comment: "It tastes good."

It is the wider contexts that will redefine this act on the part of Bill Clinton. The most extensive context in *The Starr Report* for this act is obviously that of orality. The reader is already at home with the predominance of oral sex, especially given that this particular encounter is the seventh of ten such events. Cigars are also, of course, a privileged item in the referral. Americans surely know that President Clinton is very fond of cigars, and for those innocent of this knowledge the *Report* had already made it clear that some of the gifts he received from Lewinsky reflected his interests in, among other things, cigars.

But, lo and behold, Monica Lewinsky seems to be interested in cigars as well. The president had given her one of his earlier. Even more provocative is that in a previous encounter, that of January 7, a cigar had surfaced very suggestively. On that occasion and once the overtly sexual escapades concluded, the narrator continued: "Afterward, she and the President moved to the Oval Office and talked. According to Ms. Lewinsky: '[H]e was chewing on a cigar. And then he had the cigar in his hand and he was kind of looking at the cigar in . . . sort of a naughty way. And so . . . I looked at the cigar and I looked at him and I said, we can do that, too, some time.'" So when, in the March 31 incident, the cigar is there as a "sexual aid," to quote a "Note" in *The Starr Report*, the reader should not be overly surprised. It is in a sense a fulfillment of Monica Lewinsky's suggestion in the earlier encounter. The "some time" she mentions is here and now and not some future.

This sexual prank with the cigar also speaks to the various summaries of the sexual encounters, as these surface and resurface in the *Report*. The summary cited from the "Narrative" mentioned that "On one occasion, the President inserted a cigar into her vagina." In the summary from the "Note" in the "Grounds," this insertion is clarified: "On one occasion, the President inserted a cigar into her vagina to stimulate her." Clearly, this is the "occasion." But the telling of the encounter itself speaks no word about the goal of the insertion from the "Grounds": "to stimulate" Monica Lewinsky.

In fact, the situation is exactly the opposite. It is the president who, according to the text, seems to derive gratification from the event. It is he who "then put the cigar in his mouth and said: 'It tastes good.'" The narrator of *The Starr Report* has, once again, fabulated, this time about female pleasure. In the process, this narrator has also pulled the action away from the male perpetrator, the president, and deprived him of his own oral sexual activity. The male voice, not to forget, is the one that utters the phrase, "It tastes good."

Other games — some chronological, some not — can also hide behind what may superficially appear to be a linear developmental mode. Such is the case with the "February 4 Sexual Encounter and Subsequent Phone Calls":

> On Sunday, February 4, according to Ms. Lewinsky, she and the President had their sixth sexual encounter and their first lengthy and personal conversation. The President was in the Oval Office from 3:36 to 7:05 p.m. He had no telephone calls in the Oval Office before 4:45 p.m. Records do not show Ms. Lewinsky's entry or exit.
>
> According to Ms. Lewinsky, the President telephoned her at her desk and they planned their rendezvous. At her suggestion, they bumped into each other in the hallway, "because when it happened accidentally, that seemed to work really well," then walked together to the area of the private study.

There, according to Ms. Lewinsky, they kissed. She was wearing a long dress that buttoned from the neck to the ankles. "And he unbuttoned my dress and he unhooked my bra, and sort of took the dress off my shoulders and . . . moved the bra. . . . [H]e was looking at me and touching me and telling me how beautiful I was." He touched her breasts with his hands and his mouth, and touched her genitals, first through underwear and then directly. She performed oral sex on him.

After their sexual encounter, the President and Ms. Lewinsky sat and talked in the Oval Office for about 45 minutes. Ms. Lewinsky thought the President might be responding to her suggestion during their previous meeting about "trying to get to know me." It was during that conversation on February 4, according to Ms. Lewinsky, that their friendship started to blossom.

When she prepared to depart, according to Ms. Lewinsky, the President "kissed my arm and told me he'd call me, and then I said, yeah, well, what's my phone number? And so he recited both my home number and my office number off the top of his head." The President called her at her desk later that afternoon and said he had enjoyed their time together.

The opening paragraph provides the standard information that introduces the sexual encounters in the "Narrative." The details of the encounter itself will be heralded with another "According to Ms. Lewinsky." Notice first the interplay between the third-person narrator and the first-person narration by Monica Lewinsky. Her voice intrudes on the text when and if the third-person narrator permits. What is most provocative is that the narrator relegates the narration of the sexual events to her to tell in the first-person. And perhaps that is how it should be. After all, it could be argued, Lewinsky is the best one qualified to lend that air of romance novel to the entire event, beginning with the steamy description of his removing her dress and ending with his declarations about her beauty.

To return to the February 4 encounter, once the encounter is on its way, it moves forward in a fairly straight line, going from the setting up of the meeting, to the meeting itself with all its lurid details, to the discussion between the two in the Oval Office, and then to a concluding phone call.

The exchange in the Oval Office is the only locus in the narration where there is any hint of an overt chronological intrusion into the text. Here, the narrator, commenting on the forty-five-minute conversation, notes that "Ms. Lewinsky thought the President might be responding to her suggestion during their previous meeting about 'trying to get to know me.' " Sure enough, a look back to the earlier sexual encounter, that of January 21, will verify that this is indeed the case. There:

> According to Ms. Lewinsky, she questioned the President about his interest in her. "I asked him why he doesn't ask me any questions about myself, and . . . is this just about sex . . . or do you have some interest in trying to get to know me as a person?" The President laughed and said, according to Ms. Lewinsky, that "he cherishes the time that he had with me." She considered it "a little bit odd" for him to speak of cherishing their time together "when I felt like he didn't really even know me yet."

The allusion to this earlier conversation in the later sexual encounter intertwines the two events, forcing them to be read one through the other.

This reference also calls attention to other such intrusions in the telling of this particular encounter. The two culprits decide, "at her suggestion," to bump "into each other in the hallway." The text continues: "because when it happened accidentally, that seemed to work really well." If the two of them planned this on the phone at Lewinsky's suggestion, the meeting can hardly be happening "accidentally." The clue here lies in the simple word "when" combined with the past tense of the verb and the following phrase: "when it happened . . . that seemed to work really well." This implies other happenings, also accidental bumpings into one another, that redefine this particular planned chance meeting and transform it into but one of other such meetings.

Notice also the differences, both with the beginnings and with the endings, between the two encounters presented. The text of the February 4 encounter does not show entry or exit records for Monica Lewinsky, whereas that of the March 31 meeting places her squarely in the White House, down to the minute. In the seemingly linear incident of March 31, Monica Lewinsky "after they were finished . . . left the Oval Office and walked through the Rose Garden." To say that she "walked through the Rose Garden" implies not only that she made it her business to go into an area where she might be seen but that she did not exit the White House, which, of course, she must do eventually. But this ending also adds a touch of the romantic, a sort of a lady-of-the-manor action that transports Lewinsky from her identity as a furtive mistress of the president into that other role. The second incident displays circularity in its structure, beginning and ending with a phone call. Both calls are made by the president. And whereas the first "planned their rendezvous," the last represents the president's statement of enjoyment.

Not all descriptions of the sexual encounters in the "Narrative" end on a note of pleasure for the male participant. Other narrations of the sexual escapades can display more complex structures, in which the narrator moves back and forth between chronological events. The "January 7 Sexual Encounter," a "bathroom encounter," would be such an example. Beginning with the evidentiary material, the story moves on to a call from Clinton to Lewinsky at her home. Since he was going to the office, she offered her company, and he accepted. Another pretext was used, this time his leaving the door open and her passing by with some papers, this to be followed by his invitation to enter. Lewinsky does as planned and sees a Secret Service officer, Lew Fox, "on duty outside the Oval Office." She stops and speaks to him and then, on the president's invitation, enters the Oval Office. Conversation between the two is followed by the sexual activity, including Monica Lewinsky's suggestion, already analyzed, about the possibilities for the cigar the president was chewing.

Once the sexual materials are concluded, the narrator returns with "corroborating aspects of Ms. Lewinsky's recollection," among them, Officer Fox's testimony. This testimony includes an exchange the officer had with the president about the latter's expecting to see young congressional staff members. The reader gets Officer Fox's understanding of the "reference to 'congressional staff members,'" followed by a conversation he had with a Secret Service agent in the hallway, in which "Officer Fox speculated on whom the President was expecting." He then describes Monica Lewinsky. Officer Fox, it turns out,

> had gotten to know Ms. Lewinsky during her tenure at the White House, and other agents had told him that she often spent time with the President.
>
> A short time later, Ms. Lewinsky approached, greeted Officer Fox, and said, "I have some papers for the President." Officer Fox admitted her to the Oval Office. The President said: "You can close the door. She'll be here for a while."

The President's words end the narration of the encounter.

What is clear here is that the narrator has shifted between Monica Lewinsky's presence in the White House and the evidence for this presence. In the process, he or she has offered the encounter and then moved backward in time to the earlier chronological period of the president's statement. This statement, chronologically preceding the sexual events in the encounter itself, seals the narration of that encounter. Along the way, and in between, the reader receives a physical description of Monica Lewinsky as well as what various agents are saying about her.

The Starr Report is comfortable with the narrative structure of the encounters, as they move from evidentiary documentation to the sexual events, along the way perhaps including other materials that help redefine a specific encounter. That this is the case can be seen when one looks at an event like the May 24 breakup:

On Saturday, May 24, 1997, according to Ms. Lewinsky, the President ended their intimate relationship. Ms. Lewinsky was at the White House that day from 12:21 to 1:54 P.M. The President was in the Oval Office during most of this period, from 11:59 A.M. to 1:47 P.M. He did not have any telephone calls.

According to Ms. Lewinsky, she got a call from Ms. Currie at about 11 A.M. that day, inviting her to come to the White House at about 1 P.M. Ms. Lewinsky arrived wearing a straw hat with the hat pin the President had given her, and bringing gifts for him, including a puzzle and a Banana Republic shirt. She gave him the gifts in the dining room, and they moved to the area of the study.

According to Ms. Lewinsky, the President explained that they had to end their intimate relationship. Earlier in his marriage, he told her, he had had hundreds of affairs; but since turning 40, he had made a concerted effort to be faithful. He said he was attracted to Ms. Lewinsky, considered her a great person, and hoped they would remain friends. He pointed out that he could do a great deal for her. The situation, he stressed, was not Ms. Lewinsky's fault. Ms. Lewinsky, weeping, tried to persuade the President not to end the sexual relationship, but he was unyielding, then and subsequently. Although she and the President kissed and hugged thereafter, according to Ms. Lewinsky, the sexual relationship was over.

Three days after this meeting, on May 27, 1997, the Supreme Court unanimously rejected President Clinton's claim that the Constitution immunized him from civil lawsuits. The Court ordered the sexual harassment case *Jones v. Clinton* to proceed.

Observe that the breakup displays the same textual plan as the encounters. The evidentiary material on time, phone calls, and so on, appears first. Monica Lewinsky is invited to the White House and arrives bearing gifts. But rather than the sexual contact, this incident details the breakup, instigated by Clinton, of the relationship. The two may kiss, they may hug, but "according to Ms. Lewinsky, the sexual relationship was over." This, the reader assumes, heralds Lewinsky's exit from the White House, but this time she does not walk through the Rose Garden or elsewhere. The declaration of the end of the relationship dismisses her from the text altogether.

Yet the section label "May 24: Break-Up" is incomplete. A chronological game is played here as well, this time a jump to the Supreme Court decision that "the sexual harassment case *Jones v. Clinton*" proceed. This decision is dated "three days after this meeting, on May 27, 1997." The section label makes no allusion to this crucial but later event. This chronological and thematic intrusion tells the reader that the president is only ending the affair because the law is closing in.

These accounts of the sexual encounters in the "Narrative" section of the *Report* may well be formulaic. But they are not devoid of the humorous or at least of indications that one or both parties found a particular situation humorous. In the description of the "*Easter Telephone Conversations and Sexual Encounter*," the narrator quotes Monica Lewinsky. "I think he unzipped [his pants] . . . because it was sort of this running joke that I could never unbutton his pants, that I just had trouble with it." At times, the account of a sexual encounter reads like a comedy routine, with people moving in and out of the rooms, phone calls coming in that leave the president indicating "that Ms. Lewinsky should perform oral sex while he talked on the phone."

But perhaps the most humorous incident, partly because it is compromising to the president and to the dignity of his office, is the one related in the "January 21 Sexual Encounter": "At one point during the encounter, someone entered the Oval Office. In Ms. Lewinsky's recollection, '[The President] zipped up real quickly and went out and came back in. . . . I just remember laughing because he had walked out there and he was visibly aroused, and I just thought it was funny.'" Whether the reader finds this situation humorous depends on associations with power, the body, sexual arousal, and notions of the public and the private.

The ability of the encounters to expand the textual possibilities into areas such as humor is undoubtedly related to the nature of the storytelling in the "Narrative" section of the *Report*. Here, the encounters receive lengthy descriptions, seemingly unhampered by issues of space.

Such is not the case in the "Grounds." There, the encounters, by virtue of the fact that they are shorter, are restricted to the bare (if this word be appropriate!) essentials: the dates and sometimes the location of the contact, as well as a summary description of the corporal activity, including fondling and oral sex, if that occurred. Nor does the third-person narrator share the text with a first-person narrator, be it Monica Lewinsky or Bill Clinton. Their two voices are absent in the versions in the "Grounds."

The third-person narrator, however, does make an effort at narrative variety, as with the Sunday, January 7, 1996, incident. Here, the narrator begins with the end of the meeting, Monica Lewinsky's performing oral sex on the president, and then effects a chronological shift as the events backtrack to the arrangement of this encounter by the president and the movement into the bathroom.

But there is a sense in the narration in the "Grounds" that the president is moving almost on automatic during his "intimate contact" with Monica Lewinsky. It is quite possible that the narrator sees this particular repetition of the encounters as a mere reminder for the reader of the salacious events that have already received ample detail in the "Narrative" section. Whatever the reason, from one incident to the next, the president, in the "Grounds," seems to be merely running through the paces with no advance thinking: the fondling and possible kissing of Lewinsky's breasts, the possible unzipping of his pants, the oral sex, and whatever else may have been done, such as the insertion of the "cigar into Ms. Lewinsky's vagina."

The narrator does not want to take any chances. He or she wants to make sure before presenting the descriptions in the "Grounds" that the reader is aware that these are not innocent escapades. The narration of the first encounter ends with a statement defining the types of activities indulged in by the culprits as "acts clearly within the definition of 'sexual relations' used at the *Jones* deposition."

The presentation of the sexual contacts in the "Grounds" is greatly enriched by the accompanying "Notes." The précis of the Sunday, December 31, 1995, encounter in the "Grounds" is three sentences long: "Ms. Lewinsky testified that she met with the President on New Year's Eve, Sunday, December 31, 1995, after the President invited her to the Oval Office. Once there, the President lifted Ms. Lewinsky's sweater, fondled her bare breasts with his hands, and kissed her breasts. She stated that she performed oral sex on the President in the hallway outside the Oval Office study." In that sense, it is not untypical of the other accounts in the "Grounds." But gracing the last sentence is a "Note" adding that "after the sexual encounter, she saw the President masturbate in the bathroom near the sink."

When the "Note" states "after the sexual encounter," it is clearly delineating the boundaries of the sexual encounter as only the totality of the events that took place between Clinton and Lewinsky, culminating in the "oral sex on the President in the hallway outside the Oval Office study." But, in fact, the masturbation "in the bathroom near the sink," an activity restricted by the narrator to "after the sexual encounter," could easily be seen as part of the encounter itself. Not only does it represent the corporal conclusion to the oral sex but Lewinsky's act of seeing the masturbation is part of that powerful game with the gaze.

The same phenomenon occurs with the encounter of Sunday, January 21, 1996. There also, the text of the "Ground" ends with: "The President unzipped his pants and exposed his genitals, and she performed oral sex on him in the hallway outside the Oval Office Study." The "Note" attached to this last sentence adds that "as Ms. Lewinsky departed, she observed the President 'manually stimulating' himself in Ms. Hernreich's office."

That this masturbation is clearly part of the sexual encounter can be reinforced by the testimony of Monica Lewinsky's aunt, "Debra Finerman." In the text of the "Grounds," Finerman "testified that Ms. Lewinsky described a particular sexual encounter with the President." A "Note" explains further that "she testified that the encounter concluded with the President masturbating into a bathroom sink." The reader does not learn if this is the same encounter. But what is of interest are the precise boundaries of what constitutes an encounter. The sexual limits transcend the chronological and social confines of when Clinton and Lewinsky were actually together. It is not simply the president's masturbation that expands these perimeters but Monica Lewinsky's voyeuristic gaze as well.

The two sections of *The Starr Report* that are under the obligation of repeatedly presenting these sexual adventures are the "Narrative" and the "Grounds." The reader knows by now that the fundamental project of each of these sections differs, with the "Grounds" laying out the evidence for the impeachment of President Clinton. The differences in content between the two sorts of texts have already been adduced: greater detail and length in the "Narrative," the absence of first-person narration in the "Grounds," and so forth.

Remember that textual neighbors are important in defining a text. The texts of the sexual encounters are no exception. In the "Narrative," these encounters are embedded in a chronological framework, one that dictates that the Clinton-Lewinsky meetings be placed in the order of events as these took place. The narration of the encounters begins after an initial chapter on the "Nature of President Clinton's Relationship with Monica Lewinsky," a chapter that, for the record, already summarizes the relationship down to the gifts, the encounters, the phone sex, the breakup, and so on. Once that beginning is made in chapter 2, the chronological mode takes over, and the escapades become dispersed throughout the other happenings in the text.

In the "Grounds," on the other hand, the encounters are all placed together under the title of "*Monica Lewinsky's Testimony*," which itself is a division that sits under the heading of the "Evidence that President Clinton Lied Under Oath During the Civil Case." The legal purpose needs no commentary. But their being subsumed together turns the individual sexual experiences into one event in which the reader observes the same actions occurring over and over again. This is undoubtedly what contributes to the effect mentioned earlier, in which the president seems to be moving on automatic pilot in this rendition of the intimate contacts. The act of placing the encounters together at once dispenses with them and renders them but one element in the relationship between Bill Clinton and Monica Lewinsky, no matter when they occurred.

The "Grounds" does the same with the phone sex, placing it directly after the encounters. It will be remembered that in its summary of the encounters in a "Note," the "Grounds" had attached phone sex to the actual meetings: "The President and Ms. Lewinsky also had phone sex on at least fifteen occasions," a number worth remembering. In the "Narrative," the narrator explains that Clinton and Lewinsky had phone sex on "10 to 15 occasions." In the "Grounds," the number is transformed into "approximately fifteen times." Certainly, while *The Starr Report* is obsessive about repetition — and the numbers are a good case in point — it does not seem to be overly worried about being specific or consistent.

Phone sex. If some American readers may not quite know what phone sex is, *The Starr Report* is more than willing to remedy their ignorance. In her December 22 meeting with Vernon Jordan, Monica Lewinsky informed him that she and the president had had phone sex. In a "Note," the narrator adds: "Mr. Jordan asked what 'phone sex' was. . . . Ms. Lewinsky stated that she may have explained it this way: 'He's taking care of business on one end and I'm taking care of business on another.'" For those obtuse readers who may wonder just what kind of "business" is being transacted, *The Starr Report* will be more explicit. In yet another "Note," this time in the "Grounds," a more precise definition appears: "Phone sex occurs when one or both parties masturbate while one or both parties talk in a sexually explicit manner on the telephone." In a "Note" appended to the testimony of one of Monica Lewinsky's friends, yet another definition of phone sex is enunciated: "They were like phone sex conversations. They would, you know, talk about what they wanted to do to each other sexually."

Now, at least, the reader comprehends what phone sex is. Notice, however, how the first part of this lesson is transmitted. Vernon Jordan asks what phone sex is. The reader understands this to mean that ignorance on this topic is perfectly acceptable, if a sophisticate like Vernon Jordan was not familiar with this practice either. The second part of the lesson can afford to be more explicit, if not consistent. After all, masturbation "while one or both parties talk in a sexually explicit manner on the telephone" is not necessarily the same as talking "about what they wanted to do to each other sexually." But the reader gets the idea.

And just in case there is a problem with knowing exactly what all this talk means, more information will be given. After the first mention of phone sex in the opening chapter on the "Nature of President Clinton's Relationship with Monica Lewinsky," an appended "Note" explains that "Ms. Lewinsky gave the President a novel about phone sex, *Vox* by Nicholson Baker." But this is not just any copy of *Vox*. In the "Grounds," the narrator explains that Monica Lewinsky had given President Clinton "her personal copy of *Vox*, a novel about phone sex." The intertextual power of *Vox* helps to transform this contemporary novel into a commentary on the relationship between Clinton and Lewinsky.

This technological long-distance sexual exchange seems to have its limits, however. One cannot imagine the speakers in Baker's *Vox* doing what President Clinton did: "After phone sex late one night, the President fell asleep mid-conversation." This event is only mentioned once, and this despite the narrator's mania for repetition. Perhaps Clinton's falling asleep serves too well to distance him from some of the sexual escapades and raise the possibility that his involvement was not all that intense.

One of the most provocative discourses that emanates from the phone sex ties it into an element already discussed, the aspect of masquerade. In the context of the "March 29 Sexual Encounter," the narrator mentions that the president and Monica Lewinsky "had a lengthy conversation." President Clinton "told her that he suspected that a foreign embassy (he did not specify which one) was tapping his telephones, and he proposed cover stories. If ever questioned, she should say that the two of them were just friends. If anyone ever asked about their phone sex, she should say that they knew their calls were being monitored all along, and the phone sex was just a put-on."

The phone sex as "a put-on": what an intriguing notion! Something "put on" is something fake. It is a pretense. Of course, phone sex by its nature constitutes a sort of a pretense, the difference, if you will, between "doing it" and "talking about it," which is what phone sex plays on. What Clinton is suggesting to Lewinsky is that she turn the sexual masquerade that phone sex already is into another level of masquerade, in other words the masquerade as masquerade. This would in itself only reinforce the element of masquerade already observed in *The Starr Report*.

The notion of masquerade is only one way that the phone sex imbricates itself into the larger discourses of sexuality in *The Starr Report*. Phone sex also participates in a larger linguistic discourse, a discourse of the sexual relationship itself, with all its internal stratagems and plots. The process of communication between the two participants in the relationship creates its own dynamics, its own language, some not necessarily verbal. When Monica Lewinsky complained about her job and wanted to talk about it, the president said he did not wish to talk about her job that night. Instead he stated that he wanted "to talk about other things," meaning phone sex. When he unzipped his pants and exposed his genitals, Monica Lewinsky "understood the President's actions to be a sign that he wanted her to perform oral sex on him."

More goes on, however, with the president's words about the "foreign embassy," just cited. The "foreign embassy" "tapping" the president's telephones is a symbol of evil, of an un-American force out to spy on the country's leader. In an odd twist of fate, however, it turns out that the pretense, the put-on, the "proposed cover stories" will have nothing to do with a "foreign embassy" but will be exposed by an organ of the United States Government itself, the Office of the Independent Counsel.

The sexual encounters serve *The Starr Report* well. With their lurid details, they guarantee that no matter what form they take, be it as independent units within a chronological setting or be it in a series, they will accentuate the adventures of a middle-aged president and a younger woman. And if some of his contemporaries are not attuned to modern-day sexual mores and practices, such as phone sex, they need not worry, the *Report* will teach them.

6

FALL INTO THE GAP; OR, *THE STARR REPORT*
INTRODUCES POPEYE TO BILL CLINTON

By the time *The Starr Report* appeared, everyone around the world who wanted to know knew that Bill Clinton's semen was on Monica Lewinsky's dress. How that semen got there is fairly clear: this is one of the sexual encounters during which the president actually ejaculated. But what is interesting about this incident is not so much that it provides the clear physical evidence of Clinton's involvement, evidence whose political consequences overshadow the mere spots. Equally, if not more, provocative is the way *The Starr Report* shapes the telling of the episode, in the process constructing a complex narrative in which numerous discourses operate and intersect, discourses dealing with gender, notions of public and private, orality, masculinity, and popular culture.

The reader of *The Starr Report* already knows that virtually no incident can appear in this textual drama only once. The February 28 encounter is no different from its textual relatives in this regard. In the summary preceding chapter 6 in the "Narrative," "Early 1997: Resumption of Sexual Encounters," mention is made of the February 28 encounter. Then a more detailed version graces the "Narrative," with a more summary variant presented in the "Grounds."

The striking role that repetition plays in *The Starr Report* has already been demonstrated. For now, however, a critical distinction needs to be remembered between the story — that is, the events as they took place in chronological sequence — and the narrative — that is, the way these events are constructed in a text. The story and the narrative need not be identical.

The importance of this encounter, the fact that it provided solid proof of the nature of Clinton's relationship with Lewinsky, means that its multiple appearances in *The Starr Report* hide a multiplicity of discourses. This chapter dissects the longer account in the "Narrative" section of *The Starr Report*. (Chapter 7 will examine the variant and its echoes in the "Grounds.")

What follows is the barest outline of the case: Monica Lewinsky attends President Clinton's radio address, at his invitation, relayed by Betty Currie. At the address, Lewinsky has her picture taken with Clinton. After the address, Monica Lewinsky accompanies Betty Currie and Bill Clinton because he "wanted to give her something." Once in the private study, Currie does a disappearing act, saying "I'll be right back." Now alone, Clinton gives Lewinsky the gifts, "a hat pin and a special edition of Walt Whitman's *Leaves of Grass*." Then follows the sexual encounter, whose results will be the semen on the blue dress. But the culmination of the sexual activity does not end the narrative of the February 28 encounter. Instead, the reader learns about the discovery by Monica Lewinsky of the "stains" on the dress and of the results of the laboratory tests confirming that these stains were indeed the president's semen. The closure of the narrative comes with the president and his grand jury testimony.

This account can be broken into a series of events that propel the narrative forward:

1. The establishment of the presence of the two protagonists in the White House

2. The radio address, with its relayed invitation and the official photograph

3. The movement into the Oval Office and the study

4. The presentation of gifts by the president to Ms. Lewinsky

5. The sexual encounter

6. The later discovery by Monica Lewinsky of the stains on her dress

7. The president's testimony and words on the encounter

Like the recounting of its other literary cousins in the "Narrative," the encounter of February 28 begins with a placement of the encounter in the chronological list of sexual events. "According to Ms. Lewinsky, she and the President had a sexual encounter on Thursday, February 28 — their first in nearly 11 months." This important tidbit sets the context for the ensuing developments. Although Monica Lewinsky is the source behind this information, it is that ubiquitous third-person narrator who, in fact, controls the beginning of the narrative. Lewinsky, whose presence the reader knows to be embodied in the words "According to," is, however, significant as the ultimate source of the story. The phrasing reinforces in the reader the notion that the female speaker is behind the upcoming account. But, in fact, the female speaker loses this power immediately, as the report changes narrative registers and moves to a more documentary register, that of "who was where when," using "White House records." The presence of this governmental source creates a narrative parallel to that of Lewinsky, at once affirming her account and substantiating it. In this way, the personal testimony becomes grounded in its official verification, lending credence and support to the account that follows.

But the allusion to "White House records" does more. It facilitates the entry of the president into the narrative. There is no "according to the president." There is simply the documentation that while Lewinsky was in the White House from "5:48 to 7:07 P.M.," Clinton "was in the Roosevelt Room (where the radio address was taped) from 6:29 to 6:36 P.M., then moved to the Oval Office, where he remained until 7:24 P.M. He had no telephone calls while Ms. Lewinsky was in the White House." At this point, the president is not an active speaking voice in the narrative but simply the object of the transmission from the official records.

Now that the text has established the presence of the two parties, the narrator can move forward with the plot. But before the reader can be privy to the sexual details, he or she must clear yet more hurdles. The first of these is the radio address, an event whose telling embodies a host of discourses.

The beginning will be the starting point. "Wearing a navy blue dress from the Gap, Ms. Lewinsky attended the radio address at the President's invitation (relayed by Ms. Currie), then had her photo taken with the President." This simple sentence sets the background for the all-important ensuing incidents. The three central characters are there to play their preprogrammed roles: Monica Lewinsky, President Clinton, and Betty Currie. As with the opening segment of the sexual encounter, where time was such an important factor, the text foregrounds Monica Lewinsky.

But this is not just any Monica Lewinsky. Rather, this is Monica Lewinsky the physical being defined first and foremost by her dress ("Wearing a navy blue dress"). The dress corporalizes her, at the same time that it feminizes her, a dress being a clearer symbol of the feminine than a pair of pants would be. And it signals what will happen to this clothed female body, since most readers already know what the blue dress signifies. Yet Lewinsky's attendance at this important political occasion is not accomplished at her own instigation but "at the President's invitation (relayed by Ms. Currie)." Betty Currie's role has been examined in detail, and this particular incident simply reasserts her functions as mediator. The president's appearance in the background is not unimportant, since he instigates the invitation but does not transmit it directly. The photograph concretizes Monica Lewinsky's appearance and turns that appearance into an official event, in much the same way that the White House records confirmed her presence in the White House in the opening paragraph.

The photograph, to which the reader of *The Starr Report* is not privy, combines with the dress to provide the third-person narrator with the evidence that this narrator needs to buttress the information in the official records, in the process guaranteeing Monica Lewinsky's presence on that fateful day. But the physical description has the added benefit of permitting the reader to imagine Monica Lewinsky in her Gap dress, a garment that will reemerge below.

Once this presence is clearly established, Monica Lewinsky, the object of the narration, can now speak in the first person. Her opening words are: "I was really nervous." Is she nervous about the invitation relayed by Betty Currie that she has answered, or about the radio address to which she listens, or about the photograph that is taken? Actually, it is none of these. Monica Lewinsky, it turns out, "had not been alone with the President since she had worked at the White House, and, she testified, 'I was really nervous.'"

The narrator is jumping the gun here. The young woman's nervousness should logically appear after she finds herself alone with the president, rather than in the narration of the radio address. It is highly unlikely that she would be "alone" with the president during the address. One would expect the presence of at least a few technicians or perhaps even the photographers who will take the picture of Lewinsky with Clinton.

It would seem, then, that the insertion of Lewinsky's emotional state at this point in the narrative is an anachronism, since it is followed directly by more material on the radio address: "President Clinton told her to see Ms.

Currie after the photo was taken because he wanted to give her something."
In fact, nothing in the narrative itself — speaking here about the text and not
about any extratextual material to which the reader might be privy — indicates that Lewinsky should have been expecting to be alone with the president.

The anachronism is a reminder that *The Starr Report* is not a straightforward account of events. The third-person narrator's anachronistic slip also
alerts the reader that what is at issue is being alone with the president, a fact
that was indirectly alluded to even before Lewinsky's entrance with the blue
dress, when the narrative was careful to add in the opening segment that "he
had no telephone calls while Ms. Lewinsky was in the White House," meaning that he was not disturbed by any kind of communication.

This motif is the familiar one of "being alone with the president," and it
appears and reappears in the narration of the February 28 sexual encounter,
not only where it might conceivably belong, as with the opening statement
about the nonexisting phone calls, but where it is inserted anachronistically,
as with the mention of Monica Lewinsky's nervousness. The motif comes
into full flower in the text as the geographical location of the events changes.
When it is time to move from the Roosevelt Room, the space of the radio address, to the Oval Office, it is the duo of Lewinsky and Clinton, accompanied
not surprisingly by Betty Currie, that makes the trek. In Lewinsky's words,
"Betty and the President and I went into the back office."

So far so good. But then another chronological intrusion enters the text,
this time a prolepsis, to use a technical term that refers to narrating an event
in a text before its actual occurrence in the story. This prolepsis represents
knowledge acquired by Lewinsky after the event — an unspecified "later" —
and explaining Currie's presence as the party moves from one location to the
next. "She later learned that the reason Ms. Currie accompanied them was
that Stephen Goodin did not want the President to be alone with Ms. Lewinsky, a view that Mr. Goodin expressed to the President and Ms. Currie."

The irony, of course, is that despite Mr. Goodin's best intentions, the presence of Betty Currie, as the move is made from one location to another, is but
a fleeting event, a superficial pretense. "Being alone with the president" is
what Goodin does not wish to see happen but "being alone with the president" is precisely what happens as Betty Currie performs her disappearing
act: "Once they had passed from the Oval Office toward the private study, Ms.
Currie said, 'I'll be right back.'" It is Currie's subsequent absence that per-

mits the sexual transgression to occur. This facilitator is quite conscious of her role. In this incident, Betty Currie is a strong advocate of this role: "Ms. Currie (who said she acted on her own initiative) testified that she accompanied the President and Ms. Lewinsky out of the Oval Office because 'I didn't want any perceptions, him being alone with someone.'" Not only has Currie enunciated the "being alone" syndrome, but she is, in her own way, attempting to circumvent it.

The "being alone" motif continues to be important as Bill Clinton and Monica Lewinsky proceed. Once in the study, Monica Lewinsky's first-person narration is telling: "I was pestering him to kiss me, because . . . it had been a long time since we had been alone." And, as if this were not enough, Bill Clinton, in his own words at the end of the narration of this encounter, adds: "I do believe that I was alone with her."

The repetition of "being alone" shows not only the centrality of this motif in the sexual encounter but its inevitability as well. Moreover, there is an interesting game taking place, a game that involves the articulation of the familiar "being alone" and consequently the "who is alone with whom." Presidential aides are concerned about the president being alone with Monica Lewinsky. When Lewinsky speaks about being alone, she uses the first-person plural pronoun, "we," turning herself and the president into one unit: "it had been a long time since we had been alone." The president, on the other hand, breaks this unit by his use of the first-person pronoun, "I": His "I do believe that I was alone with her" separates the two individuals and creates a split in the "we" of Lewinsky.

The entire physical migration from the Roosevelt Room to the quarters where the sexual encounter will take place also signals a crossing from the public to the private. As this crossing is accomplished, the trio of Currie, Clinton, and Lewinsky will be defined separately. Betty Currie, as she excuses herself and declares "I'll be right back," walks on "to the back pantry or the dining room." Not accidentally, these are spaces that evoke domesticity and food. What an interesting addition to Betty Currie's function in this ménage. The transgressing couple, on the other hand, ends up "in the study," denoting not only the secluded but the serious.

And it is there that Clinton gives Lewinsky the presents he had for her: "a hat pin and a special edition of Walt Whitman's *Leaves of Grass*." The narrative, in the context of the gift giving, adds Lewinsky's response describing the Whitman book as "the most sentimental gift" the president had ever given her.

The sentimentality extends further, however: "During this visit, according to Ms. Lewinsky, the President said he had seen her Valentine's Day message in the *Washington Post*, and he talked about his fondness for 'Romeo and Juliet.'"

Perhaps the most significant element in these games is the one that seems to be slipped in, as it were, without much ado by the savvy narrator of *The Starr Report*. And this is yet another chronological intrusion, this time involving the president's comment about the Valentine's Day message and his "fondness for 'Romeo and Juliet.'" Look closely at the time issue. Clinton speaks about the message and Shakespeare's play "during this visit." The visit, of course, stretches from the moment Monica Lewinsky walked in "wearing a navy blue dress from the Gap" until the completion of the sex act that led to Clinton's ejaculation. The alleged statements by the president could have been made therefore at any point in the sequence of events, including before or after the gift giving or even during the sexual adventure itself. Their placement here is not accidental.

In fact, the entire gift-giving segment has been constructed to stress the sentimental and gendered aspect of the event. The hat pin is mentioned in the text but receives more attention in the "Notes." First, Betty Currie "testified that the President later asked her, 'Did Monica show you the hat pin I gave her?'" This emphasizes the prominence of the pin as a gift, underlining at the same time its nature as a feminine accessory, one presumably that the woman receiving the gift would discuss with, or show, another woman. Even more importantly, the pin resurfaces in another "Note" in a "draft of Ms. Lewinsky's thank-you note (to 'Dear Mr. P') . . . found in her apartment" (ellipsis added). In this missive, Lewinsky writes about the pin: "My only hope is that I have a hat fit to adorn it (ahhh, I see another excuse to go shopping)! I know that I am bound to receive compliments on it." The focus on the appearance of the pin, the ability to find the appropriate hat for it, the pin's capacity to create an excuse for shopping, the compliments that this pin will generate, the fact that two women, Lewinsky and Currie, should have feasted their eyes on it: these are all fundamentally gendered concerns that also highlight the superficial nature of Lewinsky's interests.

As for Whitman's *Leaves of Grass*, it is also sexualized and eroticized in the text. First, the work picks up an emotional attribute: "Ms. Lewinsky described the Whitman book as 'the most sentimental gift he had given me . . . it's beautiful and it meant a lot to me.'" This is clearly a depiction of the work that is made after the gift-giving event. First, that intrusive third-person narrator introduces Lewinsky's comment. Second, and more important, this comment is not addressed to the president. Instead, the president's action of giving becomes that of an individual outside the narrative space, a textual space inhabited by Lewinsky and the third-person narrator. Whatever the reader's understanding of *Leaves of Grass*, Lewinsky is there to put a "sentimental" twist on it.

But the sentimental is not enough, as Whitman's work becomes the subject of yet another discourse. This transformation occurs in the same thank-you note to Clinton. Here, Lewinsky writes: "Like Shakespeare, Whitman's writings are so timeless. I find solace in works from the past that remain profound and somehow always poignant. Whitman is so rich that one must read him like one tastes a fine wine or good cigar — take it in, roll it in your mouth, and savor it!"

With three seemingly simple sentences, Monica Lewinsky has transported the reader — and Whitman — into a fundamentally oral and sensual universe. The first sentence, "Like Shakespeare, Whitman's writings are so timeless," is a straightforward statement that seems initially to be a commentary on literature. But note that Whitman's writings are compared to Shakespeare and not to Shakespeare's writings. One might initially wish to attribute this to faulty grammar or a clumsy metonymy. But, in fact, more is taking place, as the thank-you note creates a confusion between the writings of Whitman and Whitman himself. In the second sentence, "I find solace in works from the past that remain profound and somehow always poignant," the "I" of the first-person narrator, intrudes to provide a global judgment, couched in emotional vocabulary, on the "works of the past." From the more general nature of the timelessness of these works, the reader has moved into a more personal universe, that of the narrator who finds comfort in these works.

The third sentence is, without doubt, the most provocative: "Whitman is so rich that one must read him like one tastes a fine wine or good cigar — take it in, roll it in your mouth, and savor it!" Whitman starts out as the initial subject. This is not Whitman's works, but no matter, since one could argue that this is merely a rhetorical device that allows the substitution of an author for his works. Yet this substitution is crucial since it provides the possibilities for the games played with Whitman. The reading act is not just any act but the act of reading "him," placing the emphasis on the male author. The maleness is not insignificant since it will facilitate the next jump, in which the reading act is rhetorically assimilated to the oral activity of tasting "a fine wine or good cigar." But the narrator does not stop here, rather amplifying the meaning of this tasting: "take it in, roll it in your mouth, and savor it!" The experienced reader is quite aware of the implications of these three activities that highlight and stress the oral aspect of the enjoyment of the wine and the cigar, in the process sexualizing them. Whitman, the man who is read, becomes like wine or a cigar, to be consumed. In the context of a sexual encounter in which Monica Lewinsky performs oral sex on President Clinton, this discourse is highly suggestive, to say the least. Even more important, prior to the presentation of the February 28 encounter, the text of *The Starr Report* had already informed its reader that "on one occasion, the President inserted a cigar into her vagina," an incident discussed above. Orality and sexuality are inextricably tied together in this incident, as one sexual encounter is reinvoked in another, a familiar technique in the *Report*.

In fact, it is not only Lewinsky who injects the emotional into the gift-giving segment but the third-person narrator as well, as this narrator constructs this section of the encounter. The textual neighbors to Whitman's work are the Valentine's Day message and *Romeo and Juliet*. The Valentine's Day message signals, by its nature, romantic content. And, of course, *Romeo and Juliet* is a story of lovers, albeit star-crossed ones. Despite the passing of centuries, Lewinsky draws herself and the object of her desire into the same universe as that of Shakespeare's characters. She does this first through her Valentine's Day message, quoted in *The Starr Report*. This message, labeled as a "Love Note," is addressed to "Handsome" and signed "M." True, the message is not repeated in the narrative detailing the February 28 sexual encounter. No matter, because by reviving it, and this according to Monica Lewinsky, Bill Clinton unwittingly brings the message into the narrative web of the sexual encounter itself.

These discourses revolving around the gift-giving activity signal that the bestowal of the hat pin and the *Leaves of Grass* is devised as a romantic prelude to the sexual encounter itself. The text plays coy here: "In the study, according to Ms. Lewinsky, the President 'started to say something to me and I was pestering him to kiss me, because . . . it had been a long time since we had been alone.' The President told her to wait a moment, as he had presents for her." Clearly, Lewinsky has the sexual in mind, as the President delays her desire for a kiss. In a sense, the kiss becomes irrelevant since the text subverts the President's delaying tactic, turning his delivery of the gifts into a quasi-erotic prelude, a type of foreplay if one wishes.

By these twists and turns in the telling of the gift-giving segment of the February 28 encounter, that segment is turned into a narrative gold-mine manipulated and controlled by that external narrator. A quick glance at *The Starr Report* will easily demonstrate that the prose that transforms the gift-giving into an erotic prelude is, from the point of view of the events themselves, completely superfluous. In fact, the narrative flow could have been maintained easily without that commentary. This is how *The Starr Report* tells it:

> In the study, according to Ms. Lewinsky, the President "started to say something to me and I was pestering him to kiss me, because . . . it had been a long time since we had been alone." The President told her to wait a moment, as he had presents for her. As belated Christmas gifts, he gave her a hat pin and a special edition of Walt Whitman's *Leaves of Grass*. Ms. Lewinsky described the Whitman book as "the most sentimental gift he had given me . . . it's beautiful and it meant a lot to me." During this visit, according to Ms. Lewinsky, the President said he had seen her Valentine's Day message in the *Washington Post*, and he talked about his fondness for "Romeo and Juliet."
>
> Ms. Lewinsky testified that after the President gave her the gifts, they had a sexual encounter.

Eliminate the extra section, and the text would read this way:

> In the study, according to Ms. Lewinsky, the President "started to say something to me and I was pestering him to kiss me, because . . . it had been a long time since we had been alone." The President told her to wait a moment, as he had presents for her. As belated Christmas gifts, he gave her a hat pin and a special edition of Walt Whitman's *Leaves of Grass*. . . .
>
> Ms. Lewinsky testified that after the President gave her the gifts, they had a sexual encounter. . . .

The omission of that provocative segment makes it clear that the manipulation of materials by the external narrator is far from innocent.

Another advantage of this manipulation is that it paves the way for the text to set up a complicity between Lewinsky and Clinton for the strictly sexual encounter that will follow. This encounter is rife with gender innuendoes. Here is the entirety of the way this encounter is transmitted in *The Starr Report*.

Ms. Lewinsky testified that after the President gave her the gifts, they had a sexual encounter:

[W]e went back over by the bathroom in the hallway, and we kissed. We were kissing and he unbuttoned my dress and fondled my breasts with my bra on, and then took them out of my bra and was kissing them and touching them with his hands and with his mouth.

And then I think I was touching him in his genital area through his pants, and I think I unbuttoned his shirt and was kissing his chest. And then . . . I wanted to perform oral sex on him . . . and so I did. And then . . . I think he heard something, or he heard someone in the office. So, we moved into the bathroom.

And I continued to perform oral sex and then he pushed me away, kind of as he always did before he came, and then I stood up and I said . . . I care about you so much; . . . I don't understand why you won't let me . . . make you come; it's important to me; I mean, it just doesn't feel complete, it doesn't seem right.

Ms. Lewinsky testified that she and the President hugged, and "he said he didn't want to get addicted to me, and he didn't want me to get addicted to him." They looked at each other for a moment. Then, saying that "I don't want to disappoint you," the President consented. For the first time, she performed oral sex through completion.

Striking in this description is the prominent role played by Lewinsky's direct first-person narration. The reader had heard the young woman speaking in the first person throughout the previous segments. But her narrative presence in the first person was always intermittent and, more important, intercalated with that of the dominant third-person narrator. This is not the case in the description of the sexual encounter. The third-person narrator is there but only to introduce the subsequent descriptions: "Ms. Lewinsky testified that after the President gave her the gifts, they had a sexual encounter." This statement by the third-person narrator makes it appear as if the gift giving and the encounter were separate stages in the process and that as one was completed so the other began. But this narrator's statement is a quasi-mechanical presentation and oversimplification of the events that constitute the gift giving and its setting in motion of the sexual encounter.

This third-person narrator may be attempting to demonstrate neutrality and facilitate Lewinsky's narration in the first person. Yet there is also a sense in which the third-person narrator must be viewed as sexually demure and unwilling to get involved in the prurient and provocative details of the young woman's story. At the same time, some might wish to interpret the third-person narrator's receding into the background and handing the narration over to Lewinsky as a statement that her testimony is more conclusive, more spontaneous, and hence more injurious to President Clinton.

Whatever the case, this narrative disappearance paves the way for Monica Lewinsky's dramatic story of the sexual encounter. This story begins exactly where it left off: kissing. The reader will surely remember that prior to the gift giving Lewinsky "was pestering" the president to kiss her. This desire will be fulfilled, but not before another geographical displacement: "[W]e went back by the bathroom in the hallway, and we kissed." And the fulfillment is even more dramatic than the initial desire, since it involves a reciprocal action, signaled by the first-person pronoun "we." It is no longer the woman who is requesting that the man kiss her but a mutual action in which the two individuals participate.

This act of kissing will lead to the more sexually explicit acts. Clinton's participation, according to Lewinsky's tale, begins with the unbuttoning of her dress and the fondling and kissing of her breasts. A movement has been made from the mutual "we" to the president's action. As for Lewinsky, there is an uncertainty in her actions as she begins to recount them. "And then I think I was touching him . . . and I think I unbuttoned his shirt . . ." (ellipses added). In a context such as this, in which the behavior of the president of the United States is coming under close scrutiny, the formulation "I think" is odd indeed. The uncertainty is soon, however, turned into something much more absolute: "And then . . . I wanted to perform oral sex on him . . . and so I did." Without much ado, the woman moves forward to the fulfillment of her desire: the performance of oral sex on the president. He is not asked if he wishes this to happen. And Lewinsky does not inform the reader that she undressed Clinton, though she was careful to recount how he unbuttoned her dress and took her breasts out of her bra. True, if one looks at the published transcripts of Monica Lewinsky's testimony to the grand jury, one can see that the House Judiciary Committee deleted certain materials that formed part of the original testimony on this topic. However, keep in mind that *The Starr Report* must stand as an independently constructed literary text, responsible for its own imbalances. Missing here is the reverse act of uncovering the male body.

In fact, there is a sort of predatory action here, about which the female first-person narrator seems to be completely unaware. Simply put, what she wants ("I wanted to perform oral sex on him"), she does ("and so I did"). The male seems to be the completely passive object: his desires are not articulated, nor is he even asked about them. This feat of hers, about which she is so certain and so adamant, is followed by the same type of textual uncertainty that preceded the act. "And then . . . I think he heard something." Put differently, the narrator thinks she touched the president on his genitals, then thinks she unbuttoned his shirt and kissed his chest, but wishes to perform oral sex on him and does, but then thinks that he heard something. This fluidity and uncertainty in the events framing the performance of oral sex foreground this act as the one concrete event about which there is no doubt.

Lewinsky's thinking that the president "heard something" remains just that, a suspicion. Why is it that she herself heard nothing? That is itself a silence. Nevertheless, the couple makes yet another spatial displacement, this time to the bathroom. This move does not signal the end of the sexual act but rather the opposite, as she continues "to perform oral sex." The president pushes her away, but she makes her plea about caring for him and the importance of the completion of the sexual act: "I care about you so much; . . . I don't understand why you won't let me . . . make you come; it's important to me; I mean, it just doesn't feel complete, it doesn't seem right."

These are the last words in the woman's soliloquy in the narration of the February 28 sexual encounter as she pleads her case with the president. Needless to say, his own urges are not at issue, only what she wishes and what is important to her. In fact, other than the words she will attribute to the president in indirect speech, these are Lewinsky's last words in the text of the February 28 sexual encounter.

Lewinsky has raised a critical question about completion. She herself is only concerned about the completion of the sexual act itself, that is, the physical ejaculation by the president. Yet there is another completion, that of the narration of this ejaculation. Reenter the third-person narrator, who will see to the narrative completion of the sexual act: "Ms. Lewinsky testified that she and the President hugged, and 'he said he didn't want to get addicted to me, and he didn't want me to get addicted to him.' They looked at each other for a moment. Then, saying that 'I don't want to disappoint you,' the President consented. For the first time, she performed oral sex through completion." Once again, Monica Lewinsky's words become intertwined with those of the third-person narrator.

In fact, this will be the last narrative appearance of Lewinsky as speaking subject. Instead, another voice will enter the text: that of Bill Clinton. His voice emerges gradually, appearing first as the subject of indirect speech: "he said he didn't want to get addicted to me, and he didn't want me to get addicted to him." This, of course, is not the first time indirect speech has been attributed to Clinton. In the preceding segments, he, for example, "told her [Lewinsky] to see Ms. Currie after the photo was taken" and he "told her [Lewinsky] to wait a moment," when she was "pestering him" for a kiss (brackets added).

In the narration of the sexual escapades themselves, the president's direct speech is embedded in the midst of prose that one might expect to read in a romance novel: the hugging, the looking at each other. All this is a preamble to his direct words: "I don't want to disappoint you." Despite the attribution of these words to Bill Clinton and despite the fact that they are recounted in the first person, his sentence nevertheless centers on Lewinsky's wishes expressed in the first person. Clinton declares nothing about his own disappointments or his own physical needs. What he does he does for Monica Lewinsky. And yet that first-person intrusion also means that Clinton is sharing the responsibility with Lewinsky for what will occur.

Or, at the very least, that is how the text paints this encounter. Despite her desire to have the president ejaculate, the narrative thunder about this ejaculation is stolen from the female and reappropriated by the third-person narrator. It is this narrator who closes the escapade: "For the first time, she performed oral sex through completion." But perhaps it is only logical that Lewinsky not have the last word here, since she herself is still involved in the sexual process that only culminates at the end of the sentence. While she is busy performing "the oral sex through completion," the narration is recounting it. Sexual completion and textual completion are not one and the same, yet they come together in the closure to the sexual event itself.

The absence of articulated desire in Bill Clinton should perhaps not surprise the reader. True, he invited Monica Lewinsky to the radio address. But she herself plays the aggressor as soon as they are alone. It is in the first person that she declares that: "I was pestering him to kiss me." It is she who wants to perform oral sex and does. It is she who pleads for the completion of the sexual act after the president pushed her away. It is as though the male body loses complete agency in this process. It is not surprising then that he should tell her — in indirect speech — that "he said he didn't want to get addicted to me, and he didn't want me to get addicted to him." Addiction is a strong term indeed, with its implications that transcend the sexual to enter the domain of the legal. More than that, addiction is also a physical and corporal matter, and that is precisely the area where the male seems to lose control: over his body.

One might think that the president's ejaculation, the performance of the "oral sex through completion," would signal the end of the narrative detailing the February 28 sexual encounter. But that is resolutely not the case. The reader will now be transported directly into the world of the Gap dress as well as the president's testimony regarding this encounter: "When Ms. Lewinsky next took the navy blue Gap dress from her closet to wear it, she noticed stains near one hip and on the chest. FBI Laboratory tests revealed that the stains are the President's semen."

This two-sentence paragraph is the shortest of all the paragraphs that constitute the February 28 encounter in the "Narrative" section of *The Starr Report* and represents perhaps the most powerful segment of the encounter. Along with its accompanying "Notes," it brings together the conclusive evidence of the sexual impropriety of the Lewinsky-Clinton couple. Not only does this impropriety boast physical evidence, but this physical evidence itself is defined officially through a government agency. At the same time, the "Notes" accompanying this short segment enlarge its referential base, in the process permitting it to reinforce and underline a host of discourses already present in the telling of the February 28 sexual encounter.

Nor is the grammatical construction of this segment haphazard: the two sentences play with verbal tenses in a suggestive and provocative way. The FBI tests confirm that the stains on Lewinsky's dress "are" the president's semen. Notice that the reality of the president's semen is transmitted in the present tense. The use of the present tense here is incredibly jarring. If one rereads the entirety of the encounter with the verb tenses in mind, one can see that the dominant verbs are in the past tense. The use of the present tense is quite restricted. On the one hand, it appears in some of the direct speech, where it is very rare, as, for example, when Lewinsky states, "I think I was touching him . . . and I think I unbuttoned his shirt . . . I think he heard something," or when Clinton tells Lewinsky, "I don't want to disappoint you." Outside the few examples of the present tense in direct speech, only one other case of that tense appears. This is in the opening segment as the narrator is establishing the presence of the two protagonists in the White House. In the second sentence, the text reads: "White House records show that Ms. Lewinsky attended the taping of the President's weekly radio address on February 28."

The two uses of the present tense, outside direct speech, are then both associated with official documents: White House records and FBI laboratory tests. Both these documents are used by the third-person narrator to establish the facts of the case and to argue the incontrovertible nature of the evidence against William Jefferson Clinton. The present tense adds to the force of the argument, transforming this evidence into an element that is immediate and authoritative, whose validity does not expire with time. It is not an accident, of course, that these two present tenses with their ties to the official documents are strategically placed so that they can inscribe into the record both the beginning and the ending of this historic encounter.

At the heart of this brief segment with the stains is "the navy blue Gap dress." The reader will surely remember that this by-now-famous dress is what signaled the beginning of the actual encounter between Monica Lewinsky and Bill Clinton, and this directly following the establishment of the two protagonists in the White House: "Wearing a navy blue dress from the Gap, Ms. Lewinsky attended the radio address." Once the encounter itself is concluded, Lewinsky will take the dress out of the closet to wear it again. This action by Lewinsky represents the last narrative act in which she will be the subject of the action. The dress that paved the way for her sexual encounter will now help to seal that encounter.

But the dress as physical object that opens the encounter is not identical to the dress as physical object that seals that encounter. The initial dress was one worn by Lewinsky, whereas the later appearance signals a dress that was to be worn but apparently will not be. The reasons for this change of status are the stains on the garment, noticed by Lewinsky. The narrative moves directly from the stains to the FBI Laboratory tests and their findings that "the stains are the President's semen."

Rather than moving as quickly as the narrative does from the stains to the FBI tests and results, the critical act should let the stains speak for themselves not only in the text of the "Narrative" but in the attached "Notes." The stains first enter the narrative as the objects that Monica Lewinsky noticed when she "next took the navy blue Gap dress from her closet to wear it." These stains are "near one hip and on the chest." Do dresses have hips and chests? Hips and chests normally refer to parts of a body and not to parts of clothing. With this seemingly simple placement of the stains, the third-person narrator has effectively transported the reader from the blue Gap dress to Lewinsky's body. This should perhaps not come as a surprise since the initial appearance of the dress had served to corporalize and feminize Lewinsky. The stains on the dress become stains on the female body.

And just as the stains can make the jump to the female body, so they also demarcate the male body. There is no better way to allude to this body than through that essentially male fluid, semen. The knowledge from the FBI has already been shared with the reader: "the stains *are* the President's semen" (emphasis added). The-stains-are-the-semen is a strong assertion of identity that creates a complete equivalence between the stains and the semen, in the process leaving no possibility that there might have been semen elsewhere.

The discourse of the body is, however, not the only discourse generated by the stains. The stains on the dress also participate in a discourse of public and private. In a sense, the trajectory of the stains reflects a reverse trajectory of the dress itself that the stains inhabit. The stains first appear as Monica Lewinsky takes the dress out of her closet. From the closet, the stains are then careened into national and international visibility as they become identified with Bill Clinton's semen. Theirs is a clear trajectory from the private to the public. This trajectory, in turn, reverses the trajectory of the dress, which moved instead from the public to the private: making its debut at the radio address and then progressing through the recesses of the White House to find its resting place in Lewinsky's closet.

The discerning reader may well wonder how it is that these stains seem to have maintained their existence well beyond the oral sex incident with Bill Clinton. Fortunately, Monica Lewinsky is there in the *Report* to explain this strange occurrence. In a "Note," the text states: "Ms. Lewinsky testified that she did not keep the soiled dress as a souvenir. She said she does not ordinarily clean her clothes until she is ready to wear them again. 'I was going to clean it. I was going to wear it again.' . . . She also testified that she was not certain that the stains were semen. She had dined out after the radio address, '[s]o it could be spinach dip or something.'"

Superficially, this information seems to be nothing more than an explanation of how it was that the dress in Monica Lewinsky's closet still had Bill Clinton's semen on it. But, in fact, these assertions, shared between the third-person narrator and Lewinsky, open up a host of discourses not the least of which concern the body. The initial sentence creates what Arthur Koestler calls in *The Act of Creation* a bisociation, or the association of two elements not normally found together, because they belong to two different patterns of thought. Lewinsky "testified that she did not keep the soiled dress as a souvenir." The bisociation here results from the notion that a soiled dress could be a souvenir. A souvenir by its nature is something one treasures and keeps, and the fact that a soiled dress could become a souvenir stretches the imagination. At the same time, Lewinsky's denial that she would have kept the dress as a souvenir lends an element of absurdity, of camp, to the entire episode with the dress.

Whatever the veracity of this initial statement, however, it opens the narrative door for what follows. Only, this time, the "Note" will expand the physical universe to which the reader has become accustomed into wider areas, the first of which is that of cleanliness. The blue dress from the Gap that was the repository of the stains in the text now becomes "the soiled dress" in the "Note." Is this soiling a moral stain, a physical stain, or both? If the reader should sense that something is not quite as it should be here, this reader is quickly reassured about Lewinsky's personal habits: "she said she does not ordinarily clean her clothes until she is ready to wear them again." The imaginative reader might well visualize a closet full of "soiled" clothes waiting to be cleaned when their owner decides to wear them.

But how practical would it be for an ambitious young woman on the town with an active social life to wait to clean a garment until the invitation or occasion for its wearing presented itself? Either Monica Lewinsky has the world's finest one-hour cleaning service, or she is not as credible as *The Starr Report* repeatedly insists. Perhaps the narrator is aware in advance of the disbelief this statement will generate so the text immediately follows up with Lewinsky's words: "I was going to clean it. I was going to wear it again." These two sentences parallel one another, down to their grammatical construction, even repeating the vocabulary about her intentions, "I was going to." Her own internal repetition mirrors the statement by the third-person narrator, and the entirety of the explanation about the order of cleaning and wearing functions as a protest accounting for the fact that that "soiled" dress was kept in the closet.

The reader is asked to stretch his or her imagination still further as the "Note" continues. Monica Lewinsky "also testified that she was not certain that the stains were semen. She had dined out after the radio address, '[s]o it could be spinach dip or something.'" With one stroke, the third-person narrator, working in tandem with the female voice, has moved into other discourses. Lewinsky's testimony is meant to create uncertainty about the identity of the stains as semen (note again the use of the verb "to be": "she was not certain that the stains were semen"). But not to worry. The narrator will add that "she had dined out after the radio address," in this way facilitating Lewinsky's speculations delivered in her own words: "[s]o it could be spinach dip or something."

Dining out and spinach dip transport the narrative directly into an already familiar discourse, that of orality. To the orality of the oral sex has been added the oral activity of eating. The narrator says Lewinsky "had dined out after the radio address." This temporal element embellishes on the sexual interlude with the president. Lewinsky and Clinton, after all, went off directly after the radio address to have their sexual encounter. Is the narrator being coy in not mentioning that it would have been after oral sex that Monica Lewinsky would have dined out, or have the oral sex and the dining-out simply been conflated? Besides, who dines out on "spinach dip"? That food is something one more commonly associates with a cocktail party, unless, of course, it is a stand-in for another liquid. By the same token, the text has added to the color and complexity of the Lewinsky closet, filled as it is now with clothes whose stigmata could represent alternatively the residues of feasts or of trysts.

This explanation is certainly both amusing and psychologically revealing. Its legal relevance is hardly evident. Aside from showing again *The Starr Report*'s taste for prurient detail, this incident plays a crucial role in characterization. This tortured tale is meant to replace another that might form in the reader's mind: the notion of a Monica Lewinsky who lures the president into oral sex, blackmails him emotionally into ejaculating, then arranges for the stains to fall on her dress (it is a long way from mouth to hip), which she subsequently saves as a trophy. Reducing Monica Lewinsky's agency in the encounter increases that of Bill Clinton and hence his culpability.

But Monica Lewinsky is also responsible in this account for conflating orality and masculinity. The spinach dip speaks a great deal in this context. Eating spinach calls up that popular comic-strip character Popeye, whose consumption of spinach was linked to his muscle mass and his masculinity. The representation of Popeye's arm swelling up with visible strength after he ingests the magic vegetable is a part of American popular culture. This could be why the "spinach dip" has been transformed into the less improbable "guacamole" in *Monica's Story*.

In a recently recycled image (from the Indiana University *Home Pages*), Popeye is shown offering a flowering plant labeled as spinach to the object of his desire, Olive Oyl, who laughs demurely. This cartoon of Popeye with his spinach offering has not been chosen randomly. In the opening sections of the February 28 sexual encounter, President Clinton had "told her [Lewinsky] to see Ms. Currie after the photo was taken because he wanted to give her something" (brackets added). He, indeed, wanted to give her something: ostensibly, the hat pin and Whitman's *Leaves of Grass*. But the reader now knows that he ends up giving her much more: he leaves her with his semen firmly planted on her dress. Lewinsky conflates this semen with spinach. Unlike Olive Oyl, she accepts the offering given to her, at her insistence, of course, by President Clinton. That the actual sexual encounter should then take place between the initial gift giving and the discovery of that other "gift," the semen, is no longer accidental.

The inherent corporality in the stains segment continues as the narrative progresses to the closure of this sexual encounter, a closure provided by the president's testimony.

> In his grand jury testimony, the President — who, because the OIC had asked him for a blood sample (and had represented that it had ample evidentiary justification for making such a request), had reason to suspect that Ms. Lewinsky's dress might bear traces of his semen — indicated that he and Ms. Lewinsky had had sexual contact on the day of the radio address. He testified:
>
> > I was sick after it was over and I, I was pleased at that time that it had been nearly a year since any inappropriate contact had occurred with Ms. Lewinsky. I promised myself it wasn't going to happen again. The facts are complicated about what did happen and how it happened. But, nonetheless, I'm responsible for it.
> >
> > Later the President added, referring to the evening of the radio address: "I do believe that I was alone with her from 15 to 20 minutes. I do believe that things happened then which were inappropriate." He said of the intimate relationship with Ms. Lewinsky: "I never should have started it, and I certainly shouldn't have started it back after I resolved not to in 1996."

Once again, that familiar third-person narrator introduces the testimony. And what an introduction! In its attempt to bring together the corporal with the legal and the sexual, it becomes entangled in its own rhetoric. The narrator wants the reader of the *Report* to know that what follows is from the president's grand jury testimony. But the narrator also wants to prejudice the reading of this testimony in advance by ascertaining that the testimony is the result of actions taken by the OIC, actions centered on corporal elements. Not only does the president appear to have been forced to provide a blood sample, but he "had reason to suspect that Ms. Lewinsky's dress might bear traces of his semen." In the transition from the discovery of the stains to the president's testimony, the dress has evolved yet again into something that now "might bear traces of his semen." A movement has been effected from the reality that "the stains are the President's semen" into possible "traces of" this semen.

No matter. The corporal is there to ascertain the president's guilt, not only through one bodily fluid, the semen, but through another, the blood. It is hardly surprising then that the narrator is anxious to add that the president "indicated that he and Ms. Lewinsky had had sexual contact on the day of the radio address." Once assured that the reader knows that the president is guilty of sexual impropriety, the narrator can turn the text over to Clinton for his first-person tale: "I was sick after it was over and I, I was pleased at that time that it had been nearly a year since any inappropriate contact had occurred with Ms. Lewinsky. I promised myself it wasn't going to happen again. The facts are complicated about what did happen and how it happened. But, nonetheless, I'm responsible for it."

"I was sick after it was over." Is Clinton referring to a physical reaction, such as vomiting, or is he attempting to pull the reader away from the body and into an emotional universe that expands the horizons of the sexual? This initial situation is left ambiguous. But as the first-person narrator progresses, it becomes clear that the emotional component is critical. Clinton is "pleased" about the lapse of a year since "any inappropriate contact" with Lewinsky. He ends with "I'm responsible for it."

Once that responsibility is declared, the third-person narrator can reenter the narrative and intercalate the third-person voice with Bill Clinton's first-person voice. That intrusive narrator can then comment on Clinton's words: "I do believe that I was alone with her from 15 to 20 minutes. I do believe that things happened then which were inappropriate." The "I do believe" parallels the "I think" in Lewinsky's narration of the sexual interlude, leaving just the shadow of a doubt about what transpired.

But more than that, the president's testimony, functioning as it does as closure to the entire incident, harks back to the beginning of the narrative detailing the February 28 sexual encounter. Being alone "with her from 15 to 20 minutes" recalls the beginning, in which the text states that the president "was in the Roosevelt Room . . . from 6:29 to 6:36 P.M., then moved to the

Oval Office, where he remained until 7:24 P.M." (ellipsis added). The precision in the time at the beginning counters the later — and seemingly false — perception that it was "15 to 20 minutes." The phrase "I certainly shouldn't have started it back after I resolved not to in 1996" echoes and clarifies the opening paragraph in which the reader learned that this sexual encounter was "their first in nearly 11 months." This closure with time and chronology translates into a narrative circularity for this important event. But it is a circularity whose beginning is the official records and whose ending is the personal testimony.

The importance of this personal testimony is that, unlike the official records, it can be made to translate into a moral conclusion. And that is precisely what the third-person narrator does with it. "He said of the intimate relationship with Ms. Lewinsky: 'I never should have started it, and I certainly shouldn't have started it back after I resolved not to in 1996.'" Bill Clinton ends the narrative with a statement of contrition, one that applies initially to the entire relationship with Monica Lewinsky: "I never should have started it." No sooner is that declaration made about the entirety of the relationship than Clinton, in the first person, redefines it by limiting his liability: "I certainly shouldn't have started it back after I resolved not to in 1996."

President Clinton may well regret this "intimate relationship." Notice, however, that the definition of this relationship as "intimate" is that of the third-person narrator. This is a narrator who has already demonstrated to the reader that he or she is quite proficient at manipulating the narrative. And it is these manipulations that help generate the discourses ranging from orality to sexuality and from the public to the private, in the process enlarging and expanding the narrative range of *The Starr Report*.

As the February 28 sexual encounter resurfaces in the "Grounds" section of *The Starr Report*, it will be transformed yet again. Not surprisingly, this mutation will redefine both Clinton and Lewinsky's relationship and their sexuality.

7
_____

HOW IS A SEXUAL ENCOUNTER A SEXUAL ENCOUNTER?

The third-person narrator of *The Starr Report*, working in tandem with Monica Lewinsky and Bill Clinton, constructed a fascinating and provocative rendition of the February 28 sexual encounter. The three voices, when added to that of Betty Currie, accomplish this feat in the "Narrative" section of the *Report*. As the text evolves in the "Grounds" section, the incident with the blue dress stained with semen reappears, this time in slightly different narrative guises. Orality, sexuality, and the body loom large here as well. More important, the examination of the "Grounds" version of the February 28 sexual incident will deepen the understanding of repetition in *The Starr Report*, a project that calls for multiple readings as it creates textual variants of the same incident. In the process, these readings will permit the investigation of corporal geographies that exacerbate the gender games so important in *The Starr Report*.

Here is how the sexual encounter appears in the "Grounds" section:

Ms. Lewinsky testified that her next sexual encounter with the President occurred on Friday, February 28, 1997, in the early evening. The President initiated this encounter by having his secretary Betty Currie call Ms. Lewinsky to invite her to the White House for a radio address. After the address, Ms. Lewinsky and the President kissed by the bathroom. The President unbuttoned her dress and fondled her breasts, first with her bra on and then directly. He touched her genitalia through her clothes, but not directly, on this occasion. Ms. Lewinsky performed oral sex on him. On this day, Ms. Lewinsky was wearing a blue dress that forensic tests have conclusively shown was stained with the President's semen.

Perhaps the first element that should strike any reader is the brevity of this version of the February 28 encounter. And, unlike the account in the "Narrative" section of *The Starr Report*, this version is the sole property of a third-person narrator and stripped to what appears at first glance to be a bare minimum. Gone are the dramatic interjections of the first-person voices of Bill Clinton and Monica Lewinsky. This is, of course, consistent with the way in which the narratives of the sexual encounters are created in the "Grounds."

Yet the two characters are present, along with their intermediary, Betty Currie. This is the only encounter in the "Grounds" in which Currie appears. The third-person narrator leans on the two protagonists in provocative ways, and the brevity of this narrator's story helps to redefine the nature of the February 28 sexual encounter. This shorter variant, like its literary sibling, can be divided into segments:

1. The chronological setting of the encounter

2. The invitation and the radio address

3. The sexual encounter

4. The blue dress and the semen

The first segment, the chronological setting, serves to delineate the time of the encounter. Notice, however, that the information on when the adventure occurred is based on Monica Lewinsky's testimony. She may not speak in the first person in this version, but her name and title, Ms. Lewinsky, are the first elements the reader encounters on beginning this sexual voyage. As with the longer version of the February 28 encounter, this appearance foregrounds Lewinsky. Unlike that earlier presentation, however, no official documentation is necessary to verify Lewinsky's words.

At the same time, the initial establishment of Monica Lewinsky's testimony in the first sentence will be the last time any information is attributed to her by the third-person narrator. Once she has paved the way with the chronological setting, that narrator can pick up the thread of the story and tell it without any help from either Lewinsky or Clinton.

Beware, however: this is not to say that the two protagonists have no role to play. President Clinton emerges in the second segment, that with the invitation and the radio address. Here, Clinton is painted as the individual who "initiated this encounter," as he asks his secretary, Betty Currie, to call Monica Lewinsky and invite her to the White House for the radio address. The critical words are: "this encounter." The demonstrative "this" qualifies the event and harks back to the first time the encounter was mentioned. There, this was not simply an encounter but a "sexual encounter." By stating that President Clinton "initiated this encounter," the narrator is strongly implying that Clinton set the sexual adventure in motion as well. The reader already knows from the previous version of this incident that Bill Clinton had asked Betty Currie to invite Lewinsky to the radio address, after which "he wanted to give her something," an ironic turn of phrase already analyzed above. But to say that Clinton "initiated this [read: sexual] encounter" is not an innocent statement. It places the responsibility for the subsequent events squarely at his feet. He becomes the aggressor, not one who was pestered by Monica Lewinsky's desire for a kiss. And, in fact, this is precisely how the text will paint the president: as the aggressor. This is concordant with his portrayal in the other sexual encounters in the "Grounds." True, "Miss Lewinsky and the President kissed by the bathroom," a mutual act. But not to worry. The president will soon enough regain the active role in these corporal antics.

The third-person narrator provides the details in the "Grounds": "The President unbuttoned her dress and fondled her breasts, first with her bra on and then directly." The adventure with the breasts will not be unfamiliar to the reader, since the longer account has already revealed it. The difference, of course, is that the longer account in the "Narrative" foregrounds Monica Lewinsky's direct first-person narration: "We were kissing and he unbuttoned my dress and fondled my breasts with my bra on, and then took them out of my bra and was kissing them and touching them with his hands and with his mouth." Remember that in the longer account, the sexual escapades are preceded first by Lewinsky's "pestering" the president to kiss her and second, and more important, by the gift giving, whose role has already been demonstrated to be that of an erotic prelude or foreplay.

The scenario of the sexual encounter in the "Grounds" has up to this point been following in the textual tracks of the longer scenario in the "Narrative." The two parties kiss and then the president explores Lewinsky's breasts, albeit in greater detail in the "Narrative." It is at this point, however, that the third-person narrator in the "Grounds" goes off on his or her own path. Monica Lewinsky can fortunately remind the reader of the earlier account: "And then I think I was touching him in his genital area through his pants, and I think I unbuttoned his shirt and was kissing his chest. And then . . . I wanted to perform oral sex on him . . . and so I did." The narrator in the "Grounds" tells it differently: "He touched her genitalia through her clothes, but not directly, on this occasion. Ms. Lewinsky performed oral sex on him."

At first glance, the two accounts seem to be delineating the same sexual process, that of touching the genitals. The critical difference lies in the identity of the individual doing the touching. In the "Narrative" account, it is Lewinsky who touches the president "in his genital area through his pants," whereas in the "Grounds," it is the president who touches Lewinsky's "genitalia through her clothes." Both perpetrators perform the action through the clothing, an odd coincidence, indeed. Still more significant is the fact that in each of the two variants the touching goes in only one direction; there is no reciprocity. Strikingly, however, since the direction is the opposite in each rendition, a virtual reciprocity is created between the two versions, but one that is only visible if the two variants are superimposed one on the other. The "Narrative" does not say, for example, that Lewinsky touched the president's genital area only to have him follow her action by a reciprocal one in which the president touches her genitalia. And the reverse would be true in the "Grounds" where the president is the toucher with no touching by Monica Lewinsky of Clinton's "genital area."

The transformation of the perpetrator exploring the genitalia from Lewinsky to Clinton has more reverberations than that of merely creating a possible confusion between who did what to whom. The change of identity conforms with, and reinforces, the project of culpability and desire. In the "Narrative," Monica Lewinsky is unable to control her passion: she is portrayed as the one playing the role of aggressor with the president pushing her away. This is not the case in the "Grounds," where that role falls to Bill Clinton. This is in complete conformity with the initial opening segment, in which he was portrayed as the initiator of the "encounter." It would seem that both parties are equally unable to control their passions, though this mutual attraction is only visible when one places the two accounts next to each other.

Other repercussions lie hidden behind the differences in the two accounts. When the narrator states that "he touched her genitalia through her clothes, but not directly, on this occasion," that narrator is saying more than simply that the president touched Lewinsky's "genitalia." By adding the time element "on this occasion," the sly narrator has also extended Clinton's touching activity beyond this encounter in such a way that the reader assumes that Clinton was in the habit of touching Lewinsky's genital area, sometimes directly and sometimes not.

Time is also a weapon in the arsenal of the *Report*. In the "Narrative" version of this encounter, it is Lewinsky who plays with the element of time: "And I continued to perform oral sex and then he pushed me away, kind of as he always did before he came." The key word here is "always," meaning a familiar action on the part of the president. "Always" also extends the action into a limitless space, one in which actions can exist in permanence and become normalized. The summary text in the "Grounds" is busy painting a consistent image of the president as the initiator and perpetrator of the sexual encounters. These chronological references fulfill the same function: they add to the president's responsibility.

Throughout the "Grounds," verbal cues abound to point to the guilty party. There is no mystery in this version that Clinton is the winner in the culpability sweepstakes. A look at the active subjects of the verbs and sentences in this shorter version of the encounter will uncover a great deal. The grammatical task turns out to be extremely easy, since the third-person narrator in this incident does not indulge in much stylistic variation. What dominates is the simple, straightforward sentence in which the subject begins the sentence, to be followed directly by the verb. This is the rhetorical structure of four out of the seven sentences that constitute the account. The seven sentences in the "Grounds" account begin:

Sentence #1: "Ms. Lewinsky testified . . ."

Sentence #2: "The President initiated . . ."

Sentence #3: "After the address . . ."

Sentence #4: "The President unbuttoned . . ."

Sentence #5: "He touched . . ."

Sentence #6: "Ms. Lewinsky performed . . ."

Sentence #7: "On this day . . ."

Of the five sentences structured with a solitary subject, Clinton is attached to three (#2, #4, and #5).

Sentences #3 and #7 are grammatically a bit more complex, both beginning with temporal clauses. The grammatical complexity signals, in both instances, something unusual and important in the narrative. Sentence #3 reads: "After the address, Ms. Lewinsky and the President kissed by the bathroom." The temporal introduction, "After the address," signals a stylistic break in the way the third-person narrator has thus far constructed the narrative. This break heralds not only a change in the subject of the verb but a change of venue as well. Now both Lewinsky and Clinton are performing the action of kissing. Not only that, but there has been a move from one location, that of the radio address, to the bathroom. This kissing, of course, is what will lead to the oral sex, to the presence of the semen, and the proof of the president's guilt.

The result of this kissing will be confirmed in sentence #7: "On this day, Ms. Lewinsky was wearing a blue dress that forensic tests have conclusively shown was stained with the President's semen." Notice, once again, the temporal element with which the sentence begins: "On this day." Like the grammatical structure in sentence #3, that in sentence #7 also points to something crucial, here the inconvertible and solid proof of the sexual encounter. The words "On this day" hark back to the first sentence of the narrative, in which the testimony of Monica Lewinsky established the timing of the encounter. The similarity in the grammatical structure of the sentences with the temporal element inextricably links the act of kissing to that of the discovery of the semen. There is also circularity, as the last sentence moves the reader back to the first.

But one should not be misled into thinking that the construction of this version of the encounter in predominantly simple sentences means an absence of other discourses. Reigning supreme in this is the discourse of the body. This particular discourse complements the one in the "Narrative" section, in the process generating a corporal geography of the male and female. Bodily acts in both the "Narrative" and the "Grounds" begin at the top of the body and move downward gradually. In both tellings of this sexual encounter, the escapades begin with mutual kissing. Once this is accomplished, the text can begin on its corporal trajectory, in the process creating this gendered geography of the body.

Traveling the bodies in both accounts shows the divergences between the two. In the simpler account, that in the "Grounds," the mutual kissing leads the president to unbutton Lewinsky's dress and fondle her breast, first with her bra on and then directly. Then he touches her genitalia through her clothing, and she performs oral sex. In the longer account, that in the "Narrative," the mutual kissing once again leads the president to the breasts, but this time his fondling is described as involving both his hands and his mouth. Lewinsky now touches the president's "genital area through his pants" and proceeds to unbutton his shirt and kiss his chest. This is followed by oral sex.

Mapping the corporal activities and their respective accounts reveals the following:

"Narrative"	"Grounds"
mutual kissing	mutual kissing
unbuttoning dress	unbuttoning dress
fondling breasts (with hands and mouth)	fondling breasts
exploring male genitals	—
—	touching female genitalia
unbuttoning shirt	—
kissing chest	—
oral sex	oral sex

The differences between the two accounts are telling. Perhaps the most visible distinction is that of the genitals. Whereas Lewinsky explores Clinton's genitals in the "Narrative," he explores hers in the "Grounds." "Narrative" also displays an interesting movement in its depiction of the corporal explorations that will lead to the oral sex. The unbuttoning of Lewinsky's dress followed by the fondling and kissing of her breasts is paralleled by her unbuttoning Clinton's shirt and kissing his chest. The delineation of these activities in the "Narrative" and the absence of Lewinsky's parallel exploration in the "Grounds" confirms the portrait painted of the president as predator in that variant.

The male body and the female body are turned into sexualized objects in the narration of this encounter in *The Starr Report*. There is a dominant orality to the description of the corporal exploration, as one party and then another uses the mouth. The body becomes nothing but the sum of the body parts, as these are uncovered and then fondled. Missing, of course, from this corporal delineation is the unzipping of Clinton's pants. The text tells the reader about the unbuttoning of Lewinsky's dress and his shirt but reveals nothing about that most essential of all undressing activities. Yet the president's sexual organ and its semen are vital players in this encounter. This is extremely odd considering that the third-person narrator regales the reader with detailed descriptions of the fondling of the breasts, as these body parts first appear dressed and then not. The male body loses, as it were, one of its major corporal players.

That the "Narration" and the "Grounds" must be seen as complementary versions of the February 28 sexual encounter is reinforced in the ubiquitous "Notes." The first "Note" in the "Grounds" adds yet another sexual element to this already explosive mix: phone sex. This "Note" is attached to the first sentence of the version in the "Grounds," the sentence sketching the time of the encounter, and states: "They had engaged in phone sex a number of times in the interim." The longer version of this incident, that of the "Narrative," made no mention of phone sex, either in the text or in the attached "Notes."

The phone sex is by definition oral and aural at once. In its oral function, it reinforces the orality already so prevalent in the tellings of this encounter, analyzed in great detail above. It also adds different layers of signification to the encounter. There is a hidden intertextual layer, one that remains unarticulated in the text. The reader of *The Starr Report* is already aware by the time he or she reaches this point in the story that Monica Lewinsky had given President Clinton a copy of the novel *Vox*, by Nicholson Baker, "a novel about phone sex." The intertextual echoes are there, albeit not as directly as with *Romeo and Juliet* or Whitman's *Leaves of Grass*.

But the reference to phone sex does much more. It expands the sexual universe not only of the text in the "Grounds" but of the text and the "Notes" in the "Narrative" as well. Now the reader knows that in addition to the corporal fondling and the oral sex that led to the president's ejaculation there was that elusive phone sex as well.

More important, however, the addition of the phone sex redefines the long absence of sexual encounters the "Narrative" section was so careful to mention: "According to Ms. Lewinsky, she and the President had a sexual encounter on Thursday, February 28 — their first in nearly 11 months." Thanks to the "Note" in the "Grounds," the February 28 encounter is no longer an event that follows an extended period of abstinence on the part of the two protagonists. Rather, this decisive episode with the semen on the blue dress is transformed into a culmination of sexual encounters, some of which involved phone sex. The reader is now facing a connected series of events. This transformation, in turn, redefines the yearning and nervousness on Lewinsky's part, so marked in the "Narrative" account. True, she has not seen the president in eleven months, but they have carried on a phone relationship.

Yet this "Note," inserted seemingly as an afterthought, does much more. "They had engaged in phone sex. . . ." The "they" redefines the sexual relationship as being a mutual activity on the part of Clinton and Lewinsky. At the same time, the "Note" recasts the president's role. Perhaps he is not so much the aggressor he appears in the text attached to that very "Note." The allusion to the phone sex also plays games with the president's contrition, an element textually so critical to the telling of the encounter in the "Narrative." The reader would be correct in questioning the sincerity of that contrition, which turns the president into a fallen man, trapped after eleven months of sexual abstinence.

It is not, however, only the "Notes" attached to a specific event that redefine that event. The documentary nature of the *Report* permits "Notes" that are appended to one event to recast another, in the process creating complicated intertextual echoes and games. In her testimony in the "Grounds," Betty Currie "testified that President Clinton and Ms. Lewinsky were alone together in the Oval Office area a number of times." In this testimony, she "specifically remembered three occasions when the President and Ms. Lewinsky were alone together," including February 28, 1997, the day of the sexual encounter with the blue dress. But, lo and behold, a "Note" appended to this date redefines the infamous encounter yet again. A parenthetical aside has Currie now "recalling that after the President's radio address, the President told Ms. Lewinsky he wanted to show her his collection of political buttons and took her into the Oval Office study for 15 to 20 minutes while Ms. Currie waited nearby, in the pantry or the dining room." The information here is not only relegated to a "Note," that is, placed outside the text of both the "Narrative" and the "Grounds," but even within the "Note" the material that Betty Currie adds is placed in parentheses, setting it aside once again.

This recollection of Betty Currie is, however, extremely significant, adding critical information to the February 28 encounter that appears nowhere else but at the same time contradicts earlier facts. The key question concerns precisely what occurred after the radio address. In this crucial "Note," the president tells Monica Lewinsky that "he wanted to show her his collection of political buttons and took her into the Oval Office study for 15 to 20 minutes." There is something almost comic about this invitation, which smells like the old line: "Can I show you my etchings?" To do this showing, the president takes Lewinsky into the Oval Office while Betty Currie "waited nearby, in the pantry or the dining room."

And yet, comic though it may be, this showing of political buttons appears nowhere in the other two accounts of this seminal (if the word be permitted) sexual encounter. The account in the "Narrative," already analyzed, chronicles the events in the following way:

> Ms. Lewinsky attended the radio address at the President's invitation (relayed by Ms. Currie), then had her photo taken with the President. Ms. Lewinsky had not been alone with the President since she had worked at the White House, and, she testified, "I was really nervous." President Clinton told her to see Ms. Currie after the photo was taken because he wanted to give her something. "So I waited a little while for him and then Betty and the President and I went into the back office," Ms. Lewinsky testified. (She later learned that the reason Ms. Currie accompanied them was that Stephen Goodin did not want the President to be alone with Ms. Lewinsky, a view that Mr. Goodin expressed to the President and Ms. Currie.) Once they had passed from the Oval Office toward the private study, Ms. Currie said, "I'll be right back," and walked on to the back pantry or the dining room, where, according to Ms. Currie, she waited for 15 to 20 minutes while the President and Ms. Lewinsky were in the study.

In this rendition, one moves from the radio address to the photo. Then Clinton tells Lewinsky to "see Ms. Currie after the photo was taken because he wanted to give her something." This is followed by the trio moving "into the back office." Betty Currie disappears from the scene and into "the back pantry or the dining room," once "they had passed from the Oval Office toward the private study." The text of the "Grounds" goes to the point: "After the address, Ms. Lewinsky and the President kissed by the bathroom."

Different possible scenarios, some more provocative than others, some even tending to the comic. Essential information hides in the "Notes" and then not even in "Notes" that address a specific incident. All this merely confirms the view that *The Starr Report* is more than just a record of a relationship gone awry. The various renditions, even when contradictory, are the strokes that put the finishing touches on a portrait not only of a secret relationship between a president and a White House intern turned government employee but also of the gendered sexual conceptions and fascinations of the Office of the Independent Counsel — and surely of many other Americans as well.

8

"I LOVE THE NARRATIVE!"

Commenting on the work that would bear his name, Kenneth Starr declared — at least according to Bob Woodward and his sources — "I love the narrative!" Of course, in Woodward's account, Judge Starr is referring to the section of the referral labeled "Narrative." Yet Kenneth Starr's statement implies the existence of a unified narrative, "the" narrative. But, in fact, the referral to Congress displays textual tensions precisely because different narratives, different stories, intervene in what could be called the primary narrative that relates the sexual exploits of Bill Clinton and Monica Lewinsky. Narratives of denials, narratives of secrecy, and narratives of aggression and concomitant narratives of victimization will sit side by side with the narratives that secondary characters tell. All these narratives, though they owe their existence to that primary narrative, will redefine that primary narrative as stories are told in different ways, in the process setting up different expectations on the part of the reader. One can even speak of "his" and "hers" narratives. And this is not to mention a hidden narrative of desire not only on the part of Clinton and Lewinsky but also on the part of *The Starr Report*. These narratives often function as narratives of resistance to the primary narrative bent on arguing the guilt of the president of the United States. "The narrative" is not one narrative but a multiplicity of linked and interdependent narratives to which different parties are at one or another time attached.

The relationship between Monica Lewinsky and Bill Clinton in the *Report* revolves around a set of sexual encounters. These accounts are Lewinsky's narrative, digested and regurgitated by the narrator of the *Report*. Because of various factors inherent in such a relationship, not the least of which is the fact that one of the parties is the president of the United States, secrecy plays an important role.

But secrecy is not a simple element. It engenders different discourses, creates other narratives, other stories. The narrator concludes in an opening section of the *Report* that sets out its contents: "The nature of the relationship was the subject of many of the President's false statements, and his desire to keep the relationship secret provides a motive for many of his actions that apparently were designed to obstruct justice."

This assessment placing the responsibility for secrecy squarely in the president's lap is at best misleading. Indeed, the *Report* informs its public in the introductory chapter to the "Narrative" that both parties "testified that they took steps to maintain the secrecy of the relationship." Secrecy is so central that it receives its own section in the chapter, with subheadings. In the "Grounds," the narrator makes it clear that "from the beginning, President Clinton and Monica Lewinsky hoped and expected that their relationship would remain secret. They took active steps, when necessary, to conceal the relationship. The President testified that 'I hoped that this relationship would never become public.'"

But there was also a certain naïveté on the part of the participants. Monica Lewinsky, for example, "expressed confidence that her relationship with the President would never be discovered. She believed that no records showed her and the President alone in the area of the study." The records, however, not only exist but become an essential part of the description of the sexual encounters in the "Narrative."

There is even a certain irony in these secrecy attempts that was clearly not apparent to the two players, involved as they were with themselves and with the relationship. In a section labeled "*Observations by Secret Service Officers,*" the *Report* explains:

Officers of the Secret Service Uniformed Division noted Ms. Lewinsky's 1997 visits to the White House. From radio traffic about the President's movements, several officers observed that the President often would head for the Oval Office within minutes of Ms. Lewinsky's entry to the complex, especially on weekends, and some noted that he would return to the Residence a short time after her departure. "It was just like clockwork," according to one officer. Concerned about the President's reputation, another officer suggested putting Ms. Lewinsky on a list of people who were not to be admitted to the White House. A commander responded that it was none of their business whom the President chose to see, and, in any event, nobody would ever find out about Ms. Lewinsky.

The behavior that was "like clockwork" obviously speaks volumes about the inefficacy of the attempts at secrecy.

The irony is compounded by the commander's statement to an officer that "nobody would ever find out about Ms. Lewinsky." The commander's prediction is as false as the ideas of the two culprits about the possibility of secrecy. Far from "nobody . . . ever find[ing] out about" Monica Lewinsky, the entire world has found out about her.

But perhaps the conjecture by the commander would not have been so far off the mark if the two parties had actually maintained the secrecy of their association. While Bill Clinton, according to Lewinsky, may have "from the outset stressed the importance of keeping the relationship secret," that does not mean that his female coparticipant in the escapades felt that necessity as strongly as he did. "According to Ms. Lewinsky, the President sometimes asked if she had told anyone about their sexual relationship or about the gifts they had exchanged; she (falsely) assured him that she had not." And "In April or May 1997, according to Ms. Lewinsky, the President asked if she had told her mother about their intimate relationship. She responded: 'No. Of course not.' (In truth, she had told her mother.)" In this same conversation, it becomes clear that the president is on to something because he "indicated that Ms. Lewinsky's mother possibly had said something about the nature of the relationship to Walter Kaye, who had mentioned it to Marsha Scott, who in turn had alerted the President." The web of intrigue is clearly multilayered, with secrecy sacrificed at the altar of gossip. As one moves backward from the president to Marsha Scott, the "Deputy Director of Personnel," to Walter Kaye, a "Family Friend of Monica Lewinsky," to Lewinsky's mother, it becomes evident that although secrecy was a desideratum, that wish was just that, a wish and not a reality.

So it is hardly a surprise that Monica Lewinsky, who assured the president, on one hand, that she had not revealed their relationship but, on the other, had told family and friends about this relationship, should then write the president a letter that "obliquely threatened to disclose their relationship." This is in the context of her "inability to get in touch with the President to discuss her job situation." This letter was dated July 3, 1997. On January 15, 1998, Monica Lewinsky "encouraged" Linda Tripp not to "disclose" her relationship with Bill Clinton. Lewinsky did not consider herself "a 'big issue' like Gennifer Flowers and Paula Jones. In contrast, she regarded herself as nothing more than 'rumor and innuendo.'" A rumor can, of course, be verifiable and this is precisely the sort of rumor that Monica Lewinsky turns out to be. By encouraging Tripp to do her bidding, Monica Lewinsky is really encouraging her to lie.

Lying functions as a narrative layer in *The Starr Report* that redefines the primary narrative of the encounters. Its power to function in this way relates to its ability to attach itself to different characters in this melodrama, including the two principals, Monica Lewinsky and Bill Clinton.

A "Note" in the "Narrative" states that

> the negotiations in January and February 1998 (which produced the written proffer) did not result in a cooperation agreement because Ms. Lewinsky declined to submit to a face-to-face proffer interview, which the oic deemed essential because of her perjurious *Jones* affidavit, her efforts to persuade Linda Tripp to commit perjury, her assertion in a recorded conversation that she had been brought up to regard lying as necessary, and her forgery of a letter while in college.

This information relegated to a "Note" is quite telling. What is significant is not just Lewinsky's "perjurious *Jones* affidavit" nor is it her attempts to "persuade Linda Tripp to commit perjury." No. It is her "assertion . . . that she had been brought up to regard lying as necessary." So then to say that she lied to the president when she assured him that she had not revealed their relationship would be consistent with what "she had been brought up to" do. And her lying to the president transcends the relationship, extending to the gifts, in particular a hat pin that was mentioned in the subpoena. Clinton "asked whether she had told anyone about the hat pin, and she assured him that she had not." In a "Note" to this passage, the narrator clarifies that "Ms. Lewinsky acknowledged in the grand jury that she had in fact told others about the hat pin." The relegation of the lying to a "Note" turns it into an aside, an irrelevant fact that might well be overlooked.

All this the reader of the referral knows. So when the "Notes" also bring in testimony from Lewinsky's acquaintances about her credibility, this is bound to create tensions in the story. Not only does Kathleen Estep, "Counselor to Monica Lewinsky," consider Monica Lewinsky "credible," but Lewinsky's family and friends repeatedly assert that she would not lie (e.g., "I never had any reason to think she would lie to me," or "I have no reason to believe that [Ms. Lewinsky's statements] were lies," or "There were so many reasons why I believed her"). And this is not to speak of the recurring assertions of her credibility that the narrator of the *Report* freely provides. Perhaps the most inventive of these is the link made in the "Grounds" between Lewinsky's unfulfilled desire for intercourse with the president and her credibility. Here, the narrator's logic is at best not evident: "Ms. Lewinsky's statements to some that she did not have intercourse with the President, even though she wanted to do so, enhances the credibility of her statements."

While Monica Lewinsky's credibility is a constant topos in the *Report*, credibility of a different sort attaches itself to President Clinton. His is credibility connected to the existence of "substantial and credible information" regarding his having committed various legal sins that should all lead to his impeachment, such as lying under oath and obstructing justice.

The narrative of lying differs between Clinton and Lewinsky. Lewinsky's link to lying seems almost predetermined (e.g., the allusions to lying and her upbringing) and therefore becomes something to be countered with consistent assertions of credibility. Clinton's lying, on the other hand, has to be created and attached to him by the Office of the Independent Counsel. He is transformed into someone who lies by virtue of the material amassed against him.

There is no question that the judicial system plays a role in this as well. In a typical scene from a courtroom drama, the president is pitted against Lewinsky in the lying game:

There still was the question of his contact with Ms. Lewinsky's breasts and genitalia, which the President conceded would fall within the *Jones* definition of sexual relations. The President denied that he had engaged in such activity and said, in effect, that Monica Lewinsky was lying:

Q: The question is, if Monica Lewinsky says that while you were in the Oval Office area you touched her breasts would she be [sic] lying?

A: That is not my recollection. My recollection is that I did not have sexual relations with Ms. Lewinsky and I'm staying on my former statement about that. . . . My, my statement is that I did not have sexual relations as defined by that.

Q: If she says that you kissed her breasts, would she be lying?

A: I'm going to revert to my former statement [that is, the prepared statement denying "sexual relations"].

Q: Okay. If Monica Lewinsky says that while you were in the Oval Office area you touched her genitalia, would she be lying? And that calls for a yes, no, or reverting to your former statement.

A: I will revert to my former statement on that.

Notice that despite what the narrator claims, Clinton did not say "in effect, that Monica Lewinsky was lying." Clinton, as is normal in these situations, evades the questions, not accusing himself or anyone else. The "lying" is attached to Lewinsky by the questioner and, subsequently, by the narrator. The assertion is obviously being made that either Clinton was lying or Lewinsky was lying.

This instance in the "Grounds" is but one example of a repeated argument in favor of motivations for the president to lie. The proclamations of this need to lie are constructed in a most provocative way: conditional sentences that lead to likely conclusions that therefore make it necessary for the president to commit his evil deed. One example will suffice, though others could be adduced as well: "The President's motive to lie in his civil deposition on the subpoena issue is evident. Had he admitted talking to Ms. Lewinsky *after* her subpoena, that would have raised the specter of witness tampering, which could have triggered legal and public scrutiny of the President."

The narrative of lying may distinguish between Bill Clinton's lying and Monica Lewinsky's. In this way, it is similar to the narratives of denials, in which one can speak about his denials and her denials. The act of denial is one of the most popular ones in the *Report*. Monica Lewinsky's most significant act of denial is the affidavit drafted for her by her attorney, Francis Carter. Her affidavit was used by Clinton's attorney, Robert Bennett, who told "Judge Susan Webber Wright that Ms. Lewinsky had executed 'an affidavit which [Ms. Jones's lawyers] are in possession of saying that there is absolutely no sex of any kind in any manner, shape or form, with President Clinton.' In a subsequent colloquy with Judge Wright, Mr. Bennett declared that as a result of 'preparation of [President Clinton] for this deposition, the witness is fully aware of Ms. Lewinsky's affidavit.'" This written act of denial stands in contrast to Lewinsky's having shared her adventures with family and friends.

At the same time, Monica Lewinsky stated that she told President Clinton that "I would always deny it, I would always protect him." Her denial is defined as protection of the president, a protection she seems to be willing to lift when it comes to particular parties. Soon enough, however, the narrator adds that "the two of them had, in her words, 'a mutual understanding' that they would 'keep this private, so that meant deny it and . . . take whatever appropriate steps needed to be taken.' When she and the President both were subpoenaed to testify in the *Jones* case, Ms. Lewinsky anticipated that 'as we had on every other occasion and every other instance of this relationship, we would deny it.'" Observe here the use of the first-person plural, the attempt to define the denial of the relationship as an act perpetrated by the couple as a unit.

This may be the way that the narrative of denial is articulated with Monica Lewinsky. Clinton's narrative of denial in *The Starr Report* is much more fundamental in its consistency and its repetition. His voice rises early on in the "Narrative" to deny:

> In the *Jones* deposition on January 17, 1998, the President denied having had "a sexual affair," "sexual relations," or "a sexual relationship" with Ms. Lewinsky. He noted that "[t]here are no curtains on the Oval Office, there are no curtains on my private office, there are no curtains or blinds that can close [on] the windows in my private dining room," and added: "I have done everything I could to avoid the kind of questions you are asking me here today. . . ."

Interestingly enough, the president's first act of denial is linked to the geography of space. As the specific domains of denial — the "sexual affair," the "sexual relations," and the "sexual relationship" — are enunciated, they are immediately followed by a statement about the absence of curtains and/or blinds on the various windows. The spatial configurations also redefine the denial in terms of what can be seen, of the all-powerful gaze. In addition, linking the denial to the absence of curtains transforms the private space, the one that would be enclosed, into an open and more public space.

Unlike the narrative of lying that had to be grafted onto President Clinton, that of denial seems to attach itself to him quite naturally, surely a corollary of the fact that denial is his default position in the *Report*. The president's denials move from the geography of space to that of the female body, as he denies touching various parts of Monica Lewinsky's body.

From space to the body, the denials are flexible entities as they move outward. The conversation with Betty Currie in which the president makes the four statements analyzed in chapter 4, above, is a case in point. Whether one wishes to take these statements from the "Narrative" or the "Grounds," they cover substantially the same territory, spanning the range from being alone with Lewinsky to rejecting her sexual advances. And whatever their implications for the game of memory, Bill Clinton's assertions to Betty Currie are exercises in the creation of a narrative of denial. But as this narrative of denial expands, it comes eventually to englobe a much wider spectrum, moving through the president's aides to the American public.

The narrator of *The Starr Report* will not let the president's denials, be they in private (as with Betty Currie) or in public (as to the American public), simply speak for themselves, however. They must perforce be interpreted. Commenting on the president's testimony, the "Grounds" posits that

> the President's testimony strains credulity. His apparent "hands-off" scenario — in which he would have received oral sex on *nine* occasions from Ms. Lewinsky but never made direct contact with Ms. Lewinsky's breasts or genitalia — is not credible. The President's claim seems to be that he maintained a hands-off policy in ongoing sexual encounters with Ms. Lewinsky, which coincidentally happened to permit him to truthfully deny "sexual relations" with her at a deposition occurring a few years in the future. As Ms. Lewinsky noted, it suggests some kind of "service contract — that all I did was perform oral sex on him and that that's all this relationship was."

And again:

> The President's "hands-off" scenario — in which he would have received oral sex on nine occasions from Ms. Lewinsky but never made direct contact with Ms. Lewinsky's breasts or genitalia — is implausible. As Ms. Lewinsky herself testified, it suggests that she and the President had some kind of "service contract — that all I did was perform oral sex on him and that that's all this relationship was." But as the above descriptions and the Narrative explain, the nature of the relationship, including the sexual relationship, was far more than that.

President Clinton's denials, addressed initially to a physical relationship with Monica Lewinsky (e.g., "I did not have sexual relations with that woman, Miss Lewinsky") are effectively hijacked by the narrator and redefined corporally as a "hands-off" scenario. The expression "hands-off," which by definition extends from the physical to the metaphorical, is then used to withdraw the credibility from the president's denials, this time based on a logic of eroticism. The narrator finds it "implausible" and "not credible" that President Clinton should receive oral sex and not make "direct contact with Ms. Lewinsky's breasts or genitalia." In the process, the narrator in the "Grounds" plays a game of self-referral, as that text buttresses its arguments by a play on the "description" presented in the "Narrative."

Once that improbability is posited, the narrator can then move from the physical to the emotional, in the process redefining Clinton's noncredibility and the legal discourses in the "Grounds." Monica Lewinsky's words will be used to effect the transitions from the corporal universe already established by the narrator into a broader discourse that transforms the president's denials. "As Ms. Lewinsky noted, it suggests some kind of 'service contract — that all I did was perform oral sex on him and that that's all this relationship was.'" Whatever the specific arguments in favor of or against the position that Lewinsky enunciates, it remains that the narratives of male denial are not only different from those of the female but they also redefine her sexual function — and her emotional universe.

The narratives of denials, like the narratives of lying, are gender-specific in *The Starr Report*. Such is not the case with the "cover stories," as they are called in the *Report*. The cover stories create a unified front between the couple. The referral recognizes the importance of the cover stories and appropriately gives them their own sections, both in the "Narrative" and in the "Grounds."

The "cover stories" changed as Monica Lewinsky's position changed, moving from the White House to the Pentagon: "When Ms. Lewinsky worked at the White House, she and the President agreed that Ms. Lewinsky would tell people that she was coming to the Oval Office to deliver papers or to have papers signed, when in truth she was going to the Oval Office to have a sexual encounter with the President." Once the transfer to the Pentagon occurred, "Ms. Lewinsky testified that she and the President formulated a second 'cover story': that Ms. Lewinsky was going to the White House to visit Betty Currie rather than the President. Ms. Lewinsky testified that she and the President discussed how 'Betty always needed to be the one to clear me in so that, you know, I could always say I was coming to see Betty.'"

These "cover stories" are not at all convincing to the narrator of the *Report*. Taking on the president's civil deposition and his argument that he "had a general recollection that Ms. Lewinsky may have brought him 'papers to sign' on certain occasions when she worked at the Legislative Affairs Office," the narrator in the "Grounds" minces no words: "This statement was false. Ms. Lewinsky did not bring him papers for official purposes. To the contrary, 'bringing papers' was one of the sham 'cover stories' that the President and Ms. Lewinsky had originally crafted to conceal their sexual relationship." This appreciation turns both cover stories into "sham" narratives, a strong qualifier, indeed. The word "crafted" increases the strength of the "sham," as the reader imagines the two culprits sitting and plotting their ruses. Certainly, there was reinforcement of these narratives as the relationship developed and eventually ended: "Ms. Lewinsky said that the President told her that she might be able to sign an affidavit to avoid being deposed. According to Ms. Lewinsky, the President also told her, 'You know, you can always say you were coming to see Betty or that you were bringing me letters.' Ms. Lewinsky took that statement to be a reminder of the false 'cover stories' that they had used earlier in the relationship."

These ruses, these cover stories are, in effect, ways to facilitate Monica Lewinsky's entry into the space that will allow the transgressions to take place. Their nature as "cover stories," however, permits them to expand their function and become "part of their mutual concealment efforts," as Monica Lewinsky testified. Or, literally, a way to "cover" the illicit affair with an alternate reality. Simply put, the "cover stories" become narratives of deception. And, as such, they enter a moral universe. Not surprisingly, it is President Clinton who, as he did earlier, injects the moral dimension into the text of the *Report*. In a section entitled "The President's Grand Jury Testimony on Cover Stories," the "Grounds" adduces the following:

> The President testified that *before* he knew that Ms. Lewinsky was a witness in the *Jones* case, he "might well" have told Ms. Lewinsky that she could offer the cover stories if questioned about her presence in the West Wing and Oval Office:
>
> **Q:** Did you ever say anything like that, you can always say that you were coming to see Betty or bringing me letters? Was that part of any kind of a, anything you said to her or a cover story, before you had any idea she was going to be part of Paula Jones?
>
> **WJC:** I might well have said that.
>
> **Q:** Okay.
>
> **WJC:** Because I certainly didn't want this to come out, if I could help it. And I was concerned about that. I was embarrassed about it. I knew it was wrong.

The concern, the embarrassment, the knowledge that it was wrong delineate the moral universe. Observe, however, that the "it" that is the cause of embarrassment is the same "it" that was wrong but that neither of these pronouns has an antecedent. The only possible antecedent would be the "this" that the President did not want "to come out." The reader will certainly assume that Bill Clinton is alluding to the illicit relationship, but from the textual evidence that is not necessarily the case. The reference could just as easily be to the "cover story" mentioned in the question posed to Clinton. The cover story would then be representing the relationship.

This process of covering, of altering the reality, is related to another aspect of this narrative of the cover stories. The narrator called them "sham." Sham implies something false or untrue but also something simulated. The simulation inherent in these cover stories calls attention to their theatricality, to their representing a sort of masquerade. This theatricality is alive and well in Judge Starr's referral. The "Grounds" puts it this way, "In fact, however, Ms. Lewinsky stated that her White House job never required her to deliver papers or obtain the President's signature, although she carried papers as a prop." So the character in the melodrama plays her role by carrying a stage prop.

According to Monica Lewinsky, this entire act, this "artifice" as the *Report* calls it, "may have originated when 'I got there kind of saying, "Oh, gee, here are your letters," wink, wink, wink, and him saying, "Okay, that's good."' To back up her stories, she generally carried a folder on these visits." The winking, the "Okay, that's good" from the president: all this increases the ludic, the play element in these theatrics. The backing-up of the stories with the "folder" is but another hint at the game of pretense.

Not only that, but the stage prop itself could masquerade as something else. Thus it is that in the March 31 sexual encounter, Monica Lewinsky came to the Oval Office carrying a folder in which "was a gift for the President, a Hugo Boss necktie." The folder is the prop that serves as "the pretext of delivering papers to" the president. This is one identity. But the folder enters the masquerade again as the instrument that covers the gift to be delivered to the president, in the process participating in a double masquerade.

The verbal statement "Oh, gee, here are your letters" compounded with the eye movement expressed by Lewinsky's "wink, wink, wink" signal role-playing in these encounters. Deception has become a lovers' game. In this more subtle version of dress-up, Monica Lewinsky, masquerading as a secretary delivering papers, resembles the fantasy player in a nurse's or a maid's uniform.

These are roles that are self-generated, if only because the scenario was written by the participants themselves. Being shared by the two culprits, the narrative of deception differs from the earlier narratives examined, those of lying and denial, with their "his" and "hers" components. But like the narrative of deception, the "his" and "hers" variants in the narratives of lying and denial were generated by the characters and played out by them as well.

Such is not the case for what might be called the narrative of aggression. Once again, there is a "his" and a "hers." But unlike the earlier "his" and "hers," the two versions of the narrative of aggression are not generated by the characters themselves. Instead the roles of aggressors are assigned them in this melodrama, whether they wish to act out those roles or not.

Thus it is that Monica Lewinsky becomes the "stalker." As she puts it herself:

> Some White House staff members seemed to think that she was to blame for the President's evident interest in her:
>
> > [P]eople were wary of his weaknesses, maybe, and . . . they didn't want to look at him and think that he could be responsible for anything, so it had to all be my fault . . . I was stalking him or I was making advances towards him.

Notice the vocabulary in this example, in which Monica Lewinsky speaks about stalking the president: "she was to blame," "it had to all be my fault," "I was stalking him or I was making advances towards him." This language of opprobrium is directed at Lewinsky, who draws the conclusion about her negative behavior from the opinion of others. From her point of view, "people . . . didn't want to look" at the president "and think that he could be responsible for anything."

But Lewinsky's statements here do not mean that Clinton was not also defined as the aggressor in this relationship. Walter Kaye, a "Family Friend of Monica Lewinsky,"

> testified that he told Ms. Lewinsky's aunt, Debra Finerman, that he understood that "her niece was very aggressive," a remark that angered Ms. Finerman. Ms. Finerman told Mr. Kaye that the President was the true aggressor: He was telephoning Ms. Lewinsky late at night. Ms. Finerman, in Mr. Kaye's recollection, attributed this information to Marcia Lewis, Ms. Lewinsky's mother (and Ms. Finerman's sister). Mr. Kaye — who had disbelieved stories he had heard from Democratic National Committee people about an affair between Ms. Lewinsky and the President — testified that he was "shocked" to hear of the late-night phone calls.

Will the real aggressor please stand up? This is an area in which the reader is left free to make an independent judgment. True, Monica Lewinsky in the opening stages of the first sexual encounter, before any "improper" acts had taken place, "raised her jacket in the back and showed" the president "the straps of her thong underwear, which extended above her pants." The reader also knows from the analysis of the gaze that the young woman made it her business to place herself in a visible position so that President Clinton would not forget her existence. In the course of the breakup on May 24, 1997, the narrator appends a "Note" in which the reader learns that "Ms. Lewinsky tried to initiate genital contact with the President on August 16, 1997, but he rebuffed her." On the other hand, the reader is already aware that the narrator of the "Grounds" turns the sexual encounters into quasi-automatic unzippants-for-oral-sex events initiated by President Clinton. Then there is the testimony by one of Monica Lewinsky's "counselors," Dr. Irene Kassorla. The narrator closes her contribution with the statement that "the President was in charge of scheduling their sexual encounters," once again making him the aggressor.

The testimony by Dr. Kassorla, whose ultimate position in the narrative of aggression will reappear below, has a bigger role to play. Her contribution sits alongside textual neighbors, all of whom represent testimonies by *"Ms. Lewinsky's Friends, Family Members, and Counselors."* This parade of testimonies appears in the "Grounds." And much like the version of the sexual encounters in that section of the *Report*, the testimonies come one after another, fast and furious. These testimonies, brief monologues of sorts, permit these secondary characters to get on the stage and present their own version of the Clinton-Lewinsky saga. In the process, they create their own narratives, with similarities to, but also differences from, the primary narrative. These testimonies, however, are not complete narrations of the Clinton-Lewinsky affair. They function more like a kaleidoscope that when moved gives a different view.

Here is how the testimony of Neysa Erbland, "a high school friend of Ms. Lewinsky's," redefines the parameters of the sexual encounters between Clinton and Lewinsky. In the text of the "Grounds," the narrator notes that "Ms. Lewinsky told Ms. Erbland that the sexual contact included oral sex, kissing, and fondling. On occasion, as Ms. Erbland described it, the President put his face in Ms. Lewinsky's bare chest." In an appended "Note," more is to come: "She told me that she had given him [oral sex] and that she had had all of her clothes off, but that he only had his shirt off and that she had given him oral sex and they kissed and fondled each other and that they didn't have sex. That was kind of a little bit of a letdown for her. . . . He put his face in her chest. And, you know, just oral sex on her part, you know, to him." Oral sex, the letdown for Lewinsky from the absence of intercourse: these are not a problem. His face in her chest may well be a variation on the pattern of the sexual encounters. But "she had all of her clothes off, but that he only had his shirt off"? That is nowhere else to be found in the *Report*. In fact, the contrary information is provided. "Concerned that they might be interrupted abruptly, according to Ms. Lewinsky, the two of them never fully undressed." This concern and the precaution it entails appear in the opening chapter of the "Narrative," "Nature of President Clinton's Relationship with Monica Lewinsky," in a section appropriately entitled "*Steps to Avoid Being Seen or Heard.*"

Erbland's testimony may have a fantasy component. Certainly, like a number of passages in *The Starr Report*, it could easily form a part of a pulp romance novel. But its interest does not lie so much in that as in the fact that it is participating in the creation of alternate narratives of the encounters, narratives all generated by the tales Monica Lewinsky told out of school. And these narratives are inspired by the primary narrative but nevertheless sit alongside it, like the narratives of denials, lying, and deception, those "his" and "hers" narratives already examined.

The recounting of the sexual adventures to friends, family, and counselors by a principal like Lewinsky creates these alternate narratives that redefine the primary one. Her story is that of the young woman involved in a sexual relationship with the president of the United States. It may be a tale of frustration and anger, but it is also one of success, of triumph. Told to these individuals separately, the story will then appear on the stage in a different guise, redefined by the secondary voices who put their own spin on it.

The narrator of the "Grounds" will, not surprisingly, add an additional twist to this act of storytelling, in the process transforming Lewinsky into a victim and introducing a narrative of victimization. Victimization is but the other side of aggression. And if aggression created a "his" and "hers" narrative, victimization does the same: "Ms. Lewinsky had no motive to lie to these individuals (and obviously not to counselors). Indeed, she pointed out to many of them that she was upset that sexual intercourse had not occurred, an unlikely admission if she were exaggerating the sexual aspects of their relationship." Notice the emotional baggage attached to Lewinsky. The absence of sexual intercourse with the president becomes a lack whose emotional impact is played up by the narrator. The absence of sexual intercourse in her relationship with the president has transformed her into a victim.

Monica Lewinsky's "upset," her emotional state (which includes ample anger), is something she alludes to a number of times during the course of her own narration of the relationship. But it is the hijacking of her emotions by the narrator that effects the victimization. She has "confirmed" the details of her relationship with the president, "even though it clearly has been painful for her."

Lewinsky is painted as a victim by the narrator of the *Report*. Clinton is not so fortunate: he needs to fight his own battle. He will tell his own tale, adding the "his" to the "hers" in the narrative of victimization. In paradigmatic textual position to the *"Testimony of Ms. Lewinsky's Friends, Family Members, and Counselors"* stands "The Testimony of Current and Former Aides." Hers and his: the *"Testimony of Ms. Lewinsky's Friends, Family Members, and Counselors"* is based on material provided to the individuals by Monica Lewinsky, whereas "The Testimony of Current and Former Aides" is based on material provided to the individuals by Bill Clinton.

More fundamentally, there are crucial differences between the two sets of testimonies, the two narratives produced by the confessions of the participants in the sexual escapades. His telling occurs after the relationship is complete. More important, the *Report* will not bring out a parade of Clinton friends and supporters to retell and redefine the story he has already related. In fact, as opposed to the ten witnesses attached to Lewinsky, only four are attached to the president. In addition, the heavy hand of the grand jury is much more visible in the testimonies by Clinton's "Current and Former Aides," where ample quotations are presented of actual questions and answers from the testimonies.

The difference is dramatic between the two sets of testimonies. Obviously, Kenneth Starr's *Report* is making an argument in favor of President William Jefferson Clinton's impeachment. So it is to be expected that it should present its case in such a way as to create no doubt of his guilt. If this necessitates more ample participation from the grand jury testimonies of his aides, so be it.

But another element assuredly contributes to this issue: gender. Of the ten witnesses adduced in the *"Testimony of Ms. Lewinsky's Friends, Family Members, and Counselors,"* nine are women. The four individuals who appear in "The Testimony of Current and Former Aides" for President Clinton are all men. It is certainly not accidental that the almost-all-female group is treated much more gingerly in the text. There are no questions and answers presented, no situations in which a potentially aggressive questioner can push a witness, as was clearly the case with the Clinton testimony adduced above in the narrative of lying. With the men, the situation differs, and the reader can, for example, easily watch the hostile voice examining and reexamining John Podesta, whose answers show his impatience. It is as if the courtroom game in the secondary testimonies can be more effectively played with male witnesses.

Here is Sidney Blumenthal as he appears in the Clinton list of aides with his testimony. The incident takes place both in the "Narrative" and in the "Grounds." This is the version in the "Grounds":

> Sidney Blumenthal, an Assistant to the President, similarly testified that the President made statements to him denying the Lewinsky allegations shortly after the first media report.
>
> Mr. Blumenthal stated that he spoke to Mrs. Clinton on the afternoon of January 21, 1998, and to the President early that evening. During those conversations, both the President and Mrs. Clinton offered an explanation for the President's meetings with Ms. Lewinsky, and President Clinton offered an explanation for Ms. Lewinsky's allegations of a sexual relationship.
>
> Testifying before the grand jury, Mr. Blumenthal related his discussion with President Clinton:
>
>> I said to the President, "What have you done wrong?" And he said, "Nothing. I haven't done anything wrong." . . . And it was at that point that he gave his account of what had happened to me [*sic*] and he said that Monica — and it came very fast. He said, *"Monica Lewinsky came at me and made a sexual demand on me."* He rebuffed her. He said, *"I've gone down that road before, I've caused pain for a lot of people and I'm not going to do that again."*
>>
>> She threatened him. She said that she would tell people they'd had an affair, that she was known as the stalker among her peers, and that she hated it and if she had an affair or said she had an affair then she wouldn't be the stalker any more.
>
> Mr. Blumenthal testified that the President appeared "upset" during this conversation.
>
> Finally, Mr. Blumenthal asked the President to explain alleged answering machine messages (a detail mentioned in press reports).
>
>> He said that he remembered calling her when Betty Currie's brother died and that he left a message on her voice machine that Betty's brother had

died and he said she was close to Betty and had been very kind to Betty. And that's what he recalled.

According to Mr. Blumenthal, the President said that the call he made to Ms. Lewinsky relating to Betty's brother was the "only one he could remember." That was false: The President and Ms. Lewinsky talked often on the phone, and the subject matter of the calls was memorable.

A grand juror asked Mr. Blumenthal whether the President had said that his relationship with Ms. Lewinsky included any kind of sexual activity. Mr. Blumenthal testified that the President's response was "the opposite. *He told me that she came on to him and that he had told her he couldn't have sexual relations with her and that she threatened him. That is what he told me."*

Mr. Blumenthal testified that after the President relayed this information to him, he "certainly believed his story. It was a very heartfelt story, he was pouring out his heart, and I believed him." Mr. Blumenthal repeated to the grand jury the false statements that the President made to him.

This interchange stars not only the three principals present (Clinton, Currie, and Lewinsky) but Hillary Rodham Clinton as well. More than that, Blumenthal's testimony regarding his exchange with Clinton is interpreted by the narrator of the *Report* in the opening paragraph as a narrative of denial, though this incident, as will become clear, covers a range of topics.

The denial that opens the event is a global one, addressing "the Lewinsky allegations." There are no specifics, just a generalized set of allegations. Perhaps the narrator chose to foreground the narrative of denial because that is the way Blumenthal's testimony is constructed. From the initial paragraph of denial, the narrator moves to the "conversations" in which Mrs. Clinton is present. These "conversations" also constitute denials of sorts, though they also address the "meetings with Ms. Lewinsky."

The text breaks this general atmosphere of denial by yet another statement about Blumenthal's testimony before the grand jury, this time "his discussion with President Clinton." Hillary Clinton has fulfilled her role and can exit the narrative. From the general, the reader can now progress to the more specific, and with that to a first-person narration. The first exchange the aide has with Clinton is to ask: "What have you done wrong?" to which the answer is clear and forthcoming, "Nothing. I haven't done anything wrong." Those initial denials are reasserted but this time with an already familiar moral twist (the doing "wrong").

This denial, this time in the first person (unlike the earlier ones in the Blumenthal segment), is followed by the narrative of aggression and subsequently the narrative of victimization, with the president as victim. This scenario is not simple. Lewinsky *"came at"* the President and *"made a sexual demand on"* him. But *"he rebuffed her."* Stage one: this is the aggression. *"She threatened him"* and claimed she would *"tell people they'd had an affair."* Stage two: this is the possible victimization. The president may be a victim, but he is a responsible one who turns down these aggressive sexual overtures. His reason is buttressed by the argument that he has *"gone down that road before,"* that he has *"caused pain for a lot of people."* Notice that his reason is couched in terms of the suffering others will have because of his actions, a motivation that pushes him into rejecting Lewinsky's advances.

The logic of the two-pronged scenario of aggression is the fact that the young woman *"was known as the stalker among her peers."* The *"peers"* are significant. This label, stuck to Lewinsky in this testimony by her own age group, serves to distance her and her behavior from her cohort. If this label is acquired from the *"peers,"* how would an older man, namely, the president, have heard about it? The reader already knows that Monica Lewinsky had attached that identity to herself earlier in the "Narrative." Not only that but *"she hated it and if she had an affair or said she had an affair then she wouldn't be the stalker any more."* Her dislike for that description is perfectly understandable. Unusual is the fact that this identity is malleable and can be eliminated by having an affair or saying she had an affair. These two options are fascinating, being precisely the two with which the *Report* struggles: that she had the affair or that she was merely saying that she had the affair. This choice is, in either case, moot since the "President's August 1998 speech acknowledging improper conduct with Ms. Lewinsky," in effect, could tend to clear her of the charge of being a stalker.

But the gender dynamics of this incident are far from exhausted. As Sidney Blumenthal is attempting to make sense of things, he asks President Clinton about "answering machine messages." The reply brings in Betty Currie and the death of the brother, a situation that introduces the only call "he could remember." This is by no means a simple appearance, however. Like her parallel in the triangle, Hillary Rodham Clinton, who surfaces with Blumenthal to defend against the meetings with Lewinsky, Betty Currie is evoked in the same incident, but to defend against telephone messages. The two parallel roles of the two socially sanctioned women in the president's life, his wife and his secretary, confirm the president's denials. The two supportive women are, in the process, pitted against the "stalker," Monica Lewinsky.

The narrator, interestingly enough, does not discuss these issues. In the text, it is the veracity of the claims about phone calls that takes precedence. The narrator is most anxious to provide an unequivocal opinion. "That was false: The President and Ms. Lewinsky talked often on the phone, and the subject matter of the calls was memorable." This opinion is quite intrusive, inserted as it is in the middle of Blumenthal's testimony.

Like the statements with Betty Currie examined in chapter 4, in which there was a natural progression from being alone to the sexual relationship, this discussion with Blumenthal also progresses by stages. The Currie statements, in their own way, foreshadow this incident. From the initial denial that englobes the entire relationship, one progresses to the telephone calls and from there to "sexual activity."

When Blumenthal was asked whether the president had said that his relationship with Ms. Lewinsky included any kind of sexual activity, he testified that the president's response was "the opposite. *He told me that she came on to him and that he had told her he couldn't have sexual relations with her and that she threatened him. That is what he told me.*" This response raises the narrative of aggression on Monica Lewinsky's part. This time the aggression is again expressed not only by the coming-on to Clinton but by her threats as well. Present also is his implied victimization.

The entire first-person narration by Clinton is intercalated not only with Blumenthal's words, also in the first person, but also by the third-person narrator, manipulating the text. Once Clinton has delivered his contribution, the narrator can proceed to the effect that the entire interchange had on Blumenthal. The latter comments on both the story and the storyteller. The story is "heartfelt," and the storyteller was "pouring out his heart." Blumenthal "believed" not only the story but the storyteller as well ("[the president] believed his story . . . and I believed him")(brackets added). Perhaps Blumenthal set himself up for this since he had commented in the testimony "that the President appeared 'upset' during this conversation."

By now, the reader of *The Starr Report* knows that the narrator usually likes to have the last word. This time, the last word will form part of the narrative of lying. "Mr. Blumenthal repeated to the grand jury the false statements that the President made to him." If Blumenthal was duped, the narrator wants to make sure that the reader is not. A clear signal is sent that Clinton's statements were false, in a word, that he was lying. But by ending the incident on the note of "false statements," the text has effectively negated any sympathy Blumenthal and the reader might have felt toward Clinton.

The presentation of the Blumenthal incident in the "Grounds" does not lack for narratives. Denial, lying, aggression, victimization: they are all there and repeated for emphasis. Other important elements, like being alone and the gaze, if not in the variant in the "Grounds," surface in the "Narrative" telling of the incident with Blumenthal. More importantly, the variant in the "Narrative" will add a powerful component to the narrative of victimization. The incident with Blumenthal in the "Narrative" is embedded in a section entitled "*Denials to Aides*" and ends this way: "According to Mr. Blumenthal, the President complained: 'I feel like a character in a novel. I feel like somebody who is surrounded by an oppressive force that is creating a lie about me and I can't get the truth out. I feel like the character in the novel *Darkness at Noon.*'"

This is a powerful scenario of victimization. But this time the victimization is not a direct response to the purported sexual aggression of Monica Lewinsky. Rather, the president has enlarged and expanded the web of intrigue. His comments to his aide move directly from the sexual escapades and Lewinsky stalking him to a broader political commentary on the investigation by Kenneth Starr that yields the *Report* embodying these comments. "According to Mr. Blumenthal, the President complained . . .": the president's statements are defined as a complaint. But what the president has enunciated is far more. He has denounced the investigation of which he is a victim and compared himself to the old Bolshevik in the hands of Stalin's inquisition in one of this century's most powerful novels, Arthur Koestler's *Darkness at Noon*.

Once the reader gets beyond the definitions of Clinton's words as complaints, the power of these statements comes to the fore. "I feel like a character in a novel. I feel like somebody who is surrounded by an oppressive force that is creating a lie about me and I can't get the truth out. I feel like the character in the novel *Darkness at Noon*": three sentences all uttered in the first person and all beginning with three simple words "I feel like. . . ." The first sentence makes a reference to "a character in a novel," the second addresses someone being surrounded by "an oppressive force" creating lies that the individual cannot counter, and the third makes a reference to "the character in the novel *Darkness at Noon*." From "a character in a novel," the first-person narrator, the president, moves to "the character in the novel *Darkness at Noon*," specifying the novel mentioned in the first sentence. By definition, and for the reader who knows nothing about the plot of *Darkness at Noon*, the second sentence interprets this. The president not only defines himself as victim, but he also defines Kenneth Starr's investigation as an "oppressive force," akin to the GPU. Without the interpretation, the reader would not know with which character the president identified himself. The nameless character would thus have to be Rubashov (perhaps the president forgot his name). Among the ironies of this comparison is the fact that Stalin, in the novel, is referred to only as "No. 1." Yet No. 1 in the American political system (and who flies in Air Force One) is the president. But, after all, Clinton is arguing that he has been displaced from this position.

This story of political victimization and comparison to "the character in *Darkness at Noon*" gets lost between the "Narrative" and the "Grounds," despite the narrator's openness to repetition. It could be because this argument does not fit well with the main goal of the "Grounds": to set up the case for President Clinton's impeachment. Even a reader convinced of the essential veracity of the *Report*'s tale of sex and lies might still see an analogy with a story of institutionalized and political victimization.

Certainly, the *Report* would suffer if one ignored the hidden narrative of desire that guides and manipulates the text. While desire on the part of the principals in the case is evident, desire on the part of *The Starr Report* may not appear so clearly. Nevertheless it is there: the desire to make a legal case to Congress and the American public against William Jefferson Clinton. More important, however, the *Report* is involved in a trickier game of desire, that of creating desire in its reader, a desire to enter into the story. In this context, the salacious details become textual teasers.

The lacunae in the text cease to be accidental once that textual desire is posited. The monologue on *Darkness at Noon* does not stand alone as a neglected incident in the "Grounds." An equally powerful, though different, conversation takes place in the "Narrative" with Dick Morris, "the President's former political consultant," Clinton tells him: "You know, ever since the election, I've tried to shut myself down. I've tried to shut my body down, sexually, I mean. . . . But sometimes I slipped up and with this girl I just slipped up."

What a revelation and what a confession! First, the president declares, "I've tried to shut myself down." This is transformed immediately into "I've tried to shut my body down." And the statement undergoes yet a third definition, "sexually, I mean. . . ." The reader finally understands what kinds of corporal limits the president is placing on his body. "But sometimes I slipped up and with this girl I just slipped up." This last comment transports the entire monologue into a moral universe, one in which the president seems to be comfortably ensconced in *The Starr Report*. At the same time, there is an irony in the president's choice of words. He has tried to shut himself down, to shut his body down sexually. Shut down. The reader may well remember that Bill Clinton first succumbed to the temptation of the flesh during the government shutdown, not an insignificant verbal turn of phrase as chapter 9 below will demonstrate.

The shutting-down of the body, the being surrounded by an oppressive force, these are monologues that only grace the "Narrative." These lost conversations join other lost events, like the eloquent Northwest Gate incident analyzed in chapter 4, to disappear from the "Grounds." But it would be unfair to say that the "Narrative" dominates. Rather, the "Grounds" can also play the game of one-upmanship in an attempt to guide that narrative desire on the part of the *Report*.

Speaking about the gifts, the narrator of the "Grounds" elaborates: "Ms. Lewinsky explained the point: Had they admitted the gifts, it would 'at least prompt [the *Jones* attorneys] to want to question me about what kind of friendship I had with the President and they would want to speculate and they'd leak it and my name would be trashed and he [the President] would be in trouble.'" This eloquent argument appears twice in the "Grounds," but not once in the "Narrative."

The various and differing components in the *Report* speak to the modalities of desire on the part of the *Report* itself. The multiplicity of narratives swirling around the Clinton-Lewinsky relationship when compounded by the "his" and "hers" variants on these narratives alters that hidden narrative of desire. At the same time, these complex and interrelated narratives function as narratives of resistance to the primary narrative of the sexual exploits. There is no one narrative in *The Starr Report*.

9

MY BODY, MY GENDER

Among the recurrent topics of *The Starr Report* are those relating to gender and the body. The reader becomes attuned to the body not just through the encounters themselves but through the definition of what constitutes a sexual relationship. Body parts float in and out of the *Report*, as the male body is transformed and the female body defined. The ludic, the playful, is part and parcel of the discourses of the body. The naming game also participates in this central corporal discourse, in the process creating an instability in the construction of gender. Masquerade looms large here as well. Politics, too, is at stake in the portrayal of bodies, specifically, the president's body. Ernst H. Kantorowicz's classic study *The King's Two Bodies* will provide critical constructs for the examination of the "body politic" and the "body natural" in Kenneth Starr's contemporary American *Report*.

The analysis of the body might best begin with the definition of "sexual relations" in the *Jones* case: "[A] person engages in 'sexual relations' when the person knowingly engages in or causes — (1) contact with the genitalia, anus, groin, breast, inner thigh, or buttocks of any person with an intent to arouse or gratify the sexual desire of any person. . . . 'Contact' means intentional touching, either directly or through clothing." The body parts critical to sexual relations, and therefore to arousal and gratification, are the "genitalia, anus, groin, breast, inner thigh, or buttocks." In this definition, the human body is dissected into parts, all of which, with the exception of the breast, are lower body parts. The breast, of course, is a part of female anatomy. This means that the male body is restricted to its lower torso. No fetishistic behavior allowed, no gratification for the male above the buttocks, in this essentially heterosexual definition.

President Clinton, the lawyer that he is, is made to parse the definition immediately after its appearance in the referral, thereby demonstrating its limits.

> According to what the President testified was his understanding, this definition "covers contact by the person being deposed with the enumerated areas, if the contact is done with an intent to arouse or gratify," but it does not cover oral sex performed on the person being deposed. He testified:
>
>> [I]f the deponent is the person who has oral sex performed on him, then the contact is with — not with anything on that list, but with the lips of another person. It seems to be self-evident that that's what it is. . . . Let me remind you, sir, I read this carefully.

President Clinton is absolutely correct to point out the deficiencies in the definition provided in the *Jones* deposition. He centers on oral sex and, in the process, on a body part that nowhere makes an appearance, the lips. Of course, other body parts that might provide gratification can be adduced by anyone with a little imagination. In the process of his parsing, Bill Clinton reminds his listener, and subsequently the reader of the *Report*, that he himself is a careful reader. A little irony is added by the "sir."

Once the repetitions of the encounters are set in motion, body parts will start flying all over the *Report*. Breasts, hands, mouth, genitalia, chest, face: these are the major parts of Clinton and Lewinsky's bodies that appear and reappear. Other body parts star in minor roles, such as an arm and a leg here or a forehead and hair there. Some of these parts will be important for the analysis below.

Lewinsky's breasts are featured in the narration of every sexual encounter in the "Narrative" and in the "Grounds." Perhaps this fixation on the part of the narrator is not accidental. In a discussion between Lewinsky and Clinton about the allegation of sexual harassment by Kathleen Willey, "the President responded that the harassment allegation was ludicrous, because he would never approach a small-breasted woman like Ms. Willey." While this statement speaks about Willey, it cannot help but address Lewinsky as well and the general topic of the female body.

The president's "mouth and hands" become like appendages that seem to be quasi-permanently attached to Lewinsky's breasts, breasts that are bare at times but not at others. His face is also at one time described as having been put "in Ms. Lewinsky's bare chest." But the face, mouth, and hands, like lips, do not appear in the compilation of parts that might participate in the act of "sexual relations." Nor does the chest emerge as a privileged body part. Yet the president's chest is something that Lewinsky willingly uncovers and kisses.

Clearly, the definition of "sexual relations" privileges certain body parts over others. At the same time, there is a complex body language that is prominent throughout Starr's referral. The anatomical parts used in the tortured *Jones* definition are body parts that are normally covered, unexposed. Hence the face, the mouth, and the hands can be eliminated from the definition. As for a man's uncovered chest, that is acceptable in America, at a pool or a beach. For that reason, possibly, the chest is not included in the definition. But when Monica Lewinsky, in the February 28 sexual encounter, "unbuttoned" the president's "shirt and was kissing his chest," she was most likely undertaking an act that was "done with an intent to arouse or gratify," in the words of the *Jones* definition. Or when he put his face in her chest, the intent was most likely similar. But these are the privileges of a text: it obeys its own rules and sets up its own expectations.

The body language in *The Starr Report* is also gendered in odd and interesting ways. True, the president's chest appears once. But other than his face, which appears twice in the entire *Report*, and his more popular mouth and hands, some of his other body parts, in particular specific sexual parts, are surprisingly and disturbingly nonexistent. While he may unzip his pants and expose his genitals, most often the oral sex simply takes place without that concomitant act of unzipping. The word "genitals" in the *Report* is used to refer to both male and female private parts. The vagina, however, makes an appearance. Not only is the incident with the president inserting a cigar into Lewinsky's "vagina" repeated in the *Report*, but one of Lewinsky's friends, Catherine Allday Davis, testified that "the President touched Monica 'on her breasts and on her vagina.'" It is beside the point whether this is an addition, as in the case of the testimony discussed above, in which another of Lewinsky's friends, that time Neysa Erbland, testified that Lewinsky told her "that she had had all of her clothes off." Striking is the appearance of the word "vagina." If the vagina, why not the penis? The male sexual organ never appears. It is an absent body part (a deliberate avoidance since it was available in the supplementary materials). In place of the penis are the "genitals." This linguistic usage renders the body parts gender-neutral. At the same time, this procedure has the result of obscuring the president's masculinity and transforming his sexual organs into nothing but the vehicle for the performance of oral sex. This context of emasculation adds flavor to Lewinsky's otherwise banal formulation that the president lacked "the balls" to tell her "the truth" about her job search.

The absence of the penis means that the president's sexual organs, in reality obviously made up of different organs, function in Starr's referral as one anatomical unit, be it as the "genitals" or as the "crotch." And it is as one body part that this element of the male anatomy creates a ludic, a playful discourse. This occurs, for example, when "on August 18, Ms. Lewinsky attended the President's 50th birthday party at Radio City Music Hall, and she got into a cocktail party for major donors where she saw the President. According to Ms. Lewinsky, when the President reached past her at the rope line to shake hands with another guest, she reached out and touched his crotch in a 'playful' fashion." The touching of the "crotch" in public is defined by the text as "playful." Whether the reader finds it so is almost irrelevant. The narrator sets up two parallel activities, the president's reaching past Lewinsky and shaking hands with another guest and Lewinsky's reaching out and touching the president's crotch. The male action and the female action are expressed with the identical verb, that of reaching: he reaches past and she reaches out. While his act is social and political, hers is corporal and sexual. Notice that no parts of the president's body, other than his crotch, are mentioned by the narrator, not even his hand or arm doing the reaching. In the process, the president's body has been transmuted into a crotch. There is also something bizarre about this entire incident, in which President Clinton is transformed into a desired sexualized object. While he may be performing as a political figure at his birthday party, the reader discovers that for Monica Lewinsky it is his essence as a "crotch" that counts.

This construct in which the president's sexual organs create the occasion for the articulation of the playful is more apparent in a conversation that Lewinsky has with Clinton. According to Monica Lewinsky: "[H]e said, 'I promise you,' you know, something like, 'if I win in November, I'll have you back like that. You can do anything you want. You can be anything you want.' And then I made a joke and I said, 'Well, can I be Assistant to the President for Blow Jobs?' He said, 'I'd like that.'" While Bill Clinton is apparently talking of serious job opportunities, Monica Lewinsky transports the dialogue in a different direction. She maintains the official language by speaking about an "Assistant to the President" but then takes that position and makes it one "for Blow Jobs." Clinton plays along and responds that he would like that. With this phrase, he, as a character, has agreed to the play between politics and sexuality, but expressed in a humorous way. And, of course, Lewinsky's uttering of "Blow Jobs" reminds the reader of all the sexual encounters between herself and Clinton.

While there is humor in both this dialogue and the incident with the touching of the crotch, there is also aggression and an invasion of the male body. Perhaps this is fair play in the *Report*, a text that does not shy away from perceived corporal aggression on the president's part. Chapter 8 discussed the various narratives, including that of aggression, with its "his" and "hers" variants. Certainly, the "Note" in the "Introduction" to the referral interprets Clinton's alleged incident with Paula Jones as nothing short of aggression. She "alleged that while at work at a meeting at the Excelsior Hotel that day, she was invited into a hotel room with Governor Clinton, and that once she was there, the Governor exposed his genitals and asked her to perform oral sex on him."

It is perhaps not accidental that the last "Note" in the "Narrative," and hence the last text before the "Grounds," features a "defiant President Clinton." The narrator solicitously advises the reader: "*See Chi. Tribune*, Jan. 27, 1998, at 1 ('A defiant President Clinton wagged his finger at the cameras and thumped the lectern Monday as he insisted he did not have sex with a young White House intern or ask her to deny it under oath.')." The president uses his body in aggressive ways to express his denial. His gestures are belligerent as he directs his finger that does the wagging and one presumes his hand(s) that do the thumping outward from his body. These actions redefine the alleged sexual aggression by the president, who is portrayed as someone whose body parts take on a life of their own as they move outward from his body.

The president's body also plays an active role through his fluids. Chapter 6 demonstrated the role of semen in Judge Starr's referral. But semen is more than something that dries on Monica Lewinsky's dress and identifies Clinton as the guilty party. One bodily fluid opens a path for others. Twice in the "Narrative" and twice in the "Grounds," the narrator speaks about the president's blood, crucial in determining whether the semen on Lewinsky's dress is indeed Clinton's. In the "Narrative," the incident is provided: "The OIC asked the President for a blood sample." Then "in the White House Map Room on August 3, 1998, the White House Physician drew a vial of blood from the President in the presence of an FBI agent and an OIC attorney." In the "Grounds," the narrator states that "a White House physician drew blood from the President in the presence of a senior OIC attorney and a FBI special agent."

Observe that in the process of shifting from the "Narrative" to the "Grounds" the "FBI agent" has become an "FBI special agent" and the "OIC attorney" has become "a senior OIC attorney," whereas "the White House Physician" has become "a White House physician." "The" physician who becomes "a" physician is effectively moved from being the major physician to one of a possible number of medical specialists, in the process demoting that person. Contrary to what happens with the physician, the nonmedical individuals acquire a more specific identity and a higher status: the "OIC attorney" becoming "a senior OIC attorney" and the "FBI agent," an "FBI special agent." Since the "Grounds" is the more legally minded section of the *Report*, it is no surprise that the two nonmedical officials should be endowed with more power in this retelling of the incident. Equally important is the namelessness of the individuals. Their official status takes precedence, and their personal identity becomes subsumed in that status.

This is a solemn occasion. The drawing of blood from the president's body is not simply a medical event but a legal and judicial one as well. The FBI agent and the OIC attorney are there as observers of the medical procedure, at once verifying it and ascertaining its validity. They are also, willy-nilly, participating in a voyeuristic act, in which the president's body is invaded through this medical proceeding. As they engage in this activity, the reader is invited to do so as well. The role of the officials echoes that of the American public as the president's body becomes a spectacle. One presidential bodily fluid, the semen, leads to another, the blood. The blood will identify the semen. The fluid of guilt, the semen, in the process redefines the blood as a fluid of guilt as well. And perhaps this is as it should be in the logic of the *Report*. The identity of the semen in a way recasts all the events in which the president's body as sexual entity appears.

But there is a more powerful discourse of the president's body, one that points to a weak physical entity. Early on in the "Narrative," the narrator explains that "during many of their sexual encounters, the President stood leaning against the doorway of the bathroom across from the study, which, he told Ms. Lewinsky, eased his sore back." The knowledge is now, if it were not before, available to the reader that the president has problems with his back. More important, this knowledge is conveyed during the recounting of the totality of sexual encounters between Clinton and Lewinsky.

The March 29 sexual encounter, the last in the series, engenders a host of material that reinforces the fragility of the male body. The reader learns in the "Narrative" that for this meeting, the President "came in on crutches, the result of a knee injury in Florida two weeks earlier." This last sexual encounter is also the one in which Monica Lewinsky "wanted him to touch" her genitals with his, "and he did so lightly and without penetration." An appended "Note" explains: "Ms. Lewinsky testified that their genitals only briefly touched: '[W]e sort of had tried to do that, but because he's so tall and he couldn't bend because of his knee, it didn't really work.'" The president's injured body is not just an imperfect entity, but it seems to get in the way of his sexual performance as well, blocking him from the archetypical masculine act of penetration.

The knee injury reappears in a "Note" in the "Grounds," this time in the context of the gifts that Lewinsky gave to Clinton: "after the President injured his leg in March 1997, a care package filled with whimsical gifts, such as a magnet with the Presidential seal for his metal crutches, a license plate with 'Bill' for his wheelchair, and knee pads with the Presidential seal." The narrator of the "Grounds" does not tie these gifts to any kind of body language. Rather, for the *Report*, these objects are embedded in a list of gifts.

> These included a Sherlock Holmes game sometime after Christmas 1996; a golf ball and tees on February 28, 1997; after the President injured his leg in March 1997, a care package filled with whimsical gifts, such as a magnet with the Presidential seal for his metal crutches, a license plate with "Bill" for his wheelchair, and knee pads with the Presidential seal; a Banana Republic casual shirt and a puzzle on golf mysteries on May 24, 1997; the card game "Royalty" in mid-August 1997; shortly before Halloween of 1997, a package filled with Halloween-related items, such as a pumpkin lapel pin, a wooden letter opener with a frog on the handle, and a plastic pumpkin filled with candy; and on December 6, 1997, a Starbucks Santa Monica mug and a Hugs and Kisses box.

This embedding dilutes the gifts that relate to the body in the array of other gifts and thereby diminishes their power as participants in the corporal discourse.

In a discussion between Clinton and Lewinsky in the "Narrative" about the possible future of the couple, the following exchange takes place:

[H]e remarked . . . that he wished he had more time for me. And so I said, well, maybe you will have more time in three years. And I was . . . thinking just when he wasn't President, he was going to have more time on his hands. And he said, well, I don't know, I might be alone in three years. And then I said something about . . . us sort of being together. I think I kind of said, oh, I think we'd be a good team, or something like that. And he . . . jokingly said, well, what are we going to do when I'm 75 and I have to pee 25 times a day? And . . . I told him that we'd deal with that. . . .

This interchange begins with talk about the available time Bill Clinton has as president, or might have when he is no longer president, for Monica Lewinsky. He then, in the first person, alludes to his being alone in three years. She picks up that thread and transforms his being "alone" into their being "together." This signals the appearance of the first-person plural, the "us sort of being together," in the process launching a dialogue in which that plural will dominate. Now is when Clinton can speak about his body: "And he . . . jokingly said, well, what are we going to do when I'm 75 and I have to pee 25 times a day?" to which Lewinsky responds: "And . . . I told him that we'd deal with that. . . ."

Lewinsky is thinking about a future in which the two would be "a good team, or something like that." Clinton, on the other hand, is thinking about a future in which his imperfect body plays a greater role. Not only does he address the issue of age ("when I'm 75") but also the practical problem that many elderly people have with frequent urination ("and I have to pee 25 times a day). Of course, peeing for the male is done through his penis, an organ that does not exist in *The Starr Report* as part of the president's body. The president's virility, implicit in a way in the oral sex, has been deflated through its association with the less sexual task of urination. Perhaps it should not be a surprise that Monica Lewinsky notes that Bill Clinton told her that "she made him feel young." And in an unsent missive to the president, she writes: "I want to be a source of pleasure and laughter and energy to you. I want to make you smile." This wish list highlights elements that participate at once in the emotional and the physical ("pleasure," "laughter," smiling). More central is the energy that Lewinsky will impart to Clinton, whose feeble body has become so important in the text.

The corporal discourse highlighting the president's physical fragility operates as a subtext throughout the *Report*. Neither enunciating it nor alluding to it is necessary. The subtext weaves itself through the narrative, altering incidents and events that cross its path. Monica Lewinsky sent a letter to Bill Clinton, "styled as an official memo":

> Addressed to "Handsome" and bearing the subject line "The New Deal," the faux memo proposed a visit that evening after "everyone else goes home." Ms. Lewinsky wrote: "You will show me that you will let me visit you sans a crisis, and I will be on my best behavior and not stressed out when I come (to see you, that is)." She closed with an allusion to a woman rumored to have been involved with an earlier President: "Oh, and Handsome, remember FDR would never have turned down a visit with Lucy Mercer!"

This "faux" memo (one wonders whether it came enveloped in "faux" leather or was printed on "faux" leopard skin) constitutes an invitation on Lewinsky's part to come and see the president. Her offer to visit comes guaranteed "sans a crisis." Ah! Now the reader can understand the narrator's "faux" better. Lewinsky pretentiously — and clumsily, one might add — tries out her French ("sans a" would better be "sans" without the "a"), and the narrator will not be outdone, hence the "faux."

But what masquerades as an invitation is, in fact, a lot more. With her allusions to "The New Deal," Monica Lewinsky demonstrates her knowledge of American politics. But this is politics flavored with illicit sexuality. She compares herself to Lucy Mercer, "a woman rumored to have been involved with an earlier President," and Clinton is compared to "FDR." (Those with a fascination for language games will surely notice that Lucy Mercer's initials, L.M., are the reverse of Monica Lewinsky's, M.L.) Roosevelt "would never have turned down a visit with Lucy Mercer!" implying that Clinton should not turn down Lewinsky's invitation. Then there is the phrase "when I come (to see you, that is)" that initially refers to an orgasm and is quickly redirected to the act of visiting President Clinton. In the process, this phrase redefines Lucy Mercer's visits to FDR in a sexual way.

The choice of FDR is extremely provocative. Other presidents and other women could have been selected for this argument. What distinguishes Roosevelt in this context is his disabled body, a body that was confined to a wheelchair while he was president of the United States. For the analogy of female visitor/male president to work, Clinton must be compared to FDR. True, they are both presidents. But in the body language of *The Starr Report*, Clinton becomes a physically weakened specimen of manhood much like his predecessor, Franklin Delano Roosevelt. William Jefferson Clinton, who has publicly trumpeted his admiration for the youthful and vigorous JFK, finds himself likened to the older and disabled FDR.

While the example of FDR pulls in one direction, Lewinsky's addressing Clinton as "Handsome" pulls in another. "Handsome" is the most common term that Monica Lewinsky uses when addressing Clinton directly. Needless to say, this is a term that calls attention first and foremost to the president's looks, to his body.

The president comes in for other appellations. While some are quite positive and others less so, there is a clear physical component lurking behind a number of them. He appears as "the big guy" in a communication to Betty Currie. A "Note" in the "Narrative" observes that "When angry, Ms. Lewinsky referred to the President as 'creep' or 'big creep.' " In an email message to one of her friends, Catherine Davis, Lewinsky attaches yet a different appellation to the president, "a big schmuck." A "schmuck," for those in the know, is a Yiddish term and refers to the male sexual organ. A masculine physicality is implied, but it is an englobing one whose referent is the entire President (or his character) and not his genitalia.

Name games in the Clinton-Lewinsky ordeal are crucial in the discourses of identity in the *Report.* Chapter 3 addressed the way that Betty Currie and Monica Lewinsky used the same code name, Kay, when communicating with one another. That discussion also demonstrated the issues of identity that arise from this usage, linking them to the notion of masquerade. Nor does the American public need to be reminded of President Clinton's emphatic denial that seals the text of Starr's "Narrative" and reappears in identical form in the "Grounds": "I did not have sexual relations with that woman, Miss Lewinsky." The expression "that woman" distances Monica Lewinsky and relegates her to a space alien to the president, and this despite the fact that her name appears immediately after the phrase.

The corporality that inherently exists in the president's names links to his fragility and weakness in another way. The exchange referring to urination called attention to the difference in ages between the two principals in the referral. It should not come as a surprise that this will reappear in an onomastic context. The "Narrative" text tells its readers that "on occasion," Clinton called Lewinsky " 'Sweetie,' 'Baby,' or sometimes 'Dear.' " A "Note" to this statement unconsciously links this discussion of nicknames to the already familiar subtext of the president's age and fragile corporality. In an electronic message to one of her friends, Lewinsky writes: "Jeez, I hate being called 'dear.' The creep calls me that sometimes. It's an old person saying!"

The "old person saying," the absent penis, the decrepit male body with a bad back and crutches: all these elements awaken the reader to an important gendered discourse centered around the male body that extends from that physical entity to the male gender. True, the male may be called "Handsome," but this name, related to physicality, does not detract from the essential weakness of the male gender.

And the male gender becomes the object of play in *The Starr Report*. The female gender may undergo identity through name games, but there is never a question of the stability of the female gender in Kenneth Starr's referral. Such is far from the case with the male gender.

Here is the "Valentine's Day Advertisement" discussed in chapter 6:

> On February 14, 1997, the *Washington Post* published a Valentine's Day "Love Note" that Ms. Lewinsky had placed. The ad said:
>
> HANDSOME
> With love's light wings did
>   I o'er perch these walls
> For stony limits cannot hold love out,
> And what love can do that dares love attempt.
> —*Romeo and Juliet 2:2*
>
> Happy Valentine's Day.
> M

The title "Handsome" is par for the course. It is the quotation from Shakespeare that is problematic. M generously provides the source for the words from *Romeo and Juliet*. A look at the scene in Shakespeare's play quickly reveals that the quotation appears in an exchange between Romeo and Juliet. M is the signatory to these verses, one of which includes the first-person pronoun "I." Any reader would draw the conclusion that that "I" is M. But the words in the play are spoken by Romeo, a male character. Monica Lewinsky has usurped the identity of the male lover, the aggressive character in this Shakespearean scene. The dominant image of the verses themselves is the masculine one of overcoming physical obstacles. As Romeo scales the walls to Juliet's abode, so must Lewinsky penetrate those of the White House. This provocative act of intertextuality redefines Lewinsky's pursuit of the president in gender terms.

If Monica Lewinsky can masquerade as a male, it seems only logical for the president to become a female. Not only would turnabout be fair play, but a second gender reversal would preserve the heterosexual nature of the couple. And, sure enough, in *The Starr Report*, this is what takes place. President Clinton becomes a female. Here is how a "Note" in the "Narrative" puts it: "Ms. Lewinsky also testified about various steps she took on her own to ensure that the relationship remained secret, such as using different doors to enter and depart the Oval Office area, avoiding the President at a White House party, and referring to the President as 'her' in pages to Betty Currie." Notice that these "various steps" to "ensure that the relationship remained a secret" are taken by Lewinsky on her own. But to refer to the president in the female gender as "her" in "pages to Betty Currie" would mean that Betty Currie was party to this gender masquerade.

The president may have his gender played with, but he is in excellent company. It is, once again, in a "Note" to the "Narrative" that the *Report* tantalizes the gender-conscious reader: "According to her aunt, Debra Finerman, Ms. Lewinsky used the code name 'Gwen' when discussing Mr. Jordan because 'he's an important person' and Ms. Lewinsky 'always had the feeling somebody was listening in' on their phone conversations, they did not want an eavesdropper to know that Mr. Jordan was helping her find a job." Not only is Vernon Jordan's gender changed, but he acquires a female name in the process: Gwen. The president should consider himself lucky, since his gender bending is restricted to a change in pronoun.

These games with gender are presented as essential ways for Monica Lewinsky to hide her relationship with the president. They are defined as avoidance techniques. Both, however, involve the use of electronics, in one case, the "pages to Betty Currie" and, in the other, the telephone conversations. Jordan's change in gender occurs between Monica Lewinsky and her aunt, Debra Finerman. That with the president's gender takes place between Lewinsky and Betty Currie. Two women, two men: it is the solidarity between the women that permits the gender trouble. Female solidarity and homosociality is stronger than the male/female gender distinction.

Perhaps it is not an accident that Bill Clinton and Vernon Jordan participate together in another gender articulation. At the end of a meeting with

Vernon Jordan, Lewinsky "asked [Mr. Jordan] if he would give the President a hug." The attached "Note" elaborates: "According to Ms. Lewinsky, Mr. Jordan responded, 'I don't hug men.'" Monica Lewinsky asks Vernon Jordan to transmit a greeting to Bill Clinton by hugging him. Jordan interprets this request in a sexual manner and responds that he does not "hug men." His response is a traditionally American masculine one, along the lines of "real men don't hug men," demonstrating the corporal limits of masculinity and homosocial bonding between men. Little does he know that hugging men is the least of what is going on here, where he and the president have already been transformed into females.

The sexuality of the president is, of course, what sets the entire *Report* in motion. After all, the president had confessed to Dick Morris that "ever since the election, I've tried to shut myself down. I've tried to shut my body down, sexually, I mean." Chapter 8 analyzed this incident in the context of the stories that the two principals tell others. There, also, the irony of Clinton's choice of words was mentioned, since the breakdown of his corporal shutdown coincided with the shutdown of the government.

More importantly, what this strange historical conjuncture emphasizes is the intimate relationship between the president's body and the government. This is not at all an anomaly. In *The King's Two Bodies*, Ernst Kantorowicz analyzes the relationship between the "body politic" and the "body natural" (in contemporary English, one would say the "political body" and the "natural body"). While Kantorowicz is speaking about medieval and early modern royalty, the dynamics he develops are applicable to the male principal of *The Starr Report*, President William Jefferson Clinton. The "body natural" is the "body mortal," whereas the "body politic" is a body that consists of policy and government.

At the center of Kenneth W. Starr's referral are the tensions between the president's "body natural" and his "body politic." The blood, the semen, the crutches, the wheelchair: all these are designed to foreground the corporality of the "body natural" in the text. But there is much more to it than that. Monica Lewinsky is the central character in this drama whose preoccupation with the president's "body natural" creates a clash with his "body politic." The incident at the president's fiftieth birthday party is an excellent case in point. That particular event was already examined from the point of view of the ludic. Now, the incident can elucidate the issue of the president's two bodies: "On August 18, Ms. Lewinsky attended the President's 50th birthday party at

Radio City Music Hall, and she got into a cocktail party for major donors where she saw the President. According to Ms. Lewinsky, when the President reached past her at the rope line to shake hands with another guest, she reached out and touched his crotch in a 'playful' fashion." The donors are associated with the "body politic" and the handshaking the president undertakes forms part of the functions of that body. Through her parallel gesture, Lewinsky aims for the "body natural," the president's mortal body, and touches his crotch.

At a "fundraiser for Senate Democrats," Lewinsky and Clinton "were photographed together at the event. The President was wearing a necktie she had given him, according to Ms. Lewinsky, and she said to him, 'Hey, Handsome — I like your tie.'" Once again, Lewinsky directs her attentions to one body, the "body natural," while the party fundraiser calls attention to the other body, the "body politic." In Clinton's case, it seems to be the "body natural" that prevails, because he "telephoned her that night." In the course of "The Zedillo Visit" (analyzed in chapter 2 above), Monica Lewinsky wrote Bill Clinton, "I need you right now not as president, but as a man," calling attention to those two bodies.

The dichotomy that Lewinsky raises between President Bill Clinton as a government official and Bill Clinton the "man" is a textual dialogue on the president's two bodies that appears in the *Report* and whose eloquent intermediary is, interestingly enough, Vernon Jordan, the man who becomes a woman. The relevant section in the "Narrative" appears under the heading "Second Jordan Meeting":

> At one point in the conversation, according to Ms. Lewinsky, Mr. Jordan said, "[Y]ou're a friend of the President." This prompted Ms. Lewinsky to reveal that she "didn't really look at him as the President"; rather, she "reacted to him more as a man and got angry at him like a man and just a regular person." When Mr. Jordan asked why Ms. Lewinsky got angry at the President, she replied that she became upset "when he doesn't call me enough or see me enough." Ms. Lewinsky testified that Mr. Jordan advised her to take her frustrations out on him rather than the President. According to Ms. Lewinsky, Mr. Jordan summed up the situation: "You're in love, that's what your problem is."
>
> Mr. Jordan recalled a similar conversation, in which Ms. Lewinsky complained that the President did not see her enough, although he thought it took place during a meeting eight days later. He testified that he felt the need to remind Ms. Lewinsky that the President is the "leader of the free world" and has competing obligations.

This discussion between Lewinsky and Jordan unequivocally demonstrates their two positions and in the process illustrates the dichotomy between the president's two bodies.

Jordan begins with a seemingly neutral statement about Lewinsky being a friend of the president, an assertion that could place her in a political position, much like those donors whose hands the president shakes. Jordan is trying to redefine the relationship between Lewinsky and Clinton in terms of the "body politic." But no sooner does Jordan enunciate this than Lewinsky begins her argument highlighting the president's other body, the "body natural." Notice the word "reveal," chosen by the narrator to describe this act on Lewinsky's part. "Reveal" implies the divulging, the uncovering of a secret.

And this is a secret of great import. Lewinsky does not "look at him as the President." What is the antecedent to the "him" here? The president in Jordan's previous statement? If so, this would be a most ungraceful redundancy. It does, however, call attention to an ungrammaticality (to use Michael Riffaterre's term) in the text. This ungrammaticality maintains the textual suspense of that absent antecedent not only in this discussion but in the following "similar conversation." Both of these situations omit Clinton's name. His function as "the President" (with an uppercase *P*) takes precedence; his personal name is irrelevant. The "more as a man" clinches the argument, indicating that there is a clash between being the president and being "a man and just a regular person."

Monica Lewinsky's position, including her anger, revolves around the "body natural." Vernon Jordan, adamant in his position that revolves around the "body politic," "advised her to take her frustrations out on him rather than the President." He can become the substitute "body natural" in this game, diverting the anger away from the president. In the "similar conversation," attached in Starr's *Report* directly to the previous incident, Jordan's position is more forceful, as he this time "felt the need to remind Ms. Lewinsky that the President is the 'leader of the free world' and has competing obligations." These "competing obligations" represent the opposite of Monica Lewinsky's needs. Jordan has redefined the president's "body politic" in contrast to Lewinsky's "body natural."

In an appended "Note," the "Narrative" brings in Monica Lewinsky's "handwritten proffer," in which she presents "a very similar account of her second meeting with Mr. Jordan": "At some point, Mr. Jordan remarked something about Ms. L. being a friend of the Pres. of the United States. Ms. L. responded that she never really saw him as 'the President'; she spoke to him like a normal man and even got angry with him like a normal man. Mr. Jordan asked what Ms. L. got angry about. Ms. L. replied that the Pres. doesn't see or call her enough. Mr. Jordan said Ms. L. should take her frustrations out on him — not the President."

Monica Lewinsky, in a certain sense, recognizes the important role that the president of the United States plays as president. In the message she drafted to Bill Clinton during the "Zedillo Visit," she asks the president "to please be sensitive to what I am going through," even though she knows "that what is going on in the world takes precedence."

Being treated "more as a man" obviously has some effect on Bill Clinton: "During an argument on December 6, 1997, according to Ms. Lewinsky, the President said that 'he had never been treated as poorly by anyone else as I treated him,' and added that 'he spent more time with me than anyone else in the world, aside from his family, friends and staff, which I don't know exactly which category that put me in." He speaks to the shabby treatment to which he is subjected by Lewinsky. But his response does not address his high office. Rather, he is playing Lewinsky's game and attempting to justify his use of time.

At the same time, it is clear that Clinton, like Jordan, wishes to pull Lewinsky away from defining him in her restricted category, but the "body natural" seems to spring back and take over. After she sent her "peevish letter on July 3, 1997," he met with her on July 4. Here is how the "Narrative" presents that meeting:

> In Ms. Lewinsky's recollection, their meeting began contentiously, with the President scolding her: "[I]t's illegal to threaten the President of the United States." He then told her that he had not read her July 3 letter beyond the "Dear Sir" line; he surmised that it was threatening because Ms. Currie looked upset when she brought it to him. (Ms. Lewinsky suspected that he actually had read the whole thing.) Ms. Lewinsky complained about his failure to get her a White House job after her long wait. Although the President claimed he wanted to be her friend, she said, he was not acting like it. Ms. Lewinsky began weeping, and the President hugged her. While they hugged, she spotted a gardener outside the study window, and they moved into the hallway by the bathroom.
>
> There, the President was "the most affectionate with me he'd ever been," Ms. Lewinsky testified. He stroked her arm, toyed with her hair, kissed her on the neck, praised her intellect and beauty.

This incident crystallizes the central issues of the discussion on the president's two bodies. The narrator opens the narrative with the president's "scolding" Monica Lewinsky. Scolding is an action most often performed by a parent with a child. The president seems to have the upper hand in this interchange. Then Clinton's words come in: "[I]t's illegal to threaten the President of the United States." Now Bill Clinton has adopted his appropriate role, put on the garb of the presidency as it were. But this role is quickly diluted by the narrator as the reader hears that his assumption about the threat in the letter was based on a reading of Betty Currie's face.

Rather than giving the president credit with his effort to maintain the dignity of his office, of his "body politic," the narrator inserts the parenthetical remark about Lewinsky's suspicion that he "had actually read the whole" letter. Once the disrobing of the president begins, the transfer to the "body natural" can begin as well, ushered in by Lewinsky's complaints. The emotional blackmail effected through Lewinsky's tears leads to the emergence of the "body natural" as the president gives in once again to those urges: he hugs her, they move into "the hallway by the bathroom," and, in Lewinsky's words, he "was the most affectionate with me he'd ever been."

The Starr Report foregrounds the president's "body natural" as a weak body, and, in so doing, it also destabilizes traditional notions of gender. Yet it is the "body politic" that is threatened with impeachment.

10

AN AMERICAN POSTMODERN

As Bill Clinton and Monica Lewinsky become in *The Starr Report* characters involved in lurid sexual escapades, they become embroiled in a set of discourses that transcend them and their personal adventures. The reader is by now familiar with the fact that Kenneth's Starr's referral masquerades as a literary text that in the process of presenting its legal arguments also serves up a smorgasbord of cultural and literary objects. This nature of the *Report* as a depository of Western cultural values and artifacts permits it to glide through music (from Sarah McLachlan to Billie Holiday), high literature, and popular culture. The exploitation and evocation of these cultural substrata add another level of meaning to the *Report*. With its panoply of discourses, with its multileveled, constructed, fragmented, and repetitive narrative, *The Starr Report* is symptomatic of the postmodern age that gave it birth.

Starr's referral is first and foremost a text directed to a legal and political end: the impeachment of the president of the United States. In the course of arguing its case, the *Report* exposes its reader to what can be called at best tawdry legal tactics. As the narrator intertextually adduces some of the testimonies, in the hope that these testimonies will argue the point, he or she unwittingly reveals the maneuvers and procedures used to intimidate witnesses. Chapter 8 above already noted the repeated questioning of Clinton over the issue of whether he was saying that Monica Lewinsky was lying, along with his consistent and repeated answers. As the questioner moved along Monica Lewinsky's body citing her various body parts, that questioner was perhaps hoping to convince the American Congress, and other readers of the *Report*, of the veracity of Lewinsky's testimony and the necessary falsehood of Clinton's testimony. But, in fact, that extended intertextual quotation serves more to convince the reader of the frustrations of the witness being bludgeoned by the repeated questions, couched in an identical grammatical structure. The logical flaw behind this cheap trick stems from the evident fact that, in real life, contradictory accounts do not demand that one side be lying. It is doubtful that the questioner really expected to trap a former state attorney general, law professor, and richly experienced politician. Harassment was the goal.

Other tactics that smell of petty legal intimidation grace Starr's text. "On Friday December 5, 1997, attorneys for Paula Jones identified Ms. Lewinsky as a potential witness in Ms. Jones's sexual harassment case. At 5:40 P.M., they faxed their witness list to the President's attorney, Robert Bennett." Friday is, of course, a day that signals a weekend, and faxing a "witness list" at "5:40 P.M." is guaranteed to ensure that someone will have not just one bad day but a weekend full of bad days. The late time of arrival also makes the opposing team look as though it had one more day to respond than was actually the case. But surely the attorneys would argue that there was no choice in this matter. After all, time was of the essence. And, sure enough, the "following day, President Clinton . . . discussed the *Jones* case with his attorneys and Deputy White House Counsel Bruce Lindsey" (ellipsis added).

Efficiency seems to be the order of the day with the legal team:

On Friday, December 19, 1997, sometime between 3:00 P.M. and 4:00 P.M. , Ms. Lewinsky was served with a subpoena at her Pentagon office. The subpoena commanded her to appear for a deposition in Washington, D.C. , at 9:30 A.M. on January 23, 1998. The subpoena also required the production of certain documents and gifts. Among the items that Ms. Lewinsky was required to produce were "each and every gift including, but not limited to, any and all dresses, accessories, and jewelry, and/or hat pins given to you by, or on behalf of, Defendant Clinton," as well as "[e]very document constituting or containing communications between you and Defendant Clinton, including letters, cards, notes, memoranda, and all telephone records."

Ms. Lewinsky testified that, after being served with the subpoena, she "burst into tears," and then telephoned Mr. Jordan from a pay phone at the Pentagon.

Observe, once again, the time of delivery of the subpoena: Friday, "sometime between 3:00 P.M. and 4:00 P.M." The subpoena, delivered on December 19, 1997, is for an appearance at a deposition on January 23, 1998, over a month away. The legal language of the subpoena is not quoted as the narrator begins the incident: "The subpoena commanded her. . . ." The word "command," emanating as it does directly from the mouth of the narrator and not from the text of the legal subpoena, contributes to the atmosphere of coercion that the *Report* transmits. The requirement for "the production of certain documents and gifts" is followed by a list of what constitutes these materials. The "each and every" in one case and the "every" in the other case both highlight the intensity and the specificity of the requirement: "letters, cards, notes, memoranda, and all telephone records." It is not a surprise that "Ms. Lewinsky testified that, after being served with the subpoena, she 'burst into tears.'" It was sheer luck for her, of course, that at such a late hour, and on a Friday afternoon, Vernon Jordan should be available for a consultation. And is it really necessary for the narrator to detail Monica Lewinsky's tears? True, these create sympathy in the reader and turn the president into a cad for having put Lewinsky in this position in the first place. But this is a high cost for the narrator to pay, since the other side of that sympathy is the suspicion that the lawyers are indulging in a bit of legal sadism.

The part of the American legal system that consists of frequently petty contests of harassment and intimidation is on ample display in *The Starr Report*. And this legal culture probably also contributed to the obsessive and repetitive aspects of the referral.

For these attorneys to play with time might seem only fair. If the weekend in American society is a sacred time, time often spent with one's family and friends, then perhaps breaking legally into that sacred time as far as Clinton and Lewinsky are concerned is justified. The "Narrative" makes it clear in its opening chapter on the "Nature of President Clinton's Relationship with Monica Lewinsky" that "according to Ms. Lewinsky, her encounters with the President occurred on weekends." And Monica Lewinsky stated that it was at a meeting on July 4, 1997, that Clinton was "the most affectionate . . . he'd ever been" (ellipsis added). July 4 is the quintessential patriotic national holiday, on which most Americans indulge in family and neighborhood gatherings and/or picnics. For the president to be performing illicit acts on that day makes these acts that much more objectionable.

The narrator of the *Report* is not alien to these anomalies. A "Note" in the "Narrative" makes it clear that "along with weekend visits, Ms. Lewinsky sometimes saw the President on holidays: New Year's Eve, President's [*sic*] Day, Easter Sunday, July 4. In November 1997, she grew irritated that the President did not arrange to see her on Veterans Day." Lest the reader miss this added information, the narrator kindly adds in the context of the non-meeting on Veterans Day: "Many of Ms. Lewinsky's previous visits with the President had occurred on holidays. *See, e.g.*, Lewinsky 7/30/98 Int. at 3, 13, 17 (describing visits on New Year's Eve, Presidents' Day, Easter Sunday, and July 4)." If nothing is sacred, if there is a sacrilege taking place, it is a sacrilege defined in terms that sum up American culture with its pagan (New Year's), Christian (Easter), and patriotic (July 4, Veterans Day) elements.

The "holidays" are only one way in which this local American context is articulated. Obviously, aspects of the referral are similar to developments in other Western democracies. Italian investigating magistrates have successfully taken on the executive, indeed a whole political class. In France, the parliament is debating cutting the umbilical cord between politics and prosecutors. The United Kingdom has a history of political sex scandals. Nevertheless, in its particular modalities, the Starr investigation and even more so the *Report* it produced are distinctively and typically American. It does not hurt that a little homegrown wisdom pops in here and there, such as when Monica Lewinsky's therapist "cautioned her patient that workplace romances are generally ill-advised."

Then there is, of course, the all-important question of what constitutes a "sexual relationship." In the "Narrative," the president maintained that "there can be no sexual relationship without sexual intercourse, regardless of what other sexual activities may transpire. He stated that 'most ordinary Americans' would embrace this distinction." The president's assertion is repeated in the "Grounds." Bill Clinton is absolutely intent on using "most ordinary Americans" to buttress his argument. This argument has been at least partly validated in scientific research by Stephanie Sanders and June Reinisch.

But there is perhaps nothing that makes the soil in which this story grows more American than the actual locus of the relationship between Monica Lewinsky and Bill Clinton. It is difficult to think of a quintessentially more American space than the White House. There was nothing to keep the illicit couple from meeting in another location. But they do not.

And just as the White House solidifies the American space for this intrigue, so the various games in the *Report* contribute to redefining the contemporary American cultural and political scene. As the two principals exchange gifts, they exchange unspoken cultural assumptions that emanate from those artifacts. When the president goes to Martha's Vineyard as a tourist and then brings items from the Black Dog Restaurant to give to Monica Lewinsky as a gift, he is extending the cultural reach of the restaurant beyond its narrow geographical borders but nevertheless staying within America. His role as tourist is an act that participates in larger discourses of geography and notions of place.

Monica Lewinsky gave the president, "shortly before Halloween of 1997, a package filled with Halloween-related items, such as a pumpkin lapel pin, a wooden letter opener with a frog on the handle, and a plastic pumpkin filled with candy." Halloween has only in the last few years been exported as a holiday to other Western countries. The *Report* has gone further, through Lewinsky's act, into transforming Halloween and assimilating it to birthdays and holidays like Christmas: occasions for gift giving. Pumpkin memorabilia and candy are par for that occasion. But some might wonder that "a wooden letter opener with a frog on the handle" should be a "Halloween-related" item. It may not normally be such, but the narrator has transformed it into one in the process of setting it in the middle of the other items.

While these and other gifts help to delineate the parameters of contemporary America, other more significant elements come into play. One of the most central components is without a doubt that of intertextuality. The intertextual constituent in *The Starr Report* is broad and wide ranging. Music, poetry, art, drama, fiction, history, cinema: elements from these and other domains help to characterize contemporary American culture at the same time that they recast and redefine the *Report* itself, providing the reader with alternate ways of reading that text.

More important, intertextuality in the *Report* is of different kinds. Some references instigate particular actions and emotions in the text. Other cases of intertextuality, while generated by characters in the *Report*, nevertheless remain distant from the actions undertaken by those characters. Still other examples of intertextuality involve a direct relationship between the character and the intertext. The last type of intertext will involve the body, the corporal essence of a given character.

The cultural universe created by the intertext in *The Starr Report* may well begin on U.S. soil. But sooner or later that intertext is bound to participate in broader cultural dialogues. As Monica Lewinsky and Bill Clinton expand their cultural reach, so they also expand the local to the global.

Chapter 4 already examined the range of referents that a popular film like *Titanic* can generate and how in the process its presence as an intertext redrew the emotional borders of the relationship between Clinton and Lewinsky. *Titanic*, as a film, stretches the boundaries of the *Report* in other ways. Cinema, like other cultural products, is not at the turn of the millennium — if it ever was — merely a national or regional product. Rather, all cultural production has transcended national, political, and linguistic boundaries to become part of a global cultural market. A postcard that Lewinsky gives Clinton featuring "a 'very erotic' Egon Schiele painting" does the same. The Austrian artist who died in the early twentieth century crosses national and geographical borders to inhabit an American legal document from the end of the same century. Both he and his eroticism are redefined as they help redefine the American presidency. Lewinsky gives the president this postcard along with a card on which "she had written . . . 'Wasn't I right that my hugs are better in person than in cards?'" (ellipsis added).

The narrative of the *Report* has partners who help it to produce these intertextual games. The major partners are the principals: not surprisingly, President Clinton and Monica Lewinsky, but Betty Currie as well.

On the simplest level, Clinton and Lewinsky accomplish these intertextual feats through the gifts they give one another. A Hugo Boss tie that makes a high-fashion statement sits alongside a Banana Republic shirt that makes a different one. Books about American presidents sit alongside the "antique book on Peter the Great" to link absolute monarchs with democratically elected executives. The importance of Walt Whitman's *Leaves of Grass* surfaced in the context of the analysis of the February 28 sexual incident.

But undoubtedly the most provocative of the books Monica Lewinsky gives Bill Clinton is Nicholson Baker's *Vox*. This work, which appears in the *Report* as Lewinsky's "personal copy of *Vox*, a novel about phone sex," transcends its literary universe to address and expand the sexual languages in the *Report*. Baker's novel records one extended sexual conversation between two parties, a man and a woman who do not know one another. In that sense, the situation it portrays is completely different from that between the principals in Kenneth Starr's referral.

Whatever the erotic manipulations in the fictional work, a deep sense of alienation pervades the sexual discourses in the novel. That this copy of *Vox* was referred to in the *Report* as Monica Lewinsky's "personal copy" turns it into what one could call, borrowing a phrase from the male voice in *Vox* itself, a "pre-enjoyed" book. The male character enters a "used bookstore":

> But it wasn't really the kind of place I thought it was going to be, it had hardly any old books, what it had was recently published pre-enjoyed books. A de-facto library. Shelf after shelf of these things, big thick historical romances, super neatly shelved, sometimes five or six copies of the same book side by side . . . but even though there were multiple copies of these books, they weren't identical, because every one of them had been read. They looked *handled*. *All* of their pages were turned. And turned by whom? Turned by women . . . hundreds of female orgasms could be *inferred* from the books themselves . . . you could just hold any copy and think of a woman holding it open with one hand, with her thumb and little finger. It was all there in the pliability and the thumbedness of the book itself [ellipses added].

The reader understands from this conversation how a "personal copy" becomes "pre-enjoyed."

Baker's erotic novel holds a privileged place in the *Report*, as it emerges and reemerges, both in the "Narrative" and in the "Grounds." Not only that, but this is one of the items Clinton did not produce in response to subpoenas, "though his attorney represented that 'the President has complied with [the] grand jury subpoenas.'" The text in this "Note" in the "Narrative" adds that "*Vox*, however, does appear on an October 1997 list of books in the President's private study, and Ms. Lewinsky saw it in the study on November 13, 1997."

Another book that Lewinsky gave Clinton plays on a different register but was also not produced by the president "in response to a subpoena." This work, *Oy Vey! The Things They Say! A Book of Jewish Wit*, also functions as a powerful intertextual reference in the *Report*. As a pedantic aside, it is worth mentioning that *The Starr Report* gets the title of this minibook wrong. The book is referred to as *Oy Vey! The Things They Say: [sic] A Guide to [sic] Jewish Wit*. Both the punctuation and the subtitle in Starr's referral are wrong. This little gift book advertises itself in this way: "Here is a wealth of Jewish wit and humor mined from the halls of the synagogue, the political roundtables of Israel, and the supper clubs of the Poconos. Here, too, are Groucho Marx, Albert Einstein, Joan Rivers, and Lenny Bruce — just a smattering of the famous Jewish names you'll encounter in this delightful collection."

This description from the dust jacket of the minibook does not do the work justice. Divided into sections that include "Love and Sex" and "Politics," among others, the sayings are less religious or sectarian than the book's title might imply. Some of the tidbits of wisdom provide wonderful ways to evaluate and redefine many of the machinations in the Clinton-Lewinsky scandal. Perhaps Chico Marx is best equipped to comment on Clinton's tortured explanations: "I wasn't kissing her, I was whispering in her mouth." And might not Henry Kissinger's quip "Power is the great aphrodisiac!" explain part of the attraction Lewinsky felt for the president? Perhaps she might prefer Woody Allen's opinion: "Love is the answer, but while you are waiting for the answer, sex raises some pretty good questions." And President Clinton might well have benefited from Benjamin Disraeli's advice: "Be frank and explicit. That is the right line to take, when you wish to conceal your mind and to confuse the minds of others." It is an irony of the intertext that it can manipulate people and events. Many of the quips on politics are applicable to the situation created by Kenneth Starr's investigation. Who could resist Groucho Marx: "Politics is the art of looking for trouble, finding it everywhere, diagnosing it incorrectly, and applying the wrong remedies."

As intertextuality appears and reappears in *The Starr Report*, it engages the principal characters in different ways. *Vox* and *Oy Vey!*, despite their importance, remain outside the characters, separate from them. The next level of intertextuality is much more intimate, effecting an identity between the intertext and a given character. *Romeo and Juliet* provided such a case. After all, Monica Lewinsky appropriated for herself the male role of Romeo in the quotation she used. The Shakespearean saga of star-crossed lovers redefines her modern-day romance with the president of the United States.

This intimate use of the intertext by Lewinsky differs from its parallel use by Clinton. The president's reading of his own situation through Arthur Koestler's political novel *Darkness at Noon* was already noted. Both referents are high cultural, but Lewinsky's tragic love story is paralleled by Clinton's saga of political victimization; adolescent passion versus the dark and claustrophobic world of the prison.

Other cultural objects create their own discourses. In the "Grounds," the narrator summarizes a discussion of the gifts. The reader is already familiar with the differences between Lewinsky's testimony that "Betty Currie called her to retrieve the gifts" and Betty Currie's testimony that "she believes that Ms. Lewinsky called her about the gifts." The text states that Betty Currie "has a dim memory of the events." A "Note" appended to this adds: "Ms. Currie testified that she was taking St. John's Wort to try to remember, but it was not helping." This is highly ironic given the games with memory that all the principals play. Betty Currie attempts to remedy her problem with herbal medicine. But to no avail, as the inefficacy of the remedy is highlighted. This only makes sense if one forgets that Saint-John's-wort is not normally used for memory but rather to maintain emotional balance in highly stressful situations. Seen that way, it seems to have been remarkably effective.

Nevertheless, this herbal remedy attached to Betty Currie creates its own referents that speak to the other appearances of herbal medicines in the text. In the course of the incident described in the "Narrative" as "The Zedillo Visit," the text reveals that Monica Lewinsky "left two small gifts for the President with Ms. Currie." The identity of these "two small gifts" is relegated to a "Note": "In a note to the President the next week, Ms. Lewinsky would write of the gifts: 'I forgot to tell you: . . . The Gingko Blowjoba or whatever it is called and the Zinc lozenges were from me.'" After this "Note," the narrator adds: "spelling and grammar corrected." While these and other corrections are far from an uncommon occurrence in the *Report*, in this case the results are most fascinating. Those conversant with herbal medicines will recognize that Monica Lewinsky, zinc lozenges aside, is speaking about Ginkgo biloba ("Gingko" is a variant spelling). The "biloba" has changed into "Blowjoba," a word that conflates the original name of the remedy with the term "blow job."

Monica Lewinsky pretends to excuse herself as she effects the word change: "or whatever it is called." The bisociations this usage creates are multiple. The orality inherent in the "blow job" combines with the orality of lozenges. And since both zinc lozenges and Ginkgo biloba function as products that are good for one's health, so a "blow job," by extension, also becomes good for one's health. At the same time, the entire exercise comments on the multiple incidents of oral sex, of "blow jobs," in the *Report*. This intertextual transformation of "biloba" into "Blowjoba" also speaks to Lewinsky's other allusions to blow jobs in the text. The reader will surely remember that in one instance she volunteered herself as an "Assistant to the President for Blow Jobs." And, of course, unlike Saint-John's-wort, Ginkgo biloba is taken to strengthen memory.

These games with cultural referents and intertextuality redefine the text of the *Report*. But *The Starr Report* in its essence is one big intertextual game, next to which all the other intertexts pale. The reader knows that the referral is a composite of various sorts of materials around which the "Narrative" and the "Grounds" weave their sometimes convergent and sometimes divergent tales. The existence of the *Report* as a digestion of these previously existing materials means that the intertextuality already analyzed participates in a double coding: once in the internal narrative of the *Report* as an independent work and once in the *Report* as a composite work that drew these intertexts from another source from which it is itself drawn, the multiple volumes submitted to Congress.

And who are these games for if not Congress and the American people? The intertextuality with its broad cultural sweep is designed at once to impress and intimidate the reader. If some may not recognize *Vox*, they will *Romeo and Juliet*. And readers for whom Walt Whitman's poetry is too effete a reference might be reassured by the presence of *Titanic*. The complex weave of the *Report*, its fragmentation, its multiple narrations, its intertextuality, its sexual malaise: these are all symptomatic of a postmodern American condition.

As Judge Starr's referral unfolds, America, with all its contradictions, should recognize itself in it. One major national preoccupation remains invisible, however: race. The president's two chief facilitators, Betty Currie and Vernon Jordan, are both African-Americans. If Toni Morrison felt this angle was worthy of exposure, Kenneth Starr clearly did not. And, aside from the undeveloped reference to the *Oy Vey!* minibook, the *Report* makes no reference to the fact that the Clinton-Lewinsky duo make an interfaith, and not just an illicit, couple. Black and white, Christian and Jew: these categories are shunted aside in favor of those of gender and power.

With its sexual tale that keeps repeating, the plot in Judge Starr's *Report* skips like a broken record. The work as a whole, on the other hand, with its fragmented yet repetitive construction and its variety of materials can be experienced the way one surfs with a zapper through multiple television channels. Not only can the pieces of the story line be appreciated out of order, but one never knows whether one will come upon a political or legal drama, a steamy sex scene, or a discussion of an herbal remedy.

Conclusion

THE PRESIDENT'S TWO BODIES AND THE
POLITICS OF MASQUERADE

There is no question that Judge Starr, in his government position as independent counsel and with the help of his office, has brought forth a central document for contemporary America. *The Starr Report* transcends its function as a referral submitted to the United States House of Representatives to address some issues that concern America today: public and private, sexuality and gender, sexuality and disability. These issues themselves raise other questions, fundamental to the institution of the presidency. At the same time, what emerges from all these areas that intersect in the *Report* is the significance of the notion of masquerade.

The project of *The Starr Report* was to argue in favor of the impeachment of the president of the United States and presumably also of his removal. An alternate scenario could as easily have been the resignation of the president. In retrospect, it is obvious that the project did not succeed, and the *Report*, as a goal-oriented text, has failed. True, President Clinton was impeached, but only by the narrowest of partisan margins. And in the Senate, his removal did not even receive a clear majority, coming nowhere close to the necessary two-thirds. Politically more significant, the idea of the impeachment or removal of the president never made any significant inroads into his own party, remaining thus a strictly partisan position. Behind this, clearly, was the inability of Judge Starr's referral to convince the American public, the overwhelming majority of whom consistently and forcefully rejected the calls for the president's removal or resignation.

While extrinsic factors may have played some role (the state of the economy, for example, though even this is doubtful), the particularities and textual strategies of *The Starr Report* were certainly a major factor in the final result. Surely, few Americans took the time to read the complete *Report* through, yet Judge Starr's textual creation represented and framed the anti-Clinton case. Once the OIC's imprint was placed on the case, it could not be removed.

The house managers and their allies insisted repeatedly that the case against Bill Clinton was not about sex but about perjury and obstruction of justice. If they seemed at times to be preaching to the deaf, was that not because *The Starr Report* had so foregrounded sexual description, obsessively and repetitively exposing every prurient detail? Even in the more legally minded "Grounds," it is hard to see the law through the sex. How much more so is that the case when the "Grounds" are doubled by a longer, still more sexualized "Narrative," the whole accented by frequently juicy "Notes."

Yet the other side of the coin, the strategy of sexual exposure, did not work either. It did not force a presidential resignation and it did not turn the public against its chief executive. Judge Starr clearly misjudged the American people. That Americans, as some might believe, have become more sexually sophisticated and are therefore more willing to accept the adventures of a philandering president than they might have been in the past is certainly a possibility. On the simplest level, it would appear that the same sexual revolution that permitted the OIC's frankness has also inured Americans to sex talk and broadened their understanding of the range of sexual behavior.

A popular way of defending the president's actions and explaining the American public's ultimate acceptance of them has been the distinction between private and public conduct, only the second of which should be subject to impeachment. The public and private are unquestionably important in *The Starr Report*. The *Report* even raised this distinction in order to refute it, arguing that: "the President had blended the official and personal dimensions" of his activities. But the notion of the president's two bodies better represents what is at issue in Judge Starr's opus. The critical difference is the relentless corporalization characteristic of that text. This focusing on the physical body undercuts the line of argument that appears to underlie the positions of so many of the president's critics. This line of argument whose consequences one can find in the work of Bennett and Coulter, among others, presupposes a single moral organ whose flawed state threatens all the president's actions, from the symbolic to the actual. Starr pulls the reader away from the moral universe (evoked in the text most frequently — ironically enough — by Bill Clinton) toward a world of divided corporality.

One could say that the majority of the American public, faced with Starr's dilemma, chose Vernon Jordan's understanding over that of Monica Lewinsky: the actions of the leader of the free world cast into insignificance those of the lustful middle-aged man. Such an analysis would not do justice, however, to the depth of Judge Starr's argument or to the broader cultural implications of his *Report.*

The independent counsel attempts to bring down the "body politic," that is to dissolve the president as a political entity. But his main means in the *Report* is through the "body natural," by exposing the weaknesses of the president's physical body, trying to use his "body natural" to strip him of his "body politic."

It is only through an understanding of this notion of the president's two bodies that much in the *Report* that initially seems at the very least odd becomes more understandable. Take the political first. In Starr's textual universe, the political world in which President Clinton normally functions is largely concealed. This phenomenon begins with the "Key Dates," in other words at the beginning of the *Report.* There, the reader will surely remember, William Jefferson Clinton has no existence other than that bestowed on him by the "sexual relationship."

And it is downhill from there. The reader tends not to see the president interacting directly with specific political figures, be they national or international. This certainly accounts for the discrepancy between the presence of certain individuals in the "Table of Names" and their absence in the *Report*: hence the nonappearance in the *Report* of Yitzak Rabin, "Former Prime Minister of Israel," and the presence in the same *Report* of Ernesto Zedillo, "President of Mexico," as at best stage dressing.

More importantly, President Clinton hardly ever moves out of the White House. His is more the world of the Oval Office and the windowless hallway and bathroom. There are rare occasions on which the reader hears that the president has gone, for example, on vacation to Martha's Vineyard. But this exit from the White House becomes subsumed under its role as a context for the gifts from the Black Dog given to Lewinsky. It then becomes possible for

Betty Currie to manipulate him spatially in the White House itself, as he becomes the passive object being moved and escorted from one space to the next.

What might be called this political absence is compounded by other textual factors, not the least of which is the organization of *The Starr Report*. The "Narrative," of course, highlights Monica Lewinsky and her version of the story, whereas the "Grounds" brings to the fore the legal arguments in favor of the president's impeachment. On the simplest level, this translates into the fact that the president's statements are present to verify or negate Monica Lewinsky's rendition of events. This is on the one hand. On the other hand, the more legalistic arguments simply attempt to circumvent the president's statements and argue instead for his impeachment. The president's voice in the *Report* is a background voice, almost offscreen, cinematically speaking, that is heard on the periphery of the action in Starr's text.

At the same time that the *Report* attempts to downplay the president's "body politic," that same *Report* highlights the president's "body natural." And this "body natural" is there in all its manifestations, from the most rudimentary ones, like eating (e.g., pizza), to others, like those linked to sexual activity. More importantly, the reader watches as this "body natural" has its defects laid out in the text: from the sore back through the injured knee that necessitates crutches to the urinating as this body grows old and feeble. The narrator must exploit Monica Lewinsky and her storytelling to accomplish these corporal tours de force in the *Report*. But no matter what the initial provenance of these materials, their presence and manipulation in the text remain the responsibility of the narrator alone.

The president's "body natural" is not only subjected to illness and decay but also to derision. Yet the humor and the derision directed at the "body natural" can only be effective because of the inherent clash between the "body politic" and the "body natural." Thus Monica Lewinsky can laugh when the president exits in the middle of an encounter because "someone entered the Oval Office." Lewinsky's reaction: "I just remember laughing because he had walked out there and he was visibly aroused, and I just thought it was funny." Her humor is directed at the arousal of Bill Clinton as a physical body. But it is only because of his political position, his "body politic," that he finds himself having to walk out "visibly aroused."

By her actions, Monica Lewinsky unwillingly colludes with the textual project of *The Starr Report*, but this is one that goes beyond mere derision. In its focus on the "body natural," the referral foregrounds a thoroughly emasculated Bill Clinton. It is almost as if, for the oɪc, the presidency is still a quasi-magical function that demands both physical wholeness and traditional masculinity. In this patriarchal conception, showing the absence of these qualities denudes the leader of his power and legitimacy.

Gender trouble is part and parcel of *The Starr Report*. Just as Vernon Jordan has his gender altered so does the president. Interestingly enough, they are the two males who are attempting most strongly to uphold the president's "body politic." Yet they are transformed into women by other women. The instability of the male gender then permits someone like Monica Lewinsky to take on a male identity, that of Romeo in Shakespeare's play.

The reader already knows how this athletic president has been represented as a quasi-cripple. But these physical frailties are linked to sexual performance. Remember the "Narrative" incident in which Monica Lewinsky "wanted him to touch" her "genitals with his genitals." The appended "Note" explains that this touch was brief and: "[W]e sort of had tried to do that, but because he's so tall and he couldn't bend because of his knee, it didn't really work." Lewinsky's desire is thwarted by the president's "body natural." It is not simply his knee injury that is the problem. After all, such an injury is transitory. The first reason is "because he's so tall." Height is a physical attribute that inheres in someone's body and is not subject to adjustment or medical cure. Paradoxically, this trait, normally positive in a man, is treated like a defect. The president's "body natural" is a permanently flawed object that affects his sexual performance in the most traditional of ways, by preventing sexual intercourse.

By raising this dialogue, *The Starr Report* has entered perhaps unknowingly into the current debate in disability circles on disability and sexuality. Clearly, *The Starr Report* seems to be, despite itself, attuned to the problems of the age and — dare one say? — addressing them. That does not mean that its narrator is completely comfortable with this position. Rather, the opposite. The gender bending, the sexuality of the disabled: these are articulated in the *Report* in terms of more traditional views of masculinity, views of the "real men don't eat quiche" sort.

In *The Starr Report*, the president's two bodies act out an elaborate masquerade. At his birthday party, for example, he himself is performing as a political figure as he literally — and figuratively as well — uses his "body politic" to shake the hands of "major donors." But since it is his "body natural" that the storyteller, Monica Lewinsky, emphasizes by relating how "she reached out and touched his crotch," his "body politic" is made to disappear. It becomes nothing but an actor in an elaborate masquerade in which the president is playing at being a politician.

That the president's two bodies should be made to participate in this element of masquerade is not insignificant. Masquerade is a pivotal component of *The Starr Report*, which masquerades first as one thing and then as another. Kenneth's Starr's referral masquerades as a literary text (the "Narrative"), even briefly as a theatrical one (the cast of characters), and then in the "Grounds" as a legal one, and yet it includes extensive legally irrelevant descriptive and narrative materials. The whole serves up a smorgasbord of cultural and literary objects. Even Kenneth Starr wears a variety of masks. He is independent counsel, author, and judge while acting essentially as, and relating his position to that of, prosecutor.

No matter how deeply one delves into the text, the element of masquerade always lurks there. Take the cigar incident. The narrator seems to think that the cigar is a masquerade for the penis, since it is used (according to the narrator) "to stimulate" Lewinsky. In fact, however, male pleasure is masquerading as female pleasure. The president enjoys putting the cigar into his own mouth ("it tastes good"), which means that if one were to follow the narrator's logic, the president's act would have very different implications. Then the heteronormal emasculation would be complete. But perhaps the most eloquent masquerade is that of phone sex, already analyzed in its dual role as a double masquerade. And then there are those cover stories, with their simulation that borders on theatricality.

Does this masquerade result from an unwillingness on the part of Americans to own up to the ways in which they experience and use sexuality or from a general theatricality in American politics and public culture generally? Perhaps both.

To say "masquerade" is, in a certain sense, to invoke the ludic, the playful. But *The Starr Report* is a most serious text. It is a text that argues about America, its government, and the presidency. Yet by inserting itself in the most current debates about gender, sex, and disability, *The Starr Report* has given these cultural debates new symbolic meaning. It is perhaps only fitting, then, that the holder of the highest office in the land, the president, should have his two bodies textually sacrificed on the altar of these debates.

Index

DATE DUE

GAYLORD

PRINTED IN U.S.A.